DOGS

The First 125 Years
of the American Kennel Club

Editor-in-Chief, Andrew De Prisco
Contributing Editor, Amy Fernandez
Consulting Editor, Allan Reznik
Editors, Amy Deputato and Jarelle S. Stein
Designers, Jerome Callens and Sherise Buhagiar
Photography Pre-press Specialist, Joanne Muzyka
Indexer, Melody Englund

AKC Project Editor, Marcy L. Zingler

The Publisher is greatly indebted to President Dennis Sprung and Chairman Ron Mena-
ker as well as former Chairman and Vice Chairman David Merriam and the excellent
supportive staff at the American Kennel Club, especially Executive Secretary James
Crowley, Meghan Lyons (Photography Editor), Barbara McNab (Director of The AKC
Museum of the Dog), Barbara Kolk (AKC Librarian), as well as Mary Burch, Curt
Curtis, Gina DiNardo, Erika Mansourian (*AKC Gazette* Editor), Charley Kneifel,
Doug Ljungren, Mari-Beth O'Neill, Lisa Peterson, Norma Rosado-Blake, and Sydney
Suwannarat. Special thanks to William Secord of the William Secord Gallery.

Kennel Club Books
A Division of BowTie, Inc.
40 Broad Street, Freehold, NJ 07728 USA

Library of Congress Cataloging-in-Publication Data

Dogs : the first 125 years of the American Kennel Club.
   p. cm.
  Includes index.
  ISBN 978-1-59378-648-9
  1. American Kennel Club—History. 2. Dog shows—United States—History. I.
American Kennel Club.
  SF425.D64 2009
  636.706'073--dc22
                            2009012980

Printed and bound in China.
14 13 12 11 10   2 3 4 5 6 7 8 9 10

DOGS

The First 125 Years
of the American Kennel Club

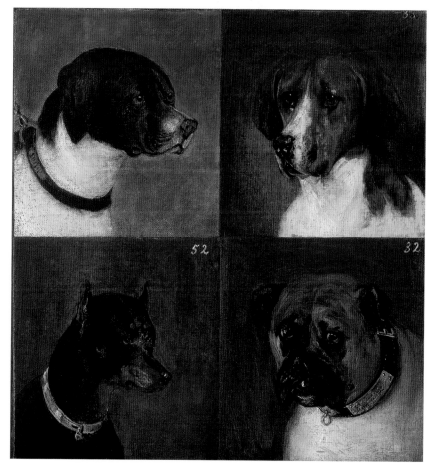

The American Kennel Club

Mission Statement

The American Kennel Club is dedicated to upholding the integrity of its Registry, promoting the sport of purebred dogs, and breeding for type and function. Founded in 1884, the AKC and its affiliated organizations advocate for the purebred dog as a family companion, advance canine health and well-being, work to protect the rights of all dog owners, and promote responsible dog ownership.

The 125th anniversary of the AKC marks the thirty-first year of the *AKC Gazette's* Annual Photo Contest. Each year six prizes are awarded for first, second, and third place in both the Color and Black and White categories. Some of the winning photographs are celebrated in this new volume, all images that excel in quality, composition, and originality. Here is photographer Carol Beuchat's First Place winner for the 2009 Color category.

CONTENTS

FOREWORD

At the American Kennel Club, we are passionate about our AKC traditions. As we reach our 125th anniversary, we are proud of our position as the world's largest not-for-profit registry and our place as the second-oldest sport-governing body in the country. As such, we are continuously striving to preserve and protect the integrity of our registry with technology as well as with our team of field inspectors throughout the country.

We have long known that dog shows and our other events are great family activities, offering participation, competition, and education for all ages. Our events invite participation from all individuals. For the youngsters, there is special competition to hone their skills as

Ronald H. Menaker, Chairman of the Board.

well as the opportunity to compete with their adult counterparts in the great variety of dog sports.

Our range of activities offers something for everyone. For those who focus on the aesthetics of form following function, there are Conformation Events, the dog shows, where judges are guided by the AKC Parent Clubs' written Standards for each breed. The outdoors people among us may gravitate to Coonhound or Performance Events. Those who are athletically inclined will most likely choose breeds with similar abilities and participate in any or all of our Companion Events, strengthening the communication and bond between dog and owner. Last year alone, our affiliated clubs held 20,000 events with more than 3,000,000 entries!

Of course, at the core of all of our programs is the concern for responsible dog ownership. Without the care and concern for all dogs, these programs would cease to exist. Through education and legislation, public awareness has been raised to new heights and continues to grow stronger.

We invite the public to visit the offices of the American Kennel Club in New York City or in Raleigh, North Carolina. Call for a tour or visit our Web site at www.akc.org.

Dennis B. Sprung, President/CEO.

AKC Gazette's Annual Photo Contest entry 2009, photographer Claire Podlaseck.

ACKNOWLEDGMENTS

As the American Kennel Club approached its centennial year in 1984, the Board of Directors agreed that an effort should be made to compile a comprehensive history of the organization and the development of purebred dog sports in America to that point. Numerous AKC staff members at that time contributed to the wealth of information contained in these pages. Charles A. T. O'Neill, then AKC Executive Vice-President, pursued the task of coordinating the efforts of many people to present the original landmark historical reference on all things AKC.

The year 2009 marks the 125th anniversary of the American Kennel Club. This 125th anniversary edition reflects the support or work for the entire project from the following people: Jim Crowley, Ron Menaker, David Merriam, Dennis Sprung, and Marcy L. Zingler, Project Editor.

Unless otherwise noted, all photos contained herein are the property of the American Kennel Club.

AKC Gazette's Annual Photo Contest, First Place Color, 2005, photographer Carol Beuchat.

INTRODUCTION

On September 17, 1884, a group of twelve dedicated sportsmen from fourteen clubs responded to a call from Major J. M. Taylor and Mr. Elliot Smith to meet at the Philadelphia Kennel Club in Philadelphia, Pennsylvania. Each was a Delegate from a dog club that had held a benched show or run Field Trials in the recent past.

The Delegates were deeply committed to the sport of purebred dogs and shared a common desire to establish a "Club of clubs." The proposed organization would consider all matters concerning Bench Shows and Field Trials. These subjects and more will be dealt with historically in the text that follows. The minutes from that first meeting are reproduced on the following pages.

This book brings you facts about the sport of purebred dogs before the founding of the American Kennel Club. It traces the sport from its early years, the evolution of Group competition, the point system, and Obedience Trials through post–World War II and into the present. It is impossible to completely detail the dynamic growth of the American Kennel Club's first century between the covers of this book. We have tried to deal with the milestones in the sport of purebred dogs as we know it.

We trust you will enjoy this book as much as we have enjoyed preparing it. We hope that facts contained in this book expand your enjoyment of the sport of purebred dogs.

Philadelphia, Pa.

"In pursuance of a call by Major J. M. Taylor &. Elliot Smith for each & every club having held a Bench Show or formed for that purpose both in the United States and Canada to be represented by a Delegate, a large number of men met at the rooms of the Philadelphia Kennel Club at the North East corner of 13th and Market Streets Philadelphia.

At 8:30 p.m. meeting called to order moved and seconded that Elliot Smith act as chairman pro tem that Samuel G. Dixon act as secretary pro tem. Objects of meetings stated to be for the purpose of forming a Club of clubs to consider all dog matters concerning Bench Shows & Field Trials. Moved by J. M. Taylor that a committee of three be appointed by the Chair to examine the credentials of those Delegates present.

The Chair appointed the following committee: Samuel G. Dixon, Geo. N. Appold, and C. M. Munhall. Moved by Maj. Taylor that a list of clubs be made and Delegates' credentials produced.

Illinois (Chicago)	represented by	J. M. Taylor
Cincinnati	"	" "
Philadelphia	"	Sam'l G. Dixon
Westminster (N.Y.)	"	Elliot Smith
Montreal	"	Jas Watson. proxy.
New England (Boston)	"	J. A. Nickerson
New Haven	"	G. E. Osborn
Kentucky (Louisville)	"	J. M. Taylor
Baltimore	"	G. N. Appold
Cleveland	"	C. M. Munhall
New Brunswick (Canada)	"	Elliot Smith
London (Canada)	"	Jas. Watson
St. Louis	"	J. W. Munson
Knickerbocker	"	R. T. Green

Moved and seconded that a recess of ten minutes be taken to allow com. to examine credentials.

Sept. 17th, 1884.

Report of Committee on Credentials: Chair. Sam'l G. Dixon reported that "The following gentlemen having appeared before us, made their respective statements and produced their credentials according to which we have formed our decisions. Mr. Dorsey from Howard County Kennel Club having stated that his club was not formed for the purpose of holding Bench Shows—our decision is that he is not a proper representative to this meeting. The following men are accepted;

St. Louis	J. W. Munson
Philadelphia	Samuel G. Dixon
Westminster	Elliot Smith
Montreal	Jas Watson proxy.
New England	J. A. Nickerson
New Haven	G. E. Osborn
Kentucky	J. M. Taylor
Baltimore	G. N. Appold
Cleveland	C. M. Munhall
New Brunswick	Elliot Smith. proxy
London	Jas. Watson. proxy
Cincinnati	J. M. Taylor
Illinois	J. M. Taylor

Mr. R. T. Green, having produced a printed form of the Knickerbocker Kennel Club's constitution and by-laws which did not mention Bench Shows, our decision is that he is not a proper representative to this meeting. Report of credentials committee was accepted. Moved, seconded and passed that Mr. Elliot Smith be elected permanent Chairman. Moved and seconded that Chair appoint a committee to draft a constitution and by-laws. Chair appointed; Maj. J. M. Taylor, Mr. J. A. Nickerson, Mr. Sam'l G. Dixon, Mr. W. B. Shattuc. Moved and seconded that chairman be added to above committee. Carried.

Moved that the meeting adjourn to meet again at 8 o'clock pm on Oct 22nd 1884 in New York City. Seconded and carried."

Sam'l G. Dixon Sec'y P.T., per p.

Edwin Frederick Holt's *Champion Dogs of the Early 1860s*, given to The AKC Museum of the Dog by Marie A. Moore. The nine breeds represented are the Pointer, the Foxhound, the Greyhound, the Black and Tan Terrier (renamed Manchester Terrier in 1874), the Bullmastiff, the White English Terrier (now extinct), the Bulldog, the Mastiff, and the Smooth Fox Terrier.

IN THE
BEGINNING

People and dogs have been inseparable since recorded time. Dogs are mentioned repeatedly in early books of the Bible, and a representation of a dog can be found at the Amten tomb in Egypt, dating from 4000 to 3500 BC. This supports the premise that the dog was one of the earliest domesticated animals.

Dog competitions of various kinds have been documented for centuries. Such events were informal, offering showcases for grading the hunting, coursing, and even fighting abilities of various strains of dogs. Dogs are competitors by nature, and, at their masters' requests, will enthusiastically enter competitive situations. This uninhibited compliance strengthens the bonding process, which has been well documented. It is no wonder, then, that today's dog is the most sought-after and trusted of all animals.

Dog shows as we know them are a relatively recent phenomenon. They follow centuries of dogs working as hunting, coursing, guard, and draft animals, and of course being our companions. Sadly, dogs have also been exploited in cruel activities such as bullbaiting, bearbaiting, and dog fights. Through all of these types of contests,

Ad for an early dog fight at the Westminster Pit, 1819.

people learned early on that selective breeding could produce offspring with predictable characteristics. It was found that traits such as shape, size, temperament, and special abilities could be predicted by selective breeding. Thus, generations of the same strain were reasonably uniform with respect to these important qualities. "Breeding in line" became the rule. Although no accurate records exist, there is little doubt that knowledgeable dog men of yesteryear knew what to expect, within limits, from specific matings. This led to the predictability of type, skills, and temperament.

EARLY CONTESTS

Competitive dog activities in England prior to 1859 suggested a pattern for Americans to follow in staging their own events (see Chapter 2). The English events were very informal affairs, without uniform rules. Strictly local in entry and attendance, they were most often held in neighborhood taverns. Townspeople responded well to the exhibitions, which grew steadily in popularity and frequency.

One such exhibition was described in an article by poet and writer Gerald Massey and portrayed by R. Marshall in an 1855 oil painting that now hangs in the offices of The Kennel Club (England). It shows a group of fanciers and their dogs at a ring formed by tables in a tavern. Jemmy Shaw, owner of the tavern, is standing in the ring. Such efforts were generally referred to as Pot House Shows.

Other, more gruesome, competitions were often staged at the same locales. In fact, Jemmy Shaw advertised "Public Ratting Sports Every Tuesday Evening," followed on Wednesdays by "Canine Exhibitions." Shaw, like many proprietors of public houses, was involved deeply in a variety of dog-related contests and sports. In fact, he had catered to the "doggy set" at a tavern he had previously owned, the Blue Anchor, which served as the headquarters for the Toy Dog Club. One of these Toy dogs was Shaw's own English Toy Terrier, Tiny the Wonder, who held the record for killing 200 rats in a rat pit in 54 minutes, no small accomplishment.

Early reports also list the Elephant and Castle, another tavern, as the site of various canine competitions, including a Specialty Show for Toy Spaniels in 1834. And the infamous Westminster Pit has gone down in history as the locale for such brutal encounters as bullbaiting and bearbaiting by dogs, fought to the death of one or more of the

A match show at Jemmy Shaw's Queen's Head Tavern, 1855. From an oil painting by R. Marshall, 1855.

unlucky participants. Such public engagements disappeared gradually, although clandestine dog fights persist even today.

In addition to public house shows and the baiting and fighting encounters, dogs were included in district fair competitions for livestock, beginning in the late 1700s. In the country, large landowners with substantial kennels of hounds put their bitches in whelp "out to walk" in the homes of tenants on their estates, where the puppies could be raised in a homelike atmosphere and receive great personal care. The contact with people, including children, nurtured the proper emotional development of the young stock. The practice of putting bitches "out to walk" continued well into the twentieth century.

In time, local contests developed to the point that these young animals met competitively. Prizes were awarded for the best developed, most promising, and so on. Although generally limited to the Hound breeds, these local competitions were important to the early development of dog shows. They alerted people to the importance of condition and uniformity of type, while at the same time sharpening the competitive urge. By the late 1850s in England, informal matches and public house shows were not enough. Forward-thinking fanciers began to seek better outlets for their interest in competition.

EARLY ORGANIZED SHOWS AND TRIALS

The first organized dog show took place on June 28 and 29, 1859, staged out of the tavern atmosphere at Newcastle-on-Tyne. Although the entry was relatively small, the event was well organized. Preshow entries were accepted, and a printed catalog was available. *The Field* advertised the show on May 28, 1859. The entry of sixty dogs was limited to Pointers and Setters, which suggests the major area of breed interest at the time. The judges for Pointers were J. Jobling, T. Robson, and J. H. Walsh (aka Stonehenge), while the Setters were passed on by Robson, Walsh, and F. Foulgar. The show at Newcastle-on-Tyne was followed the next year by one at Birmingham, which drew an entry of 267 dogs and included an all-breed classification.

Organizers of the 1860 Birmingham show broke the all-breed classification down into Division 1 breeds—Sporting—and Division 2 breeds, which included some Working, some Non-Sporting, some Toys, and a few Terriers. Division 2 at this show was the forerunner of Group divisions. A class for foreign non-sporting dogs was also offered, but there were no entries. In the years that followed, established shows grew in size and number.

The first organized Field Trial was held at Southill on April 18, 1865, with Rev. Thomas Pearce (Idstone) and a Mr. Walder as judges. The Trial was called a success, although that opinion occasioned considerable controversy in sporting papers. Only sixteen entries competed, including Pointers (large and small) and Setters (English, Irish, and Gordon). Subsequent Trials, with improved turnouts, were staged at Stafford, Bala, Shrewsbury, and several other locations. These subsequent Trials are reported in detail in the first volume of *The Kennel Club Stud Book,* which covers the years 1859–1874.

The first show staged under the aegis of The Kennel Club (England) was the Crystal Palace event of June 16–20, 1873, with an entry of 975 dogs. Following this event, attention turned to the production of a printed stud record for all registered dogs. After much discussion about an editor capable of producing such a book, Frank C. S. Pearce, the son of the aforementioned Rev. Pearce, was selected. Pearce proved to be an excellent choice. The first volume of *The Kennel Club Stud Book: A Record of Dog Shows and Field Trials* appeared in 1874. The book is quite impressive, with more than 600 pages of breeding particulars for 4,027 dogs together with show and Field Trial results dating back to 1859. The honor of being number one belonged to G. T. Rushton's Bloodhound bitch Abeille, whelped in 1865. Pearce continued as editor of the Stud Book. A second volume was issued in July 1875.

The Kennel Club (England) experienced many of the problems that plague infant organizations. However, mature thinking and careful planning prevailed. Some opposition to policies became apparent in 1875, but it was quickly resolved. Since then, The Kennel Club and its activities have progressed with minimal difficulty. Those who wish to learn more about the early development of this institution should read *The Kennel Club: A History and Record of Its Worth* (London, 1905) by E. W. Jaquet, published by *The Kennel Gazette.* This is a fully annotated volume that offers historical background, biographical sketches of many important club members, a record of actions by several committees, and much more. Jaquet was secretary of The Kennel Club at the time.

Early dog shows in England that led to the birth of The Kennel Club preceded similar actions in America by several years. The English experience served as a preview of many of the problems that confronted Americans in their desire to become part of this new and exciting sport.

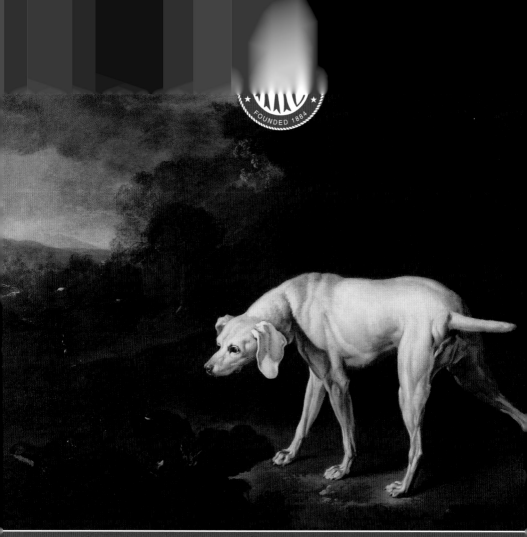

Jean-Baptiste Oudry's *Pointer Pointing at Quail,* 1726, given to The AKC Museum of the Dog by Mr. and Mrs. Philip S. P. Fell.

EARLY AMERICAN SCENE

The early American development of dog contests included dog fighting and baiting as well as hunting and general field activities. Matches and field competitions involving Pointers, Setters, and Hounds, while generally local in entry, were numerous and widespread. New World dog fanciers were both active and knowledgeable, and many wealthy landowners maintained private packs of Hounds for hunting. In so doing, they kept detailed kennel records that demonstrated knowledgeable breeding practices designed to improve their stock.

PRESIDENTIAL PARTICIPATION

George Washington had a strong kennel of Foxhounds at Mount Vernon and maintained written records of individual dogs dating to 1758. He was very particular about their bloodlines and kept detailed accounts of each of his dogs, including all new litters.

Washington's love of dogs continued through his life. In 1785, his kennel was enlarged by a gift of seven French hounds from General Lafayette. Washington hunted these dogs, and his diary contains a number of interesting observations upon their performance.

THE

AMERICAN KENNEL

AND

SPORTING FIELD.

BY

ARNOLD BURGES,

(LATE EDITOR, "AMERICAN SPORTSMAN.")

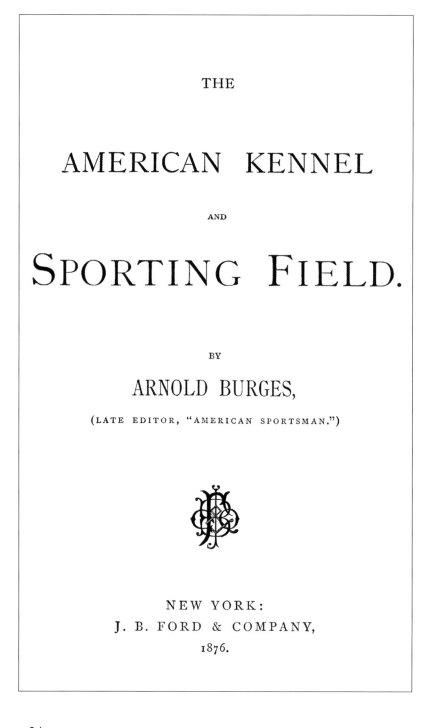

NEW YORK:

J. B. FORD & COMPANY,

1876.

FACING PAGE: Title page from the first American stud book by Arnold Burges, 1876.

George Washington's Hound pack is only one of many documented during the eighteenth and early nineteenth centuries. This was to be expected, as most American sportsmen closely followed English activity in this area. Such sporting papers as John S. Skinner's *American Turf Register,* first published in 1829, included both English and American field-sport information. Another early periodical, the *United States Sporting Magazine*, begun in 1835 and edited by C.R. Colden, had sections offering considerable information on hunting, dog care and training, and other related topics.

The most important publication in this area was *The American Kennel and Sporting Field,* by Arnold Burges. Published in 1876, it includes the first organized stud record to be published in America. The number one dog was a black, tan, and white English Setter named Adonis, owned by George Delano of New Bedford, Massachusetts. Adonis is listed as being sired by Leicester out of Doll, who was imported in whelp. Burges included breeding particulars for a total of 327 dogs: 55 English Setters, 50 Gordon Setters, 71 Irish Setters, 64 native Setters (basically, English Setters), 44 crossbred Setters (any combination of English, Gordon, and Irish), 34 Pointers, and 9 Spaniels of various breeds (Clumber, Cocker, and Irish Water).

Burges's book offers another important dividend: an annotated chronological listing of the first dog competitions in America. It begins with the Illinois State Sportsmen's Association of Chicago event held on June 2, 1874. Since no awards, only a general commendation, were given, this affair cannot be considered a true dog show. Problems plagued the second attempt, which was staged under the auspices of the New York State Sportsmen's Association in

Two Generals and Their Hounds

During the American Revolution, Washington's interest and affection for dogs led him to return a stray hound to General Howe, the British commander. This return was made by special courier, under a flag of truce. The courier also delivered this note:

"General Washington's compliments to General Howe,— does himself the pleasure to return to him a dog, which accidentally fell into his hands, and by the inscription on the collar, appears to belong to General Howe."

In his reply, General Howe recognized that dogs have always provided a common meeting ground for all persons under all and sundry circumstances.

THE
AMERICAN FIELD

THE SPORTSMAN'S JOURNAL.

Published by the American Field Publishing Co.

Four dollars a year: two dollars for six months; one dollar for three months; strictly in advance.
Money should be sent by Postal Order. Draft on Chicago, or by Registered Letter.
The AMERICAN FIELD and NEW YORK SPORTSMAN $6 a year.
The Trade supplied by the American and Western News Companies.
Manuscript intended for publication should be written on one side of the paper only.
Communications must be accompanied by the writer's name and address, not necessarily for publication, but as a private guarantee of good faith, and all communications, upon any subject, or for any department, must be addressed

N. ROWE,

Editor and Manager American Field,
155 & 157 Dearborn St., CHICAGO, ILL.

GREAT BRITAIN OFFICE AND AGENCY:—The American Exchange in Europe (limited); Henry F. Gillig, General Manager, 449 Strand, W.C., London, Eng.

WESTERN OFFICE:···155 & 157 Dearborn Street, Chicago, Ill.
EASTERN OFFICE:··Office " New York Sportsman," Tribune Building, New York.
Address all communications to Western Office.

NEW YORK AND CHICAGO, SATURDAY, JULY 2, 1881.

THE AMERICAN FIELD.

In our last issue we announced that the CHICAGO FIELD Publishing Company having consummated arrangements with the incorporators of the AMERICAN FIELD Publishing Company for the sale of the CHICAGO FIELD, its good will, patronage, and everything appertaining thereto, this issue of the paper would be under the title of the AMERICAN FIELD.

The "AMERICAN FIELD," we think, will be generally recognized as a more appropriate name than the CHICAGO FIELD, since the paper has never been local nor sectional, but national, always maintaining that the sportsmen of America were a brotherhood, whose interests are identical, and consequently the interests of one section of as much import to the paper as those of another. The word "Chicago," therefore, to the casual observer, and one unacquainted with the true characteristics of the paper, localized it, which was extremely objectionable to the best interests of the paper, which is happily obviated by the substitution of the word "American."

Stud book editorial page, 1881. Dr. Nicholas Rowe's comments regarding the journal's name change from *The Chicago Field* to *The American Field*.

Oswego, New York, on June 22, 1874. Only two dogs and one bitch were entered. Under the circumstances, no awards were given.

On October 7, 1874, a show held in Mineola, New York, under the rules of The Kennel Club (England), had entries in Pointers, Irish Setters, Gordon Setters, and "Setters of any breed." There was a satisfactory entry, and this event is considered to be the first American dog show. The very next day, October 8, 1874, the Tennessee Sportsmen's Association held a combined dog show and Field Trial in Memphis. This was the first such combined event and the first organized Field Trial in America. Once again, the dog show portion of the meeting was conducted under the rules of The Kennel Club.

A competition in Detroit followed on January 14–21, 1875. It was open to "dogs besides those devoted to field sports" and was probably the first truly all-breed event in America. Unfortunately, the report in Burges's book on the Detroit show carries results limited to the Sporting breeds, which brings up the question of whether any other breeds were involved. It is interesting to note that classes for Pointers were divided into Pointers over 55 pounds and Pointers not exceeding 55 pounds.

Other events in 1875 included the Rod and Gun Club show, Springfield, Massachusetts, April 28–29; the Watertown, New York, show, May 3; the Paris, Kentucky, show, June 3; the Mineola, New York, show, June 23–24 (its second event); and the New England Association Fair in Manchester, New Hampshire, September 7–10.

The Tennessee Sportsmen's Association staged a second annual event on October 27, 1875, in Memphis. It was an unusual affair for this early date, as it included Sweepstakes and Puppy Stakes together with the inaugural Classes for Braces and a "free-for-all" Stake open to Setters and Pointers, regardless of age, for the "Championship of America." Five entries competed for the cup, valued at $150, together with the considerable prize money of $250 for first place, $150 for second place, and $100 for third place. The entry fee was $25 per dog, which shows that high entry fees existed even then. The Memphis show had several other Stakes as well, making it an event that truly departed from the simple format used for the early events.

Burges's 1876 book was basically a stud record that also reported the results of some early dog shows and some isolated field activities. Burges did not attempt to include reports of such exhibitions as fairs and farm events that exhibited dogs along with many other animals. He contemplated updating his stud record in new editions but never did so. In 1882, a revised edition of *The American Kennel and Sporting Field* was published, correcting errors in the 1876 publication. In his preface to this edition, Burges gave the following reasons for not continuing the effort:

> [S]ince I wrote *The American Kennel and Sporting Field* and have therein the first list of canine pedigrees ever issued in this country, I stated in the Preface my intention to revise that list from time to time so as to keep pace with the importations and breeding of sporting dogs. This intention was, however, frustrated by the organization of the National American Kennel Club, in 1876, having for its object, among others, the issue of an official stud book, and as I recognized the fact that a National Club could give to such a work a character no private individual could, I withdrew *The American Kennel and Sporting Field* from the competition. The book has consequently remained unrevised until now. . . In a country where field sports have but recently come into general recognition, and where but a few years since canine breeding and selling was confined to a disreputable class, a short time naturally produces

Breeds Recognized in the Early Years

1878	Chesapeake Bay Retriever, Clumber Spaniel, Cocker Spaniel, English Setter, Gordon Setter, Irish Setter, Irish Water Spaniel, Pointer, Sussex Spaniel
1885	Basset Hound, Beagle, Bloodhound, Bull Terrier, Collie, Dachshund, Fox Terrier, Greyhound, Harrier, Irish Terrier, Mastiff, Pug, Saint Bernard, Scottish Terrier, Yorkshire Terrier
1886	American Foxhound, Bedlington Terrier, Bulldog, Dandie Dinmont Terrier, English Toy Spaniel, Italian Greyhound, Newfoundland, Scottish Deerhound, Toy Manchester Terrier
1887	Great Dane, Mexican Hairless (dropped in 1959), Poodle, Skye Terrier, Standard Manchester Terrier, Wirehaired Pointing Griffon (originally Russian Setter)
1888	Airedale Terrier, Dalmatian, Eskimo Dog (dropped in 1959), Japanese Chin (originally Japanese Spaniel), Maltese, Old English Sheepdog, Pomeranian, Welsh Terrier, Whippet
1891	Borzoi (originally Russian Wolfhound)
1893	Boston Terrier
1894	Field Spaniel
1897	Irish Wolfhound
1898	French Bulldog

great alterations, and the writer who honestly tries to keep up with the developments of the day, will find himself compelled to retract assertions, made upon the authority of different circumstances.

Burges's perception was correct, as there had been substantial activity in several areas since the first edition in 1876. The number of shows and entrants had burgeoned, and new breeds had appeared. There was also now a rival stud record, *The National American Kennel Club Stud Book.* But Arnold Burges was the first to publish a stud record in America, and in so doing emphasized the singular impact of such a record upon the growth of interest in purebred dogs. Burges died on March 10, 1888, long before he could see the results of his effort to establish a reliable record for posterity.

THE NATIONAL AMERICAN KENNEL CLUB

The National American Kennel Club rapidly became important in its field. It was founded at the Chicago show on January 26, 1876, with permanent headquarters in St. Louis, Missouri. The officers and committee elected at the Chicago meeting were Dr. N. Rowe, President; J. H. Whitman, First Vice-President; E. C. Sterling, Second Vice-President; C.H. Turner, Secretary; and Luther Adams, Treasurer. The executive committee consisted of L. H. Smith, P. H. Bryson, C. H. Raymond, L. V. Lemoyne, W. Jarvis, Arnold Burges, S. H. Turrill, E. O. Greenwood, and C. F. Demuth.

The majority of the new Club's members were Field Trial oriented and not active in dog shows. Preparation and publication of the Stud Book were the responsibility of President Rowe, who had excellent credentials for the task. Rowe, editor of *American Field*, a leading sporting paper of the time that still exists today, was a well-known writer as well as an active dog breeder and exhibitor. Unfortunately, work on the registry was slow, and it was not until 1879 that the initial volume was published. This volume includes particulars for 1416 dogs registered through 1878. The registrants are broken down into seven major divisions: English Setters, Irish Setters, Gordon Setters, crossbred Setters, Pointers, Spaniels, and Chesapeake Dogs and Retrievers. The Spaniel division embraces a number of variants, including Irish Water, Clumber, Cocker, Sussex, Retrieving, and Water Spaniels.

Typical entry information in *The National American Kennel Club Stud Book* is offered for the aforementioned English Setter dog

First Annual N. Y.

Bench Show.

Catalogue

1877.

NEW YORK:

ROGERS & SHERWOOD, PRINTERS, 21 BARCLAY STREET.

1877.

Adonis: "George E. Delano, New Bedford, Ma., breeder/owner; whelped 1875; black, white, and tan; by Leicester (by Llewellin's Dan), out of Lill III." Adonis is the same dog recorded as number one in Burges's earlier stud record. However, there he is recorded as being sired by Leicester out of Doll. The discrepancy illustrates that early records were not without error.

The first volume of this stud book includes a great variety of information. There are the constitution and bylaws of the National American Kennel Club, the club's Bench Show and Field Trial rules, breeding particulars for the 1,416 dogs registered, and results for nine Bench Shows held from 1876 to 1878. The book also includes the results of five Field Trials: Memphis (1874, 1875, and 1876), Iowa (1877), and Nashville (1877).

Among the Bench Shows reported is the Westminster Kennel Club's first dog show, held on May 8–10, 1877. What is not mentioned is that the event was extended through May 11 as a result of the crowd's desire to view the 1,201 dogs entered. This event is the second oldest continuous sporting event in the country (the Kentucky Derby is the oldest). A complete history of the Westminster show appears in *The Dog Show—125 Years of Westminster* by William F. Stifel, published in 2001.

Dr. Rowe continued to produce *The National American Kennel Club Stud Book,* publishing the second volume in 1885. This edition is marked as being "printed by N. Rowe for the National American Kennel Club" even though the club had changed its name in 1884 to the National Field Trial Club and had dropped all interest in Bench Shows.

The American Kennel Club had been organized in 1884 and had assumed full jurisdiction over Bench Shows. In 1886,

Crossbred Setters

The crossbred Setter classification is interesting since it was not unusual at the time to mix blood to gain improved performance. Crossbred Setters were rather popular, as evidenced by the 258 stud book entries that include double and triple crosses of the Setter breeds. A note at the beginning of the crossbred section suggests that the records were not always well kept. "Owing to the indefinite character of some of the pedigrees," the note reads, "it was impossible to decide to what breed certain dogs belonged. They are therefore included in the present class to save disregarding them altogether." This is indeed a frank and interesting statement.

FACING PAGE: Cover of the very first Westminster Kennel Club Show catalogue, 1877.

Dr. Rowe assembled and published the third volume of the stud record, which was issued in quarterly installments and called *The American Kennel Stud Book*. Dr. Rowe, who had full title to the stud record, subsequently offered the initial three volumes gratis to the infant AKC, which accepted them. Without Rowe's effort and generosity, the initiation of a stud book would have been delayed for many years and would not be as extensive as it is with respect to the early entries.

"Father of the Stud Book," Arnold Burges was the author of *The American Kennel and Sporting Field* (1876), and contributed vastly to the early record keeping of purebred dogs.

Dr. Rowe's effort to improve the lot of purebred dogs, particularly field dogs, never wavered, and he worked tirelessly from about 1874 toward the completion of a new endeavor, *The*

Field Dog Stud Book. This effort was approaching realization at the time of his death in 1896 at age fifty-four. Fortunately, Mrs. Rowe, who had always assisted her husband, carried on both the *American Field* magazine and the final preparation of *The Field Dog Stud Book*. Published in 1901, *The Field Dog Stud Book* has been continued from then on, enjoying reciprocity with *The American Kennel Club Stud Book*.

A third national stud record, the *American Kennel Register*, backed by the Forest and Stream publishing company, appeared in 1881 as a monthly publication. It included a stud record in the form of a stud book with much useful information: a registration number assigned to each dog, show results, and reports on important happenings. It was an excellent editorial effort. The magazine ceased publication after the January/February 1889 issue. The newly founded American Kennel Club had offered to take over this stud book to ensure continuity, but Forest and Stream refused the offer, and the *American Kennel Register* disappeared from view.

With the consolidation of the stud records into *The American Kennel Club Stud Book* and with the formation of the AKC itself, the American stage was set for the future growth and development of the sport of purebred dogs.

DRUID Nº 4287,
(Prince—Dora)
Breeder Mr. LLEWELLIN. Importer & Owner ARNOLD BURGES.

Whelped in 1873 in England and imported by Arnold Burges in 1877, the handsome blue belton English Setter known as Druid was an excellent bird dog and an important bench winner and sire in the United States.

Maud Earl's *Irish Members*, c. 1902, given to The AKC Museum of the Dog by Helen M. Best and family in memory of John S. Best. Depicted are two Irish Terriers owned by Mr. Frank Clifton.

BIRTH OF THE
AMERICAN
KENNEL CLUB

When the National American Kennel Club changed its name to the National Field Trial Club in 1884 and altered its direction to embrace field dogs only, dog shows were left without a central governing body. Regardless, many established Bench Shows continued because the public's interest in this activity grew steadily, and serious efforts to form a national kennel club came from several sources.

Major James M. Taylor, an experienced dog judge and breeder, and Elliot Smith of the Westminster Kennel Club each put forth such an effort, but both attempts failed. However, a group of twenty-five dedicated fanciers then petitioned Taylor and Smith to renew their efforts. This petition was in the form of a "Call for a Kennel Club" that appeared in the August 1884 issue of the *American Kennel Register.* It reads:

Editor *American Kennel Register:*

In view of the conflicting actions of the Westminster Kennel Club and of Major Taylor relative to the inception of a National Kennel Club, and the danger of the proposal falling through thereby, we respectfully ask you to issue a call for a meeting of exhibitors and clubs to form such a Kennel Club, and that you prepare a plan of organization, work, etc., for such a club, to be considered at this meeting. It seems very desirable that the co-operation of so respected and experienced a judge as Major Taylor, and so old and influential an organization as the Westminster Kennel Club, should both be secured to this object.

The "call" evoked a substantial response from fanciers and clubs across the United States and Canada. Taylor and Smith both backed the effort and aided its progress in every possible way. A meeting was scheduled for September 17–18, 1884, in Philadelphia, during the Philadelphia Dog Show. Delegates from American and Canadian clubs attended; these clubs included Illinois, Cincinnati, Philadelphia, Westminster (New York), Montreal, New England (Boston), New Haven, Kentucky, Baltimore, Cleveland, New Brunswick (Canada), London (Canada), and St. Louis—thirteen clubs in all. Several other groups had representatives who were not admitted to the meeting because their bylaws did not mention Bench Shows, a point of substantial importance at the time.

The major order of business at this meeting was twofold: first, to select a suitable name for the organization, and second, to appoint a committee to draft a constitution and bylaws. This committee was to make a report in New York during the week of Westminster Kennel Club's first annual show for Non-Sporting Dogs, October 21–24, 1884. The committee consisted of Elliot Smith, Chairman; J. A. Nickerson; W. B. Shattuc; Major Taylor; and S. G. Dixon.

On October 22, 1884, the newly drafted constitution and bylaws were approved at the New York meeting, and officers were elected for the ensuing year. The proposed name of the club was the National Bench Show Association. It was also proposed that membership should consist of clubs only, not individuals. The documents were approved after some changes and additions, including a change in name from the National Bench Show Association to

the American Kennel Club. The officers elected were Major J. M. Taylor (Lexington, Kentucky), President; Elliot Smith (New York, New York), First Vice-President; and Samuel Coulson, Second Vice-President.

AKC Gazette's **Annual Photo Contest entry 2009, photographer Charles Guthrie III.**

THE AMERICAN KENNEL CLUB IS FORMED

The October 22, 1884, meeting in New York marked the true beginning of the American Kennel Club as a structured organization—a club with a name, a constitution, bylaws, and a full complement of officers.

The second annual meeting of the American Kennel Club was held in Philadelphia on May 19, 1885. A hotly contested election at that meeting yielded the following results: Major Taylor, President (by a six to five vote); Elliot Smith, First Vice-President; A. W. Pope, Second Vice-President; G. E. Osborn, Secretary; and E. Comfort, Treasurer. Some friction existed in the new club, as evidenced by the close margin of Taylor's election and also by the fact that this annual meeting was convened only about seven months after the first meeting. The committee that had been previously appointed to revise the constitution and bylaws submitted a more concise version, which was accepted.

Women in the Dog Sport

Breeder, judge, and author Anna H. Whitney was the first woman invited to judge AKC shows. She judged throughout Europe and the United States, including sixteen Westminster assignments between 1888 and 1913.

In 1928, Mrs. Reginald F. Mayhew, noted expert on Pomeranians and Wire Fox Terriers, became the first woman to officiate on a Westminster BIS panel, which then consisted of five judges.

In 1933, Mrs. Geraldine R. Dodge became the first woman to officiate as the sole Westminster BIS judge. Her Giralda Farms kennel pro-

duced numerous top-winning Sporting and Working dogs including the 1932 and 1939 Westminster BIS winners, namely the Pointer Ch. Nancolleth Markable and the Doberman Pinscher Ch. Ferry von Rauhfelsen of Giralda.

Famed breeder of Blakeen Poodles Mrs. Sherman R. Hoyt became the first female owner/handler to win BIS at Westminster in 1935, with the Swiss-imported Standard Poodle Ch. Nunsoe Duc de la Terrace of Blakeen.

Breeder of Carillon Poodles Mrs. Helene Whitehouse Walker introduced obedience trials to the United States, which became an AKC event in 1936.

Noted Poodle authority Anne Rogers Clark became the first female professional handler to win Westminster in 1956, with Toy Poodle Ch. Wilber White Swan. She handled three dogs to a Westminster BIS, judged twenty-three Westminster assignments, and bred the 2002 Westminster BIS winner, Miniature Poodle Ch. Surrey Spice Girl.

Despite these accomplishments, many dog clubs did not permit women to join or hold office for decades. The Ladies Kennel Association was founded in 1900 to allow women a voice in the AKC. However, the AKC barred female Delegates

Mrs. Geraldine R. Dodge, owner of the Giralda Farms kennel and first woman to officiate as sole judge for Best in Show at Westminster Kennel Club.

until 1974, when three women were elected at the June meeting. Gertrude Freedman (Bulldog Club of New England), Carol Duffy (Mid-Hudson Kennel Club), and Julia Gasow (English Springer Spaniel Club of Michigan) were the first women to be elected. Dr. Jacklyn Hungerland became the first woman to join the AKC Board in 1985.

All-breed judge, former professional handler, and breeder, the late Anne Rogers Clark with judge the late Dr. Josephine Deubler, stalwart of the famed Montgomery County Kennel Club Show.

BELOW: All-breed judge Jane Kamp Forsyth at the first revival of the Morris & Essex Show, posing in front of a 1955 photograph of Anne Rogers and herself handling a brace of English Cocker Spaniels.

Cleanthe Carr's *Three Japanese Chins*, 1939, given to The AKC Museum of the Dog by Gilbert S. Kahn.

until 1974, when three women were elected at the June meeting. Gertrude Freedman (Bulldog Club of New England), Carol Duffy (Mid-Hudson Kennel Club), and Julia Gasow (English Springer Spaniel Club of Michigan) were the first women to be elected. Dr. Jacklyn Hungerland became the first woman to join the AKC Board in 1985.

All-breed judge, former professional handler, and breeder, the late Anne Rogers Clark with judge the late Dr. Josephine Deubler, stalwart of the famed Montgomery County Kennel Club Show.

BELOW: All-breed judge Jane Kamp Forsyth at the first revival of the Morris & Essex Show, posing in front of a 1955 photograph of Anne Rogers and herself handling a brace of English Cocker Spaniels.

At the same meeting, twenty-eight committees were appointed to consider adopting Breed Standards to be used at shows held under AKC rules. Some of the committees were confined to one breed, while others were concerned with the Standards for several breeds.

The friction within the club's hierarchy only increased after the May 1885 meeting in Philadelphia. In December 1885, after a stormy seven-month period, Major Taylor submitted his resignation, which was accepted by Elliot Smith, First Vice-President, who was then elected President and successor to Taylor. At a June 10, 1886, meeting, the offices of Secretary and Treasurer were combined, and Alfred P. Vredenburgh became the guardian of that new office, a position he held until December 16, 1919.

It also became apparent during this time that the club needed a reliable stud book. As mentioned earlier, the American Kennel Club had agreed to take over *The American Kennel Stud Book* from Dr. Rowe in 1887 and to be fully responsible for its future publication. The introduction to the fourth volume of *The American Kennel Club Stud Book* (1887) acknowledges Rowe's gift of the initial three volumes. The quarterly frequency introduced by Rowe continued through 1888 but reverted to annual frequency with the fifth volume, issued in 1889.

An additional development in AKC history was the late entry of still another national kennel club into a field already filled with unsuccessful groups. This club was organized as the National Kennel Club of America on April 3, 1888. Its President was Dr. J. Frank Perry, who wrote extensively on dogs under the pseudonym of Ashmont. Perry had been part of previous attempts to form a national club, and he was a signer of the 1884 "call" for a national kennel club. The new group was the first to offer bargain rates to early joiners. At their July 1888 meeting, they elected Dr. Frank Perry as President, Anna Whitney as Vice-President, W. S. Jackson as Vice-President, E. S. Porter as Vice-President, Dr. C. E. Nichols as Vice-President, and H. W. Huntington as Secretary/Treasurer. There was a fifteen-member executive committee elected for staggered terms of one, two, and three years.

The National Kennel Club of America is noteworthy for the election of Anna Whitney as Vice-President, perhaps the first woman to become a national dog club officer in America. The National Kennel Club of America, however, did not prosper, and gradually it faded from view as the AKC continued to gain ground.

CANADIAN CLUBS

Other important developments occurred in the 1880s. Canadian clubs had depended on the American Kennel Club for registrations, shows, and trials. Early attempts to form a national kennel club in Canada included the creation of the Dominion of Canada Kennel Club. According to the June 1883 issue of the *American Kennel Register,* the club held an annual meeting and elected officers, but no further report appeared, indicating that the club had failed.

Activity in Canada continued, however, and in 1886 three Canadian clubs resigned from the AKC, reflecting the growing schism that eventually led to the founding of the Canadian Kennel Club in 1888. An effort in this direction had begun at a meeting held in London, Ontario, in September 1887, followed by another meeting in London the next year, at which the Canadian Kennel Club was founded. Interestingly, Samuel Coulson, who had been elected a Vice-President of the AKC in 1884, was elected a Vice-President of the newly formed Canadian Kennel Club. A complete history of this club in these early years may be found in "The Canadian Kennel Club Story," an article appearing in the seventy-fifth anniversary issue of *Dogs in Canada* (February 1963).

Cleanthe Carr's *Three Japanese Chins*, 1939, given to The AKC Museum of the Dog by Gilbert S. Kahn.

EARLY GROWTH
AND INNOVATION

The last ten to twelve years of the nineteenth century were exciting for both the sport of purebred dogs and the infant American
Kennel Club. Interest in breeding purebred dogs grew tremendously, and dog shows gained popularity in all regions of the country.
Much of this progress may be attributed to the reduction of friction
between individuals and competing clubs as the AKC gained strength
and support. Furthermore, *The American Kennel Club Stud Book* was
now the sole responsibility of the AKC, as the only competing stud book,
the *American Kennel Register*, had passed into oblivion.

The American Kennel Club was strengthened further by the long-
term incumbency of President August Belmont, Jr., a post that he held
continuously from 1888 to 1915. Prior to this, the AKC had had three
Presidents: Major Taylor (1884), replaced by Elliot Smith, who served
two terms, and William Child (1887). Belmont replaced Child in 1888.
The frequent changes in this office did little to instill confidence in the
organization. Belmont's election and long incumbency, along with that

of Alfred P. Vredenburgh as Secretary and later Secretary-Treasurer, marked a change in direction and attitude, offering a stability that had previously been lacking.

THE *GAZETTE*

In 1888, August Belmont proposed that the AKC publish a magazine called the *American Kennel Gazette,* which he believed would aid the club's growth and inform people about purebred dogs and dog shows. His proposal met with some opposition. For example, several members of the Board said the cost would be prohibitive. Belmont countered with an offer to personally underwrite the effort by covering any deficit that might arise, up to $5,000 per year. The first issue of the *Gazette* appeared in January 1889 with the following statement:

> The American Kennel Club having adopted the plan of publishing a Gazette, in pursuance of your wishes in the matter, the officers have begun this, its first publication, with the new year, 1889, and they will endeavor, as much as lies in their power, to meet what they feel the Kennel World requires in the shape of an official organ; taking as their guide the expressions of opinion on the subject from breeders and exhibitors,

---

Top Ten Breeds of the 1880s

English Setters

Irish Setters

Pointers

Irish Water Spaniels

Gordon Setters

Beagles

Collies

Fox Terriers

Dachshunds

Mastiffs

The top five breeds of the 1880s were all working gundog breeds. While this is the only decade that the English Setter reigned as the number-one breed, it remained in the top ten for four decades, but hasn't been in the top ten since the 1910s. Irish Setters, the number-two breed of the decade, fell to number seven in the 1890s and then did not make the top ten until the 1970s, when it ranked number six. Three of the breeds in the decade's top ten would never make the list again: Irish Water Spaniels, Gordon Setters, and Mastiffs.

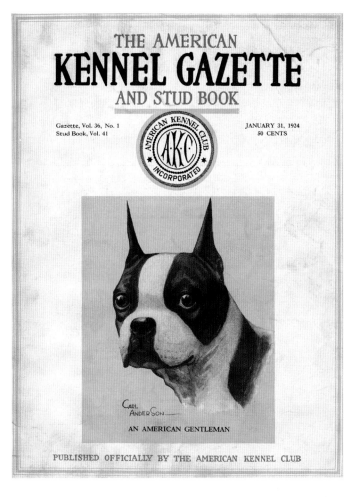

THE AMERICAN
KENNEL GAZETTE
AND STUD BOOK

Gazette, Vol. 36, No. 1
Stud Book, Vol. 41

JANUARY 31, 1924
50 CENTS

AN AMERICAN GENTLEMAN

PUBLISHED OFFICIALLY BY THE AMERICAN KENNEL CLUB

both in the past and since the adoption of the plan of publishing this *Gazette*.

Cover of the *Gazette*, January 1924, featuring the Boston Terrier.

It is proposed to afford the Kennel Club and its individual members an official medium for the publication of all proceedings and announcements bearing upon any subject embraced by the interests of the Kennel World, and to keep and publish a complete and official record of all that transpires during the year, either in connection with shows, Field Trials or matters affecting the breeding, kennel or field management of any known breed of dogs.

The new magazine had a trim size approximating today's *Gazette*, but did not carry the editorial material that has since become an important feature. In fact, there was neither an editorial nor illustrations, and the first issue had only twenty pages, but the *Gazette* slowly expanded. James Watson, an established writer, dog judge, and knowledgeable dog fancier, was appointed the *Gazette's* first editor. Watson gave the magazine a new look and began to include news items and informative articles concerning dogs as well as records of AKC affairs. Since its inception, the magazine has grown steadily in size, circulation, and quality (see Chapter 12).

INTO THE NEW CENTURY

As the sport of purebred dogs continued to gain popularity, the AKC prospered. New clubs came under the AKC's influence, and many older clubs gained in size and prestige. This growth necessitated many changes, and one of these concerned office space. In 1884 the infant group had no permanent office. The September 17, 1884, meeting that resulted in the organization of the AKC had been held in the Philadelphia Kennel Club office, with subsequent meetings held in various other locations—Baltimore, Boston, Cincinnati, Newark, and New York. As steady growth brought in new clubs, additional shows, more registrations, and an ever-expanding volume of records, the need for space grew.

THE FIRST OFFICIAL OFFICES

In 1887, the first official office was opened at 44 Broadway in New York City. It was a small room, but large enough to house the sparse early records and to be a site for Delegates' meetings, since there were fewer than twenty Delegates at that time. The first such meeting was held at this location on March 23, 1887. However, there was no quorum, so the meeting was immediately adjourned. At the next meeting, the treasurer reported a balance of $55.73. In New York City, Delegates' meetings were subsequently held at the Downtown Association on Pine Street, the Hoffman House, the old Madison Square Garden, and the New York Life Building.

By 1895, the sport had grown so much that the AKC required larger quarters, and the offices were moved to 55 Liberty Street, New York City, on May 9. This space was adequate for a few years, but it then became necessary to obtain more floor space. Additional suitable offices were rented at the same address to include separate rooms for the *Stud Book* and *Gazette* activities. At this time, the staff had expanded to nine employees. The first telephone service was installed in 1902. There was considerable discussion about the heavy financial outlay of $75.00 per year before the service was approved!

Top Ten Breeds of the 1890s

Saint Bernards

English Setters

Pointers

Collies

Fox Terriers

Accepted into AKC in 1885, the Saint Bernard swiftly rose to the position of number-one dog of the decade. To this day, the Saint Bernard is the only giant breed to secure the country's top position as well as the only number-one breed to never appear in the top ten again. In later decades, two large German working dogs did get close to the number-one position: the Doberman Pinscher rose to the number-three position in the 1970s, and the Rottweiler to the number-two position in the 1990s. The Great Dane's appearance in the top ten of the 1890s marked its only top-ten ranking in its history.

Cocker Spaniels

Irish Setters

Beagles

Great Danes

Bull Terriers

In 1909, the AKC moved its headquarters to the German-American Insurance Building at 1 Liberty Street, New York City, for a ten-year stay. There was space for a library and a meeting room together with additional rooms for several departments. In 1919, the American Kennel Club moved to 221 Fourth Avenue, later renamed Park Avenue South, where the AKC would have its longest occupancy, a little over forty-four years. The AKC offices were originally on the fifth floor of the building, and in 1928 moved to the twelfth floor of the same building.

In January 1964, with more than 300 employees and the largest canine library in the world, the American Kennel Club moved to the New York Life Building at 51 Madison Avenue, New York, New York where it remained until 1998.

AMERICAN KENNEL CLUB INCORPORATION

In 1889, the matter of incorporation was first introduced, though it was not to be resolved for a number of years.

The AKC was incorporated in 1906, but that was not the beginning of the AKC Board as we now know it. The incorporation marked the beginning of the Delegates' two-year battle against President August Belmont and others. An act of the New York State legislature ended the battle in 1908, as the law at the time did not allow for corporations com-

New Breeds for the 1900s and 1910s

1903	Chow Chow
1904	Boxer, Chihuahua, Schipperke, Standard Schnauzer
1906	Pekingese, Samoyed
1908	Doberman Pinscher, German Shepherd Dog, West Highland White Terrier
1909	English Foxhound, Otterhound
1910	Brussels Griffon, English Springer Spaniel
1911	Sealyham Terrier, Shetland Sheepdog
1912	Belgian Sheepdog
1913	Cairn Terrier, Norwegian Elkhound
1914	Welsh Springer Spaniel
1915	Flat-Coated Retriever, Papillon
1917	Labrador Retriever

posed of individual entities that continued to function as corporations themselves. The Delegates prevailed in their fight against Belmont, and it was the 1908 incorporation that made the AKC into something similar to what we know today.

Under the 1906 bylaws, there would be no more quarterly Delegates' meetings. AKC business would be conducted almost entirely by a thirty-man Board of Directors. The terms of six of the Directors would expire each year, and the Delegates' main function would be to attend the annual meetings to elect people to fill those vacancies. Other than that one function, the Delegates had been stripped of virtually all authority.

Another similar point that has been discussed by the Delegates even in the new millennium is whether Directors no longer have to be chosen from among the Delegates.

Furthermore, if the Board met four times a year, an eight-man Executive Committee was fully empowered to act for the Board between meetings, and half that number constituted a quorum. In short, decisions affecting thousands of fanciers could be made by four individuals!

On May 26, 1908, the AKC was granted articles of incorporation under a special charter from the state of New York. The new constitution and bylaws were published in the June and December 1908 issues of the *Gazette* and were approved in January 1909. The Delegates then adopted the AKC Charter in February 1909. (This Charter appears on page 2 of the AKC booklet labeled *Charter, Constitution and By-Laws*.)

DELEGATES' MEETINGS

During the American Kennel Club's early years, as the Delegate body grew, meetings were held in hotels. However, during the AKC's occupancy of 221 Fourth Avenue, the quarterly Delegates' meetings were held in the American Kennel Club offices. This practice continued until September 1946. After the September 1946 meeting, the quarterly Delegates' meetings, which had grown considerably in size, were again relocated to hotels.

Top Ten Breeds of the 1900s

Collies	The Collie, on a continual climb since its number-seven position in the 1880s, became the number-one breed of the first decade of the new century. The breed ranked in the top ten breeds for seven decades of the 20th century. The number-two breed of the decade, the Boston Terrier, is the first small companion dog to get to this position; the breed would stay in the top three for five decades, peaking at number-one in the 1910s and 1930s.	Cocker Spaniels
Boston Terriers		Bulldogs
English Setters		Airedale Terriers
Bull Terriers		Beagles
Pointers		Irish Terriers

For the December 1946 meeting, Delegates met at the Hotel Commodore in New York City, which remained the site of the Delegates' quarterly meetings until March 1954.

The June 1954 Delegates' meeting found the American Kennel Club at the Roosevelt Hotel, which remained the meeting location until December 1956. In March 1957, the meeting moved to the Hotel Biltmore, where the quarterly meetings remained until June 1981. From September 1981 to June 1988, meetings were again held at the Roosevelt Hotel. After June of 1988, the Delegates' quarterly meetings were moved to the Marriott Marquis. After that, meetings were variously held at the Hyatt, the Sheraton, and the Crown Plaza. Regardless of the hotel, the meetings were always held in New York City until the 1990s when some meetings were held in other cities.

MEMBERSHIPS

The American Kennel Club was primarily formed as a "Club of clubs," and working agreements with foreign kennel clubs, including the Canadian Kennel Club, began as early as 1889. Although there was also a time when individuals held associate memberships, after 1923 only clubs could become members of the AKC.

In 1891, a technical problem arose when the American Bull Ter-

---

Top Ten Breeds of the 1910s

Boston Terriers	The Boston Terrier, a top-ten breed for six decades of the 20th century, remains the only "made in the U.S.A." breed to reach the number-one position, a feat the breed accomplished twice. The Airedale Terrier reached the number-two position, the highest the breed would ever claim, appearing in the top ten for three consecutive decades and then never regaining its national popularity. The decade also marked the French Bulldog's only jaunt into the top ten. Recognized by the AKC in 1906, the Pekingese makes its first appearance in the top ten and would remain on the list for six consecutive decades.	French Bulldogs
Airedale Terriers		English Setters
Collies		Cocker Spaniels
Beagles		Pekingese
Bulldogs		Bull Terriers

rier Club applied for membership in the AKC, at the same time requesting recognition of the breed. The matter was tabled while an investigation was held to determine whether there was such a breed. Initially, with the request

This agile, high-flying Bloodhound performing in an Obedience Trial shatters expectations of what this heavy scenthound is capable.

for breed recognition, the alternative name of Boston Terrier had been submitted, and the breed was finally recognized under the name of Boston Terrier in 1893.

The associate membership category, which consisted of individuals rather than clubs, also caused problems. Associate members were thorns in the side of the organization, continually making suggestions and requests, often of a strictly local nature. In the 1890s, a suggestion for a clubhouse was broached by this group, but rejected. One of the most unusual proposals concerned the possibility of erecting dog kennels in New York City's Central Park. In 1923, AKC associate membership was finally eliminated.

RULES, POWER, AND PRACTICES

Several interesting practices surfaced around the turn of the century. For example, the Secretary had the power to approve or disapprove both the shows and the rules under which they were held. He had sweeping powers and the authority to decide whether or not a breed would be able to offer Winners Classes, called Open Classes at that time. In addition, it was not unusual for a breed with a small number of registrations to be relegated to the Miscellaneous Class instead of one of the breed Groups. During this same general period, many

Miscellaneous Class History

The Miscellaneous Class was created to accommodate foreign breeds and recognized breeds with entries too low to warrant separate classes, usually fewer than five dogs. Show-giving clubs were not required to offer classes for every breed, and regular classes were designated arbitrarily based on entry size and breed popularity. It was not unusual for some breeds to be in the Miscellaneous Class at one show and a Regular Class at the next.

Although the Miscellaneous Class was intended for rare and unrecognized breeds, in the early days Miscellaneous became a catchall class for hybrid types, mixed breeds, and canine oddities because AKC registration numbers were not required to enter shows.

In 1898, AKC revised regulations stated: "The Miscellaneous Class shall be open to all dogs of established breeds for which no regular class has been provided in the premium list. Entries in this class must specify the breed of the exhibit. Failure to comply with this condition shall disqualify the dog and cancel the award."

In 1905, the AKC restricted the Miscellaneous Class to breeds that were eligible for registration.

Rules did not prevent the practice of entering recognized breeds in Miscellaneous rather than the Regular Classes designated in the premium list. Since Miscellaneous winners could earn championship points and advance to the next round of competition, it was sometimes used to circumvent competition in the Regular Classes.

In 1924, the AKC again revised the rules to exclude Miscellaneous Class winners from further competition.

In 1955, the Miscellaneous Class was further restricted to specific AKC-approved breeds in the process of seeking recognition.

of the smaller events were termed "ribbon shows," which closely approximated today's sanctioned events. Fanciers complained about these practices, but it was some time before the Secretary's powers were curtailed.

In 1895, a critical situation arose on the West Coast, where clubs were becoming dissatisfied with their position within the sport. The distance between the West Coast and the New York City headquarters made communications very difficult. In an attempt to alleviate such problems before they got out of hand, Secretary-Treasurer Vredenburgh went to the West Coast in 1895 to discuss problems with club representatives in that area. The trip was quite productive and resulted in the formation of the Pacific Advisory Committee (PAC) in 1896. This committee was to act as an intermediary between the AKC and groups in the western United States.

This move proved effective for a time, but problems continued to surface, culminating in the formation of a short-lived rival kennel club, the Pacific Coast Kennel Club. This organization quickly recruited some ten clubs, suggesting that the situation had become sufficiently critical to send Vredenburgh on another trip. It was finally decided to permit West Coast clubs to elect their own advisory committee rather than have it appointed in New York, as had been the practice. This helped, but it did not eliminate all of the problems. In 1911, the Oakland (Calif.) club held a show under antagonistic rules the same day that an AKC event was held by the Golden Gate Kennel Club in San Francisco. This resulted in suspension of the Oakland club and its officers, although they were subsequently reinstated.

By 1913, the problems had grown more numerous. The PAC continually requested deviations from the rules to reduce the cost of events on the West Coast. The AKC consistently refused to grant such deviations. With no solution in sight, members of the PAC resigned in 1913, effectively eliminating that committee. In its stead, the AKC appointed a Trial Board together with a West Coast agent. This action was met with mixed feelings but accepted by the majority of clubs and fanciers.

The situation on the West Coast reached a climax in 1914, when the San Jose Kennel Club was disqualified for holding a show under the rules of a new group, the National Dog Breeders Association, which failed shortly after its inception. However, problems on the West Coast did eventually subside as modes of travel and telephone service improved.

EARLY SHOWS

Other matters of national importance also required attention, one of the most urgent involving guidelines for championship requirements. Then, as now, the making of a champion was of substantial importance, and the establishment of procedures required much study and time. Early American shows followed procedures for championship titles similar to those in England at the time, requiring three first-place wins in the Open Class, which was generally divided by sex. Several changes had been made by 1900, and the following point schedule for all-breed shows emerged, based upon the total number of dogs at the show:

fewer than 250 dogs	1 point
250 to 499 dogs	2 points
500 to 749 dogs	3 points
750 to 999 dogs	4 points
1,000 dogs and more	5 points

The schedule applied to the entire show, so the number of dogs in each breed did not matter.

All Member Club Specialty Shows were rated four points, while non-member Club Specialties were given a two-point rating, regardless of the entry size. Obviously, the system had inequities. For example, at an all-breed show with more than 1,000 dogs, a dog in a breed with few dogs entered could earn five points because of the size of the overall show entry. The same dog could defeat a relatively large breed entry at a small event—fewer than 250 dogs—and win only one point. In all instances, regardless of show or entry, an accumulation of ten points was required for a championship.

Beginning in 1904, other suggestions emerged when an attempt was made to rate shows according to the prize money offered as follows:

$2,000 in Regular Classes:	1 point
$2,500 in Regular Classes:	2 points
$3,000 in Regular Classes:	3 points
$4,000 in Regular Classes:	4 points
$5,000 in Regular Classes:	5 points

The top prize, $5,000, is valued at roughly $100,000 in contemporary dollars.

Additionally, all Specialty Shows would be automatically rated four points, and shows held on the Pacific Coast would be rated at one-half the monies in the aforementioned schedule. This proposal, while never put into effect, raises some interesting points. First, the prize monies were obviously of greater importance at that time than they were later; second, West Coast affairs were generally smaller in entry, probably because of the distance involved.

RULE CHANGES

Approximately about 1909, championship requirements were changed so that fifteen points were required, and these points had to be won under three different judges.

The year 1909 also marked the addition of Trial Boards. Until then, the AKC Board of Directors heard all controversies, settled all disputes, and levied all fines and penalties for rule infractions. Trial Boards were established to hear and rule on complaints and controversies, to levy fines, and to take care of other such business. Concurrent with this action, rules governing Superintendents were established. Until this time, anyone could assume the role—a judge, a handler, a dealer—in fact, anyone who was in good standing with the AKC. The new rule decreed that anyone serving in the capacity of Superintendent, Show Secretary, or Show Veterinarian was prohibited from exhibiting or judging at the same show.

Many other rules governing dog shows came under scrutiny. Non-member Specialty Clubs now had to obtain permission from the breed's Parent Club before giving a show. Another change concerned dog show classes—an American-Bred Class was substituted for the relatively new Graduate Class. This new class was for dogs bred and whelped in the United States and became effective on January 1, 1910.

Pacific Coast shows were originally given a lower point rating than eastern events because of the generally smaller entries at shows in the West. However, this changed in 1910. The new policy provided that all shows west of the eastern borders of Montana, Wyoming, Colorado, and New Mexico under the jurisdiction of the Pacific Advisory Council would be rated as follows:

fewer than 100 dogs: 1 point
fewer than 200 dogs: 2 points
fewer than 300 dogs: 3 points
fewer than 400 dogs: 4 points
400 dogs and more: 5 points

Show officials George Thomas and James Mortimer looking over the Wire Fox Terriers at an early dog show. Spratt's supplied the benching with straw bedding.

These new ratings were extremely helpful in building interest in the West, where the purebred dog fancy had long been hampered by rules formed for East Coast shows. Shows held by Non-member Specialty Clubs could not be rated more than two points regardless of their overall entry. Member Specialty Club shows had a four-point rating. Why this difference was applied is unclear, but it surely placed an unfair restriction on non-member Clubs.

In 1911, a rule concerning territory was created. In large cities, there was a trend toward the development of several clubs, often formed by dissident groups. The first established club had no protection if other clubs endeavored to hold a show that might be in conflict. The new rule gave sole privilege to the Member Club that had held the first show in a given area. No other event could gain show approval in the same area without first obtaining permission from the established club. However, if the existing Member Club failed to hold a show within a period of eighteen months, a show could be approved for another club without permission from the Member Club. In addition, if the Member Club failed to hold a show within twelve months of the show held by the newly

Licensed Club, an application for AKC membership from the new club would be accepted without the consent of the older existing club. This rule prevented inactive Member Clubs from selfishly holding a territory and offered other clubs the opportunity to develop.

CLASSES OFFERED

Judging procedures have undergone an amazing metamorphosis over the years. In the early days, most shows did not offer a Best in Show award. In any case, there was no official award. Actually, there was no such competition unless a trophy was offered, which made the judging necessary.

The first Best in Show award went to an imported White Bull Terrier named Count at the Western Connecticut Poultry, Pigeon, and Pet Stock Association Show in 1885. It was not unusual for awards to be offered for both Best Dog in Show and Best Bitch in Show. These awards could go to exhibits that were not in the breed competition but were entered in the unclassified Specials Class.

The Specials Class included dogs of several breeds not entered in the classes, and entries often reached seventy or eighty at some large events. This class was not even noted in many early catalogs. The number of judges for the class varied with the time period. For example, at Westminster in 1921, two judges and a referee were listed. The referee was to be used to break a tie between the two judges if necessary.

In its first thirty years, the American Kennel Club established itself as the preeminent American organization with regard to purebred dogs and dog shows. As the AKC approached the 1920s, it was found to be a club with a firm foundation and the proven ability to weather adversities and administer a body of rules that served its membership and the interests of purebred dogs.

Julian Alden Weir's *Words of Comfort*, 1887, given to The AKC Museum of the Dog by the estate of Claire L. Formidoni in memory of Jean Lemoine Formidoni. Depicted in the painting is a tender moment between a Bulldog and a Bloodhound.

THE 1920S

The pattern of dog shows in America changed greatly during the 1920s. Previously, shows had been conducted with little guidance from the AKC, and there was little standardization in the procedures for holding shows. It was not until well into the 1920s that standardized procedures began to emerge. It became apparent that uniform rules, applied equally to all dog clubs, were necessary if the sport were to prosper. As travel conditions improved and fanciers began to attend shows outside their immediate geographic areas, loose national control by more than one dog club proved inadequate.

In 1920, the AKC began Sanctioned Matches, which provided useful training grounds for more formal events, and they made dog owners more aware of correct show procedures. In 1923, after a great deal of study and discussion, the AKC initiated a nationwide remedial program. A committee of Directors was appointed to study the rules and to recommend changes. The existing rules did not enable the AKC to cope with problems that surfaced as show activity increased. At one time, for example, a dog defeated in the Breed Classes could, under certain circumstances, be eligible to enter the competition for Best Dog in Show. Surely this created an undesirable situation.

GROUPS ARE BORN

The Stud Book used two breed divisions in volumes 4, 5, 6, and 7, one for Sporting Dogs and one for Non-Sporting Dogs. Later editions, from 1891 to 1914, reverted to strict alphabetical order. Then, in 1915, two divisions appeared again.

The aforementioned committee of Directors offered a number of recommendations, particularly with respect to show rules and judging procedures. One of the most important recommendations concerned the overall structure of dog shows, which entailed separating the breeds into five Variety Groups. Entrants in each breed would compete for Best of Breed. The Best of Breed winners for the breeds in each Group would then compete for Best in Group. The five Group winners would then meet to vie for Best in Show. The dog

Sporting or Non-Sporting

At the turn of the century, some show catalogs began by grouping breeds into Sporting and Non-Sporting, and difficulties soon arose. In the April 1901 *Gazette*, Gustav Muss-Arnolt, the well-known artist, wrote a letter asking the AKC to address the problem, since a dog had been entered as Non-Sporting in one show and as Sporting in another.

RIGHT: An excerpt from the April 1901 *Gazette* letter from Gustav Muss-Arnolt.

SPORTING AND NON-SPORTING DIVISION.

March 15, 1901.

Editor American Kennel Gazette:

Dear sir: A question came up at the late Duquesne Kennel Club show, which I think should be taken up and decided once for all by the American Kennel Club, viz.: What is a sporting breed and what is non-sporting?

At said show it was left to the secretary to decide this knotty point, and, without any prejudice to this venerable officer, I think it a very unlucky way. Said official, for reasons of his own, put bloodhounds and dachshunde in the non-sporting division, forsooth! I thought, why for? If hounds are sporting dogs, why, the "prototype" of them, the bloodhound, is not in the same designated as Best in Show had then defeated all other entrants. This was the beginning of the present Group system. The five Group divisions were:

Group 1: Sporting breeds (including all Pointing breeds, Retrievers, and Spaniels as well as all Hounds)
Group 2: Working breeds (including all Working and Herding breeds)
Group 3: Terrier breeds
Group 4: Toy breeds
Group 5: Non-Sporting breeds

By 1924, the new Group system was in use across the country. Exhibitors liked the new format, as it offered standardized competition that made major awards more meaningful.

The Westminster Kennel Club was the first to include Best in Show under the new format. Ch. Barberryhill Bootlegger, a Sealyham Terrier owned by Bayard Warren, captured the award. A full review of the new show procedure, "What the New Rules Mean," by John F. Collins, appeared in the January 1924 *American Kennel Gazette.* The new rules had many virtues, the most

Group Evolution

The earliest dog shows offered classes for only Pointers and Setters, and the AKC originally provided only two group classifications: Pointers, Setters, Spaniels, Foxhounds, and Beagles were designated as Sporting breeds; all other breeds were classed as Non-Sporting.

In 1924, the AKC created three new groups. Terriers were separated from the Sporting breeds. Toys and Working breeds were separated from the Non-Sporting Group.

After 1924, only one dog representing each breed or variety could advance to Group competition. In 1927, a standardized format was instituted for show catalogs categorizing all breeds into these designated Groups and listing them in alphabetical order.

In 1930, the Sporting Group was further divided separating the Gundog breeds from Sporting Hounds. In 1937, the name Sporting Group (Hounds) was shortened to Hound Group. In 1983, the Working Group was subdivided to create the Herding Group.

The First "Official" Best in Show Winners

In 1924, the AKC put into effect the basic rules for Best in Show competition that are still in place today. Prior to 1924 "Best in Show" could be awarded in a more haphazard fashion, sometimes to dogs that had been defeated—or had not even competed—in the Breed competition on that day.

There were 154 AKC all-breed shows in 1924, but the *American Kennel Gazette* reports a Best in Show winner from only 72 of those, so the names of some early winners may be forever lost to history. (Some shows, of course, may not have organized a BIS competition at all.)

The first "official" Best in Show recorded was at Westminster Kennel Club, held over three days on February 12–14 that year: the Sealyham Terrier Ch. Barberryhill Bootlegger, owned by Bayard Warren. Wire Fox Terriers were by far the top show breed in those

The cover of the *The American Kennel Gazette* for February 1924, featuring Ch. Barberryhill Bootlegger, following his victory at Westminster Kennel Club, the first "official" Best in Show winner.

days, with 20 wins recorded that first year, and the most successful of them that year was Ch. Chappaqua Wrangler's Peggy, who is credited with six BIS wins: at Middlesex County Kennel Club, Providence County Kennel Club,

Sealyham Terrier Ch. Barberryhill Bootlegger, painted by American artist William Schnelle, circa 1924, part of the AKC Collection.

Queensboro Kennel Club, Nassau County Kennel Club, Huntingdon Valley Kennel Club and Westbury Kennel Association. Most of these clubs are still alive and flourishing today.

The only other dog credited with more than two BIS that year was the famous Greyhound Ch. Rosemont Liskeard Fortunatus, who won at the Kennel Club of Philadelphia, at the Ladies Kennel Association and at Del High Kennel Club in Pennsylvania. He went on to win even more in the following three years and had also been successful during the "pre-official" period before 1924.

Obviously most of the activity was centered in the Eastern states in those days, but AKC shows were held across the country. There even were what could be called "circuits"—e.g., the Illinois Valley Kennel Club held its show on March 25–26, the Chicago Kennel Club on March 27–29, and the Milwaukee Kennel Club on March 30–31. There were at least ten shows in California, including one hosted by the Hollywood Kennel Club and another by the Los Angeles Kennel Club; and there were shows in Texas, Florida, Nebraska, Kansas, and Georgia.

Following are some dogs that won their breed's first officially recorded Best in Show win in 1924:

BREED	NAME	SHOW	DATE
Borzoi	Prince Boris III	Willamette Valley Kennel Club	09/24/24
Boston Terrier	Ch. Kuettel's Little Sir Thomas	Fresno Kennel Club	10/04/24
Cairn Terrier	Dochfour Oliver	Englewood Kennel Club	10/04/24
Cocker Spaniel (Black)	Princess Marie	North Westchester Kennel Club	06/26/24
Doberman Pinscher	Eido vom Stresow	Detroit Kennel Club	04/03/24
English Setter	Willowbrook Bluebird	Lynnfield Kennel Club	09/20/24
German Shepherd Dog	Ch. Etzel v.d. Ettersburg		03/26/24
Greyhound	Ch. Rosemont Liskeard Fortunatus	Kennel Club of Philadelphia	04/12/24
Irish Setter	Modoc Chief	Nebraska Kennel Club	09/04/24
Old English Sheepdog	Tenacre Grenadier	Southampton Kennel Club	08/23/24
Pomeranian	Minegold Mamorn	Oakland Kennel Club	08/17/24
Scottish Terrier	Bentley Cotsol Lassie	Paterson Kennel Club	09/20/24
Sealyham Terrier	Ch. Barberryhill Bootlegger	Westminster Kennel Club	02/14/24
Smooth Fox Terrier	Ch. Self Renown	Texas Kennel Club	10/26/24
Whippet	Sloe Eyes	Los Angeles Kennel Club	12/13/24
Wire Fox Terrier	Welwire Barrington Bridegroom	Eastern Dog Club	02/24/24

important being that the dog judged Best in Show had defeated all other competitors, as is the case today.

It should be pointed out that the new format was not mandatory, and any club could elect to forgo any competition after Best of Breed if this were advertised in advance. For example, for many years the Saw Mill River Kennel Club ended all judging after Best of Breed/Variety until 1987, when the club resumed Group and Best in Show competition.

JUDGING REQUIREMENTS

The new rules seemed to encourage many more individuals to begin judging. This was due in part to the new uniformity in procedure. In any event, the May 1925 issue of the *American Kennel Gazette* carried a License Committee notice concerning the requirements for a judging license. These requirements were the result of several years' study concerning the proper procedures for screening judging applicants. This considerably reduced the number of new multibreed and all-breed licenses gained in preceding years, when there were few restrictions.

The committee suggested that each Variety Group be judged by the judge or judges who had evaluated the largest number of breeds in that Group during the Breed Classes. For Best in Show, the judge(s) had to be selected from among the Variety Group judges. These suggestions, however, have long since been dropped.

Until the early 1920s, unless prizes were offered for Best in Group or Best in Show, there was no competition at those levels. However, when such prizes were available, multiple judges officiated, sometimes as many as six.

Sealyham Terrier, Ch. Pinegrade Perfection.

In order to avoid ties, it became customary to have an odd number of judges. By 1917, the number was limited to five.

The License Committee, whose duty it was to approve judges and shows, was dissatisfied with having so many judges. These men felt that when three or more judges were involved, there was always the possibility that each would have a favorite. Thus, the winner could be determined by compromise or by the most persuasive judge rather than by merit. Basically, the committee felt that judging dogs was such a subjective matter that it was virtually impossible for three or more judges to agree totally about any single animal.

In May 1930, the Delegates approved the License Committee's recommendations, and the responsibilities of selecting winners in Breed, Group, and Best in Show competition were placed with individual judges who were selected by the show-giving club.

Drawing of the Best in Show presentation at the AKC Sesquicentennial Show, Philadelphia, 1926. Mayor W. Freeland Kendrick, of Philadelphia, presenting the Best in Show trophy to the Sealyham Terrier, Ch. Pinegrade Perfection, handled by Percy Roberts. The drawing was by B. Laurence Megargee, brother of the famous artist Edwin Megargee.

THE SESQUICENTENNIAL SHOW

In 1926, the AKC felt that the fancy should participate in the celebration of the nation's sesquicentennial (1776–1926). For the first time, the AKC sponsored its own show. The 1926 show, known as the Sesquicentennial (or Sesqui) Show, was held in Philadelphia from September 30 through October 2, 1926. It was a huge success and had a lasting effect on the public.

There were five Groups and thirty-one judges at this show. The prizes were numerous, including a specially designed gold medal offered by the Sesquicentennial International Exposition to every Best of Breed/Variety winner. The American Kennel Club itself offered solid gold medals to every Winners Dog and Winners Bitch and sterling silver medals to every Reserve Winner. In addition to these unique prizes, money was offered in all Breeds/Varieties—twenty dollars for first place, ten dollars for second place, and five dollars for third place in all Regular Classes. Each of the five Groups offered cash prizes of fifty, thirty, and twenty dollars for First, Second, and Third places, respectively. Sterling silver Best in Show trophies were offered by The Kennel Club (England) and by the dog-food company Spratts. The generous trophy list attracted an entry of 2,899 contestants.

The judging panel included some of the most respected arbiters in the country. A complete and informative biographical article on these judges appeared in the August 1926 issue of the *American Kennel Gazette*.

Best in Show at the Sesquicentennial extravaganza was captured by the Sealyham Terrier Ch. Pinegrade Perfection, an imported bitch owned by Frederick C. Brown and handled by Percy Roberts. Interestingly, Mr. Roberts had two dogs eligible for the Terrier Group competition. He opted to handle the other one, and sent in the Sealyham Terrier with Eland Hadfield. The judges saw it differently, however, and placed the Sealyham First in the Group. Roberts, of course, handled the bitch for Best in Show.

The top entry was 164 Wire Fox Terriers (there were also 48 Smooths), followed by 139 Shepherd Dogs, 117 Boston Terriers, 89 Pekingese, 82 Bulldogs, 75 in both Cocker Spaniels and Pointers, 71 English Setters, and 68 Airedale Terriers. These numbers give an idea of breed popularity at that time. (Note: *German* had been deleted from the

---

Top Ten Breeds of the 1920s

German Shepherd Dogs	Accepted in 1908, the German Shepherd Dog overtook the Boston Terrier in 1925 and became the number-one dog of the 1920s. The breed then disappeared from the top ten until after World War II, when it reemerged as the number-six dog of the 1950s and has remained in the top four breeds of the decade until the present day. The 1920s also saw the Chow Chow as its number-three breed, the highest ranking the breed would ever achieve.	Collies
Boston Terriers		Beagles
Chow Chows		Airedale Terriers
Pekingese		Cocker Spaniels
Fox Terriers (Wire)		Bulldogs

German Shepherd Dog's name during World War I and was restored at a later date. Cocker Spaniels were not separated into American Cockers and English Cockers until 1946.)

MORE CHANGES

The Sesquicentennial Show was an unqualified success and also gave purebred dogs tremendous positive publicity. However, the limits on the number of judges had not yet been imposed, and using three judges for each Group and five judges for Best in Show was an expense that few events could carry. Additionally, the restrictions placed upon judges limited those who applied to judge additional breeds and expand their licenses. For these reasons, the format was changed after this show, and in the December 1926 *Gazette*, a notice appeared that relaxed the requirements for a judging license and allowed anyone in good standing with the AKC to judge. The edict also barred persons who were commercially connected with dog-related products from judging.

Among other changes made during the late 1920s was the Board's decision to expand the number of Groups from five to six. The new Group 2 was created to include all of the Hound breeds that had been previously classified in Group 1 with the Sporting Breeds. These breeds, which had been referred to as Sporting Breeds (Hounds), were now referred to as Hounds. Group 1, the Sporting Group, continued to embrace Setters, Pointers, Spaniels, and Retrievers. The remaining Group divisions were renumbered: Working (Group 3), Terrier (Group 4), Toy (Group 5), and Non-Sporting (Group 6).

In May 1927, the AKC tried to direct more attention to American-bred dogs by offering special incentives, announcing that it would offer a fifty-dollar cash award for Best in Show, if American bred, at all Member Club events. This incentive was limited to one year and did much toward expanding interest in American-bred dogs.

The recurring complaint against ear cropping was also raised during this period. England had outlawed the practice, and the English press had arguments for and against it. The American Kennel Club Rules Committee aired the matter at a Delegates' meeting. After a lengthy discussion, it was decided that no further action would be taken on ear cropping.

The first edition of *Pure-Bred Dogs, The Breeds and Standards as Recognized by The American Kennel Club* came in 1929 in the form of a hardbound book. In 1938, the book was renamed *The Complete Dog Book*.

Edwin Megargee's *Ch. Flornell Checkmate*, 1940, given to The AKC Museum of the Dog by Mr. and Mrs. James A. Farrell, Jr., of Greenwich, Connecticut. Whelped in England in 1938, Checkmate was expertly handled in the show ring by one of the fancy's greatest handlers, Percy Roberts, himself a British import.

THE 1930s

Although the country suffered through the Great Depression, registration figures and interest in dogs and dog shows grew. The number of recognized breeds increased from 83 in 1930 to 105 in 1940. The first AKC Obedience Trials were held, and AKC Field Trials grew in popularity. In 1935, the one-millionth dog was registered in the records of the AKC Stud Book.

PROFESSIONAL HANDLERS

The practice of securing the services of a professional handler is as old as the sport of purebred dogs in the United States. In 1926, a group of professional handlers formed the Professional Handlers' Association (PHA), whose purpose was to support the handlers' general interests and standards of conduct. The association's first real assembly took place in November 1926 in connection with the American Kennel Club Sesquicentennial Show in Philadelphia. Members elected Leonard Brumby, Sr., who later became the AKC's first full-time Field Representative, as the first PHA President. The association grew and prospered. Many years later, the Dog Handlers Guild (DHG) was formed; it also garnered a substantial national membership.

The one millionth dog registered, a Shetland Sheepdog. Russell H. Johnson, then president of the American Kennel Club, presents a framed certificate commemorating the milestone.

In 1930, the American Kennel Club began requiring licenses of all persons who charged for dog-handling services. The AKC established criteria under which handlers were granted a license to engage in their profession at American Kennel Club dog shows. The AKC rule for licensing, which had been adopted at the September 1929 Delegates' meeting, stated: "No person shall be eligible to handle dogs for pay or

New Breeds for the 1930s

Affenpinscher	Bouvier des	German	Lakeland Terrier
Alaskan	Flandres	Shorthaired	Lhasa Apso
Malamute	Brittany *(registered*	Pointer	Norwich Terrier
American	*as Brittany Spaniel*	Giant Schnauzer	Pembroke Welsh
Staffordshire	*until 1982)*	Great Pyrenees	Corgi
Terrier	Bullmastiff	Keeshond	Puli
Bernese	Cardigan Welsh	Komondor	Rottweiler
Mountain Dog	Corgi	Kuvasz	Siberian Husky
Border Terrier			

act as an agent for pay at any show held under American Kennel Club Rules unless he shall hold a license granted by the said Club through its License Committee." This rule was made effective ninety days from the date of the meeting.

The License Committee subsequently established fees for handlers' licenses: for public handlers, the initial fee was fifteen dollars and the annual renewal fee was five dollars; for private handlers, ten dollars and five dollars; and for assistant handlers, five dollars and two dollars. In 1954, the fees for obtaining a license and renewal were eliminated.

The first handler's license was issued to Harold Correll. A list of the first twenty-six public handlers licensed by the American Kennel Club was published in the January 1930 issue of the *American Kennel Gazette*. Thereafter, the AKC

Established in the 1930s, Junior Handling remains a popular sport for young people. This well-dressed young man is stacking his Akita at an outdoor show.

periodically published a complete alphabetical list of licensed handlers. In 1931, at the request of the PHA, the AKC issued a directive to all clubs, stating that handlers were to be given admission to any AKC show upon presentation of the license card.

Over the years, professional handlers have played an important part in the history of the sport of dogs. They have provided the support system for the top show dogs in many breeds. Expertise in the care, conditioning, and presentation of show dogs comes only through years of dedication, hard work, and continuing education.

JUNIOR HANDLING

Another important activity that began in the 1930s was the Children's Handling Class, first held in 1932 at the Westbury Kennel Association Show. The idea of involving children in dog shows came to the forefront in the late 1920s, when dog showing was still considered to be strictly a wealthy man's sport. Children who accompanied their parents to shows

similar to that of the modern AKC booklet *Rules Applying to Registration and Dog Shows*.

An amendment dealing with the registration of litters was adopted at the December 1933 Delegates' meeting:

> All litters of dogs eligible for registration and whelped in the United States of America on or before January 1, 1932, must be registered by their breeders, owners, or lessees of the dam at the date of whelping and no single dog from any such litter will be otherwise eligible for registration. A single dog of a registered litter can be registered only by the breeder, owner of sire, owner or lessee of dam at date of whelping … No dog of such registered litter shall be eligible for exhibition until it has been registered or listed in the usual manner.

This amendment was significant because it required a statement of the number of puppies in a litter and the sex of the puppies; subsequent individual registration of the "get" was limited in number and sex to those noted on the litter registration. The registration required the signatures of the owners of both the sire and the dam. This rule is still in effect today, and it did much to eliminate dishonest practices while greatly improving the validity of the *Stud Book*.

Best American-Bred in Show

In 1927, the AKC instituted policies to encourage the exhibition of American-bred dogs, starting with fifty-dollar awards to American-bred BIS winners. In 1934, to commemorate the AKC's fiftieth anniversary, this concept was expanded. American-bred Group winners received twenty-five-dollar awards and the top-winning American-bred dog of the year received two hundred and fifty dollars. These cash prizes were awarded until 1939. AKC rules permitted clubs to award Best-American Bred in Show from 1935–1939.

AMERICAN-BRED COMPETITION

In 1935, the AKC created nationwide competition that emphasized the importance of American-bred dogs. Each year, an American-bred representative of each Group was selected based upon total Group triumphs during the year.

The effort to determine these winners generated tremendous competition among wealthy exhibitors, who journeyed to all sections of the country, often on chartered airplane flights. This situation all but eliminated dogs owned by people of more modest means. The publicity generated by

Winners of the American-Bred Group awards for 1938: Left to right: Ed Sayres, Jr., with Kerry Blue Terrier Ch. Bumble Bee of Delwin, Geraldine Rockefeller Dodge with German Shepherd Dog Ch. Giralda's Geisha, Hayes Blake Hoyt with Standard Poodle Ch. Blakeen Jung Frau, H. E. Mellenthin with Cocker Spaniel Ch. My Own Brucie, John Royce with Pekingese Ch. Kai Lo of Dahlyn, and Hans Sacher with Smooth Dachshund Ch. Herman Rinkton.

the American-bred competition was generally unfavorable, and 1939 was the last year of such competition.

BREEDS AND VARIETIES

During the 1930s, there was a change concerning breeds with Varieties, such as Fox Terriers. The rule stated that Variety winners within a breed should compete for a single Best of Breed. This reduced the number of breed representatives in the Group and caused considerable controversy among exhibitors. Even so, Fox Terriers were not recognized as two separate breeds until 1985, 100 years after the Parent Club was founded and the Breed Standard was adopted.

In 1953, all Variety winners were again permitted in the Group and at all-breed shows; Best of Breed was eliminated in breeds with Varieties. This increased the number of Varieties, so breeds gained additional representation in the Group. For example, Cocker Spaniels had had only one representative in the Group in 1937, but by 1943 there were three: Solid Color, Parti-Color, and English type. One year later, there were four Cockers in the Group, Black (including black and tan), Parti-Color, the newly established Any Solid Color Other than Black (ASCOB), and the English type. In 1946, the English type was designated a separate breed as the English Cocker Spaniel and Cockers Spaniels were once again represented by three Varieties: Black, Parti-Color, and ASCOB, as they remain today. The aforementioned rule change in 1953 caused several breeds to install Varieties where possible, thereby increasing the number of dogs eligible to compete in the Group. The last breed to be permitted to establish varieties was the Chihuahua in 1952.

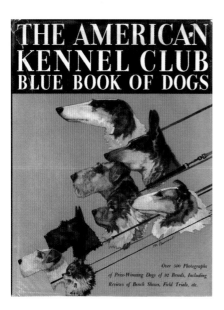

The American Kennel Club Blue Book, published in 1938.

THE BLUE BOOK

In 1938, the American Kennel Club published its first and last strictly commercial book, *The American Kennel Club Blue Book*. This book carried advertising from a host of the country's top kennels, including many of those whose dogs had captured the 1937 American-bred awards. The *Blue Book* included references to all phases of canine activity under the AKC at that time. In addition, the *Blue Book* offered a chapter on Greyhound racing, with emphasis on AKC-registered dogs, together with Field Trial and Obedience sections that included such information as the listings of 1937 winners. Since inclusion was generally dependent on the purchase of an advertisement, many worthy dogs were omitted.

THE LIBRARY

The AKC established a library at its April 1934 Board of Directors meeting. A Library Committee was formed to supervise the operation, with Hubert Brown as Chair. Brown was assisted by William Cary Duncan (a Director), Louis de Casanova (*Gazette* editor), Edwin Megargee (a widely known artist and fancier), and James W. Spring (AKC counsel). The library continued under the committee's supervision until 1958. The first full-time Librarian was appointed in 1937. The library grew tremendously during her term and after her retirement continued under the supervision of several well-schooled librarians. The AKC Library is considered to be one of the best and most complete on dogs and related subjects in the world (see also Chapter 12).

MORRIS AND ESSEX

An important milestone in dogs and dog shows took place in 1939, when the Morris and Essex Kennel Club enjoyed an all-time record entry at its May show. There were a total of 3,862 dogs on the benches, and all were judged in one day!

Morris and Essex was a most unique event. It was entirely organized and conducted by Geraldine Rockefeller Dodge on her Madison, New

Parent Clubs and Breed Standards

Each AKC-recognized breed must be represented by a national Parent Club, which is responsible for protecting its welfare in multiple capacities. The AKC provides numerous resources to assist with their formation and administration.

In addition to representing the breed's interests regarding AKC policies, Parent Clubs conduct health surveys, fund genetic research, and promote genetic testing to safeguard breed health. Parent Clubs have the authority to petition the AKC to reopen their breeds' stud book in order to enlarge the gene pool to address health issues.

Parent Clubs also devote resources to educating the public, mentoring breeders and judges, managing breed-specific rescue programs, and organizing shows and performance events.

A primary responsibility of each Parent Club is writing and revising an official description of its breed's ideal conformation, temperament, and movement— the Breed Standard. The AKC pro-

vides guidelines and assistance to clubs when formulating and revising their Standards to ensure clarity of content and phrasing. AKC regulations allow Parent Clubs the option of revising their Standards every five years if they determine a need to emphasize goals for improvement or address emerging faults or undesirable extremes of type that may arise as the breed evolves. The process requires multiple rounds of voting and approval from individual club members and the AKC Board of Directors before revisions are accepted.

The AKC publishes all standards in *The Complete Dog Book* and posts them on its Web site, www.akc.org. The AKC also furnishes judges with copies of Standards, illustrated Standards, and relevant educational material to assist them in judging newly recognized breeds.

The AKC Web site includes multiple links to each AKC Parent Club for breeder referrals, rescue, and general information.

Morris & Essex Revival

Mrs. Geraldine R. Dodge founded her Morris and Essex show in 1927, presiding over every detail with painstaking care until 1957. It was celebrated for its picturesque grounds, elegant trappings, and record entries.

Forty-three years later, in 2000, Morris & Essex was revived, along with many of its grand traditions.

The show is held the first Thursday in October near the grounds of Giralda Farms in Madison, New Jersey. The new Morris & Essex, held every five years, is next scheduled for 2010.

Nostalgia and history combine at the revival of the Morris & Essex show, making these very special shows memorable for all who attend.

Colored Bull Terrier Ch. Rocky Tops Sundance Kid, "Rufus," was judge Michele Billings's choice for Best in Show at the 2005 Morris & Essex Kennel Club Show, handled by Kathy Kirk. Also pictured are Dorothy Cherry, one of Rufus's owners, and Ernest Planck, Director, Breeder/Enthusiast Group North America, Nestle Purina PetCare.

Jersey, estate. The first show, held in 1927, had 504 dogs benched. The show grew steadily before reaching the aforementioned peak entry. Best in Show at the 1939 landmark event was the Cocker Spaniel Ch. My Own Brucie, owned by H. E. Mellenthin. Morris and Essex was suspended during the war years, 1942–1945, but resumed in 1946, limited to thirty-two breeds. Breeds were added until seventy-eight of them were represented (by 2,548 entries) at Mrs. Dodge's last show in 1957.

Overview of the original Morris and Essex show.

At the 18th annual Morris and Essex Kennel Club Show, 1948, club president Geraldine R. Dodge, with the esteemed judge Alva Rosenberg, awarding Best in Show to Bedlington Terrier Ch. Rock Ridge Night Rocket, owned by Mr. and Mrs. William A. Rockefeller. The handler was Anthony Neary.

Bernese Mountain Dog judging underway at the first revived Morris & Essex Show in 2000.

The Hon. David Merriam judging the Terrier Group at Morris & Essex show.

Franklin Brooke Voss's *Ch. Nornay Saddler*, given to The AKC Museum of the Dog by the estate of Elsie S. Simmons. An English-bred Smooth Fox Terrier, born in 1940 and imported into the United States at eleven months of age by the Hon. James M. Austin of Old Westbury, New York, Saddler was the perfect show dog, winning fifty-nine BIS awards.

THE 1940S

During the 1940s, the sport of purebred dogs in America was largely shaped by the Second World War. The hostilities that began in Europe in 1939 affected the sport in America via a continuing reduction in the number of imported dogs. After the United States became actively involved in the war, dogs did their part for the war effort. They distinguished themselves through the Dogs for Defense program, performing many heroic deeds in all arenas of action.

Throughout the war years, American dog shows, Field Trials, and breeding activities struggled, but the continuation of these activities, even on a reduced scale, was a triumph of American ingenuity. Dog shows offered relief and relaxation to many in a nation at war. These activities brought a certain sense of normality to participants in this tumultuous time, when daily life was affected by the war.

TIME AND THE WAR

The American Kennel Club's flexible reaction to the difficulties of the war permitted deviations from existing rules, allowing dog clubs to continue functioning. For example, a number of shows would be approved to be held in the same building on consecutive days, using the same equipment. This was necessary to overcome the hardships that resulted from gasoline and tire rationing.

The number of *un*benched shows increased, and geographic restrictions were relaxed. Other adjustments relaxed the strict rules governing time schedules for arriving at and leaving events, enabling exhibitors to conserve gasoline by cooperating with other exhibitors to use the same vehicle. It was not long before all those who wished to exhibit could do so.

Actually, the adversity of the war years proved a blessing in disguise, as it demonstrated that many highly restrictive rules were unnecessary and even undesirable. The new practice of clustering shows resulted in more show-giving clubs, more shows, and more entries. During this period, the AKC sought to increase sanctioned Match activity and in 1947 created a separate booklet of regulations for these events. This initiated many such informal events, which led to the entrance of many new fanciers into the sport.

In the mid-1940s, professional judges formed the Professional Dog Judges' Association, which included many of the top all-breed judges. They wanted greater input on rule changes and other matters affecting them as a group. In 1945, they met with Henry Bixby, AKC Executive Vice-President. The outcome was an experiment offered at the Maryland Kennel Club show held in February 1946.

At this show, the judges commented on the dogs as they judged, but this process was not very well received, as few exhibitors appreciated having their dogs faulted before other judges and exhibitors. The panel for this show included Anton Rost (Judges' Association President), L. J. Murr, E. L. Pickhardt, W. L. Kendrick, Alva Rosenberg, and E. D. McQuown. Best in Show was awarded to Standard Schnauzer Ch. Winalesby Vaaben.

In the late 1940s, for the first time, some two-day Benched Shows judged only three Groups each day. Many other changes were adopted during this period for the convenience of the exhibitor. Before the war, dogs were required to be benched from 10:00 a.m. to 10:00 p.m., a rule

New Breeds for the 1940s

American Water Spaniel
Basenji
Black and Tan Coonhound

English Cocker Spaniel (separated
   from Cocker Spaniel)
Weimaraner

that was strictly enforced. During the war, a 6:00 p.m. excusal time went into effect at most shows so exhibitors could leave earlier. Unbenched Shows were even more convenient, permitting exhibitors to come and go at will. If the rules hadn't changed during the war, two-day Benched Shows with hours from 10:00 a.m. to 10:00 p.m. might have remained the rule rather than the exception.

Dwight D. Eisenhower and Mamie Eisenhower at the Potomac Boxer Club Specialty Show in 1948. John P. Wagner is the judge; Walter Foster has the lead on Merry Monarch and Nate Levine is handling El Wendy.

INNOVATIONS

One important postwar move was the January 1946 appointment of the first full-time Field Representative, Leonard Brumby, Sr. Prior to becoming Executive Vice-President, Henry Bixby had attended some shows in this capacity, but Brumby was the first to serve full time in this position. Field Representatives attended shows and Trials and also observed the actions of exhibitors and judges. This was an attempt to improve the overall quality and operation of all events.

Mr. Brumby's work was well received, and an editorial that appeared in the March 1946 issue of the *Gazette* indicated, "As the Field Representative, Leonard Brumby has already done yeoman service in 'spiking'

The Dogs of War

Those who valiantly served were not only soldiers in uniform. Dogs in service to our country represented many breeds and many functions. Some of our best-known kennels contributed dogs to the war effort in defense of freedom.

ABOVE: This French Bulldog delivered cigarettes to our troops in the trenches. **BELOW:** "Honorably discharged" dogs in 1945. Smooth Fox Terrier "Red" with James Austen and Doberman Pinscher "Baron" with Herbert Byette. **FACING PAGE, top:** The first group of dogs actually inducted into the US Army. These dogs became messengers and sentries and performed countless other tasks after their four-week training course. It is particularly interesting to note the great variety of breeds utilized. In this photo, the six dogs in the foreground are, left, an English Springer Spaniel, a Pointer, and a Doberman Pinscher. On the right, we see an Airedale Terrier, an Irish Setter, and a Siberian Husky. **FACING PAGE, bottom:** Devil Dogs in training. This troop of Doberman Pinschers were specially trained to accompany Marines in landing operations as shown in this practice landing from a Marine barge. **FACING PAGE, inset left:** Chinook Kennels (NH) donated numerous Siberian Huskies during World War II. This dog is carrying a machine gun. **FACING PAGE, inset right:** Technical Sergeant Thomas Gately, USMCR, a well-known professional handler who temporarily gave up showing to train Devil Dogs for the Marines. After the war, he resumed his activity in the sport, eventually becoming a judge.

A meeting of the Professional Dog Judges' Association, November 1945, with Henry D. Bixby, then AKC Executive Vice-President. Standing, left to right: Joseph Burrell, Louis Murr, Dr. Charles McAnulty, and Leon J. Iriberry. Seated: Alva Rosenberg, Anton Rost, Henry D. Bixby, William L. Kendrick, and William F. Meyer.

ringside gossip before it had the chance to grow into the vicious rumor stage and in settling differences of opinion on the spot before they got out of hand." In 1947, Leroy Beardsley became the first Field Trial Field Representative.

The position of Field Representative grew in importance over the years as the sport grew. The Field Representative became the eyes and ears of the American Kennel Club throughout the country, keeping it in touch with the fancy.

The number of AKC Field Representatives increased steadily, especially with the great upsurge in dog show activity between 1970 and 1980. In 1970, there were 569 all-breed shows and 599 Specialty Shows, with a total of 597,170 dogs competing. By 1980, the number of all-breed dog shows had risen to 823 (an increase of 45 percent), the number of Specialty Shows had risen to 1,238 (an increase of 107 percent), and the number of dogs in competition had risen to nearly 950,000 (an increase of 59 percent). By 2000, all-breed shows had risen to 1,415, Specialty Shows to 2,049, and the number of dogs in competiton to over 1,500,000.

Judges and rules relating to them had always been difficult to administer. In October 1947, for the first time, a directory of judges who held permanent licenses was issued, with their names, addresses, and breeds. Prior to this, such information was carried only periodically by the *Gazette*. The directory also included judges who had been approved merely on a temporary basis.

Another new rule allowed prospective judges to gain experience through an Apprentice System. This involved the apprentice's being in the ring and observing the procedures of a licensed judge and possibly examining and discussing selected dogs with the judge, if time permitted. The apprentice judge was then required to inform the AKC about which and how many shows he had observed. After several such assignments, the apprentice was generally approved to judge the selected breeds applied for. Thereafter, apprenticing was not required for additional breeds.

The Apprentice System was in effect for a number of years but was dropped in 1970. It is doubtful if there will ever be a system satisfactory to all for gaining and training new judges, but this subject receives continued attention from the AKC because of its importance.

Around 1950, the Bred-by-Exhibitor Class came into being, and the Limit Class was dropped, confining the entry of imported dogs to the Open Class. Previously, imports could be entered in the Limit Class, which was for all dogs except champions. The Open Class was for all dogs, including imports and champions.

Many procedures and rules were created or revised during the 1940s. The stress of World War II brought about changes and ultimately a body of rules that served the sport of purebred dogs well.

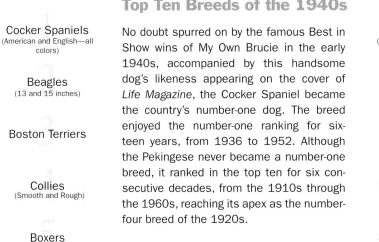

Top Ten Breeds of the 1940s

Cocker Spaniels
(American and English—all colors)

Beagles
(13 and 15 inches)

Boston Terriers

Collies
(Smooth and Rough)

Boxers

No doubt spurred on by the famous Best in Show wins of My Own Brucie in the early 1940s, accompanied by this handsome dog's likeness appearing on the cover of *Life Magazine*, the Cocker Spaniel became the country's number-one dog. The breed enjoyed the number-one ranking for sixteen years, from 1936 to 1952. Although the Pekingese never became a number-one breed, it ranked in the top ten for six consecutive decades, from the 1910s through the 1960s, reaching its apex as the number-four breed of the 1920s.

Dachshunds
(Longhaired, Smooth and Wirehaired)

Pekingese

Fox Terriers
(Smooth)

English Springer Spaniels

Scottish Terriers

T. Tashira's *Ch. Bang Away of Sirrah Crest*, 1957, given to the AKC Collection by the great champion's owners Dr. and Mrs. R.C. Harris along with The American Boxer Club. The Best in Show winner at Westminster Kennel Club in 1951, Bang Away accumulated 121 BIS wins in his six-year career and sired 90 champions.

THE 1950S AND 1960S

War-related problems that had threatened the sport were no longer a factor in the 1950s, but the AKC still needed to exercise flexibility in applying new rules and interpreting old ones. The surge of interest in purebred dogs and virtually all dog-related activities brought about many new rules and the amendment of existing ones.

Field Trials enjoyed particular growth, and many new exhibitors entered Obedience Trials, where the activity was supplemented by an influx of ex-servicemen connected with the war-dog effort.

THE QUESTION OF WOMEN

When the AKC was incorporated in 1909, the bylaws stated: "The voting powers of each Member Club can and shall be exercised only by a male Delegate selected by said club to represent it for that purpose."

There is little documentation about any movement to seat female Delegates before 1950. In December of that year, James M. Austin, Delegate of the Ladies' Kennel Association of America and owner of the famous Fox Terrier Nornay Saddler, proposed that the Delegates

New Breeds for the 1950s

Belgian Malinois (formerly Belgian
    Sheepdog)
Belgian Tervuren (formerly Belgian
    Sheepdog)

German Wirehaired Pointer
Rhodesian Ridgeback
Silky Terrier

Registration on the Rise

A glance at registration figures tells the story of AKC's growth better than words. It took fifty-one years for the AKC to register the first million dogs (1935). It took only twenty-one more years to reach the five-million mark (1956).

go on record as being in favor of making women eligible to be Delegates. There was no second to the motion, and no action was taken.

The question of seating female Delegates was one of the most controversial of the decade. Per the bylaws, all Delegates had always been men. In March 1951, the matter was revisited, but it was tabled until June, when a vote on the proposal was scheduled for the March 1952 meeting. At that time, the motion failed again. Women would have to wait more than two decades to see a different result.

Top Ten Breeds of the 1950s

Beagles
(13 and 15 inches)

Cocker Spaniels

Boxers

Chihuahuas

Dachshunds
(Longhaired, Smooth and
Wirehaired)

The only breed to rank in the top ten breeds every decade since the founding of the American Kennel Club became the nation's top breed in the 1950s: the Beagle. Not coincidentally, Charles Schultz's pet Beagle, Snoopy, made his illustrious first appearance in national newspapers on October 4, 1950, and swiftly became a pop phenomenon. The Beagle reigned as number-one from 1953 to 1959. The Boxer's rise to the number-three position may be linked to the career of one of America's most famous show dogs, Ch. Bang Away of Sirrah Crest, the Westminster winner in 1951, who made history by winning Best in Show 121 times.

German Shepherd
Dogs

Poodles

Collies
(Smooth and Rough)

Boston Terriers

Pekingese

FLEXIBILITY AND CHANGE

A long-standing rule for registration of a kennel name (affix) gave the owner sole use of the name with no time limitations. In this decade, a change limited exclusive use to a five-year term, with renewal available upon application and payment of a fee.

In 1950, it was determined that no show could extend for more than two days unless AKC permission was obtained. One-day shows became more popular, and in 1951 a rule went into effect that required judges to evaluate twenty dogs per hour to allow the show to end at a reasonable time. This was subsequently changed to 25 dogs per hour, with the total number of dogs not to exceed 175 per day at an all-breed show and 200 per day at a Specialty. Rules were instituted that required clubs to state entry limits on their premium lists.

In 1950 as well, a recording fee was imposed on each entry. The charge was only a nominal twenty-five cents per dog, but it generated considerable revenue given the number of shows and entrants. Despite the increase in revenue, the recording fee was discontinued in 1954.

Many innovations begun during the war years were held over. Two of the most significant were one-day shows and the elimination of benching at many shows. Two-day shows steadily declined in number, and those that continued initiated a format in which three Groups were judged and benched each day, with Best in Show being judged on the final day. This meant that only the previous day's Group winners had to be held over to the next day. Benching (in which all competitors were present for the entire duration of the show) had allowed fanciers to learn about dogs by spending time with others of greater experience. Leisurely benched multiple-day events became merely a memory.

Madison Avenue

Continuous growth in the sport of purebred dogs caused the American Kennel Club to outgrow its quarters at 221 Park Avenue South by early 1964, at which point the AKC moved its offices to 51 Madison Avenue. It is historically interesting to note that the new quarters were on the site of the old Gilmore's Garden, where the first Westminster Kennel Club Show was held on May 8–10, 1877.

JUDGING

Once again, judging limits were examined. As before, restrictions were needed if one-day shows were to end on time. Many clubs assigned judges too many dogs. Some events were conducted under less than satisfactory lighting, particularly when daylight hours were a factor. Schedules calling

Westminster Kennel Club, 1960. The international press gives full coverage to Best in Show Pekingese Ch. Chik T'Sun of Caversham. Clara Alford was the handler.

for a 175-dog maximum with 20 dogs per judge per hour were suggested. The possibility of a 200-dog load at 20 dogs per hour was also considered, but it was decided that the 175 per day, 25 per hour schedule was the most acceptable.

In 1962, judges who had apprenticed in one breed could apply to judge other breeds without needing to apprentice. Then, in November 1969, a new approach to approving Conformation and Obedience judges appeared—the Provisional Judging System. This was one of many ongoing efforts to improve judging by establishing more demanding requirements. New applicants with adequate breeding and exhibiting experience were permitted to officiate at three shows, after which the Board of Directors reviewed their performances. After this review, the provisional judge was either certified or required to obtain further training and experience. The approval process for new judges will never be easy, nor will the search for a better system ever end.

SHOW RULES–CLASSES AND SUCH

The Best of Winners Class was replaced by judging Best of Winners during Best of Breed/Variety in 1967. If either Winners Dog or Winners Bitch won the Breed/Variety, that dog or bitch was also automatically Best of Winners.

Shows that were limited to champions only and/or dogs having a certain number of championship points were relatively rare and did not gain much support. The same was true of other types of restricted shows.

New Obedience regulations, effective January 1969, were well received. They primarily helped make the rules more concise and brought many new entrants to these events.

The 1960s continued the pace set in the 1950s, with an emphasis on refining judging procedures as well as the certification and conduct of judges.

Top Ten Breeds of the 1960s

Poodles

German Shepherd Dogs

Beagles
(13 and 15 inches)

Dachshunds
(Longhaired, Smooth, and Wirehaired)

Chihuahuas

The Poodle, recognized by the AKC in 1887, did not make the top ten breeds until the 1950s when it ranked number seven. This glamorous show dog and companion strutted into the number-one position in the 1960s and would become the first breed to hold the number-one crown for two consecutive decades. To this day, the Poodle holds the record for being the most popular dog for twenty-three consecutive years (1960—1982). German Shepherd Dogs, the number-one breed of the 1920s, secured the number-two spot for the 1960s and the 1970s.

Pekingese

Collies
(Smooth and Rough)

Miniature Schnauzers

Cocker Spaniels
(American—all colors)

Basset Hounds

A victory lap for Best Junior at Westminster Kennel Club in 2005, Alexis Ditlow with English Springer Spaniel Ch. Preferred Stock the Natural. INSET RIGHT: Professional handler Christian Manelopoulos, gaiting white Standard Poodle Ch. Brighton Minimoto in the finals for Westminster Kennel Club Best in Show 2007. Ch. Brighton Minimoto was a back-to-back winner of the WKC Group in 2007 and 2008, following in the pawprints of her sire, Ch. Ale Kai Mikimoto On Fifth, who accomplished the same feat in 2003 and 2004. INSET LEFT: The winner of the Westminster Kennel Club Toy Group in 2005, Ch. Yakee If Only, being presented by professional handler David Fitzpatrick.

Benched Shows

Early dog shows typically ran for three to five days, and all dogs were required to remain on public display for the duration. Benching was implemented to replace the resulting clutter of chains, packing crates, and pens and create a pleasing display of exhibits for spectators. This arrangement became so popular that the AKC eventually imposed rules limiting excessive benching decorations.

As shows proliferated, five-day events became impractical. Many clubs also shifted to less costly and elaborate formats during World War II. Because of their convenience and cost-effectiveness, the switch to unbenched shows continued throughout the 1950s.

Today, six Benched Shows remain:
International Kennel Club of Chicago
Kennel Club of Philadelphia
Golden Gate Kennel Club
Westminster Kennel Club
Portland Kennel Club
Detroit Kennel Club

In recent years, many shows have begun adding "Meet the Breeds" attractions to their shows in order to provide a showcase of purebreds, which made Benched Shows so popular. The AKC's National Championship is the best example of how effective and educational such attractions can be.

TOP: A sweet Bearded Collie, receiving the final touches on a grooming table in the benching area. BOTTOM: Two lovely Borzois, waiting patiently on their nicely appointed bench at the Westminster Kennel Club show.

Frederick Thomas Daws's *Ch. The Laird of Mannerhead and Ch. Limelight of Mannerhead by Sparkling Jet of Misty Isles*, 1931, given to The AKC Museum of the Dog by Frank T. Sabella, one of the fancy's consummate Poodle handlers and judges. In the 1930s and 1940s, Mrs. Campbell-Inghis's Mannerhead Kennels of Miniature Poodles were well regarded.

THE 1970s AND 1980s

As the end of the American Kennel Club's first hundred years approached, dogs had become an increasingly greater factor in people's lives. The following verse by British poet George Crabbe from over two hundred years ago describes the nature of dogs and their relationship to humans:

> *With eye upraised his master's looks to scan,*
> *The joy, the solace, and the aid of man;*
> *The rich man's guardian and the poor man's friend,*
> *The only creature faithful to the end.*

We can be proud of the AKC for recognizing and furthering this precious, enduring, and age-old bond.

THE QUESTION OF WOMEN REVISITED

Since the AKC's formation in 1884, only men had been permitted to serve as Delegates. No women were allowed to hold this office or to vote on any rules affecting all Member and non-member Clubs, even though many women were members of those groups. This situation was criticized for many years, but the attempts to rectify the situation had always failed.

By 1970, the effects of the feminist movement had trickled down to the sport of dogs. Equal opportunity litigation was rampant. Traditional male bastions fell one by one, and the American Kennel Club could no longer hold back the future.

In June 1972, AKC President John A. Lafore advised the Delegates that the Board of Directors was considering the possibility of bringing before them a proposal to amend the bylaws to permit women to be seated as Delegates. The decision had been reached after consulting with the club's attorney.

At the September 1973 meeting, Mr. Lafore announced that the proposal would be brought before the December meeting. The form of the amendment would be published in the *Gazette* as required. At the December meeting, a motion was made to adopt the amendment by

Top Ten Breeds of the 1970s

Poodles

German Shepherd Dogs

Doberman Pinschers

Beagles
(13 and 15 inches)

Dachshunds
(Longhaired, Smooth and Wirehaired)

Irish Setters

Cocker Spaniels
(American—all colors)

Miniature Schnauzers

Labrador Retrievers

Collies
(Smooth and Rough)

Poodles retain their position as the country's top dog for a second decade and have remained in the top ten every decade since. The Doberman Pinscher made its first appearance in the top ten in the 1970s as the number-three breed; the breed would remain in the top ten for the 1980s as well. The Miniature Schnauzer entered the top ten in the 1960s as number eight and uniquely sustained that ranking for three consecutive decades. The 1970s also marked the first appearance of the Labrador Retriever in the country's top ten.

Juniors Today

Since becoming an official AKC event in 1971, Junior Showmanship has expanded to provide many resources and opportunities for young people with an interest in dogs.

The AKC's National Junior Organization was formed in 1997. Its seminars and bimonthly electronic newsletter by, for, and about Junior Handlers have been utilized by approximately fourteen thousand Juniors.

The AKC Junior Scholarship Program awards up to $100,000 in scholarships annually to deserving Junior Handlers, including a $2,000 scholarship to the Best Junior Handler at the AKC National Championship.

In 1999, the AKC established its Junior Showmanship Recognition program to recognize the accomplishments of Juniors handling dogs to Companion and Performance titles. In addition to Obedience, Agility, Rally, Tracking, Lure Coursing, Herding, and Earthdog awards and titles, Juniors receive additional certificates acknowledging their achievements.

secret ballot. The motion was defeated by twenty-five votes. However, at the Board meeting, a written notice had been submitted, requesting that the proposed change be placed before the annual meeting in March. The issue was still alive.

The March 1974 annual meeting of the American Kennel Club was a historic event. The motion to decide about the amendment to delete the word *male* from Article VI, Section 1 was to be by roll call, which left no chance for a Delegate to vote secretly and not follow his club's wishes. The amendment passed by a vote of 180 to 7.

The first female Delegates were elected in June 1974: Carol D. Duffy, representing the Mid-Hudson Kennel Club; Gertrude Freedman, representing the Bulldog Club of New England; and Julia Gasow, representing the English Springer Spaniel Club of Michigan. These three women attended their first Delegates' meeting in September 1974. In the twenty-first century, the percentage of women in the Delegate body has hovered around 60 percent.

MORE CHANGES–SHOWS, FEES, HANDLERS, AND GROUPS

A serious fuel shortage late in 1973 resulted in policy changes on territorial limits and show dates. As a result, it was not unusual for several clubs to hold their shows at the same location on consecutive days. These cluster shows minimized travel while offering additional shows, a great convenience for exhibitors. This required a more flexible approach by the AKC, a situation reminiscent of the war years. The maximum number of Specialty Shows permitted to cluster was raised from ten to twenty. The initial event approved under this new rule was that of the Combined Specialty Clubs of Dallas in 1974.

Fuel shortage again became a factor in 1977, resulting in more requests for all-breed cluster shows, particularly in the less populated regions. Shows in these areas offered an educational experience while assuring financial stability for the show-giving clubs. They also helped popularize dogs and dog shows in many regions where little interest had been apparent before these events were held.

The approval of cluster shows was a step forward. It led to more entries, allowed the most efficient use of a facility, and enabled clubs in the same general area to use the best facility in that area. By 1982, 30 percent of all-breed shows were part of cluster arrangements. The argument against cluster shows was the possible loss of individual geographic identity of the several show-giving clubs. However, many smaller clubs had experienced difficulty in holding unsupported shows in their own areas because of expenses and the absence of suitable facilities. Without cluster shows, these clubs would have had great difficulty holding independent events.

At the March 1977 Delegates' meeting, there was an attempt to reinstate the recording fee in effect during the early 1950s. This twenty-five-cent-per-dog fee had been instituted to help the AKC with show-related expenses, but it was discontinued in 1954. There was still considerable opposition to the fee in 1977, and at the June meeting the proposal was withdrawn. However, it was revived again in December.

AKC expenses for administering shows and trials had risen dramatically and were offset only by registration income. One reason for the additional expenses was the increase in the number of Field Representatives. The twenty-five-cent recording fee was reinstated on April 1, 1978, and five years later it was increased to fifty cents, effective May 1983. The AKC saw this fee as a way to gain income without having to increase registration rates.

In January 1978, the AKC stopped licensing professional handlers, which it had been doing since 1929. This change placed all professional handlers in the same category as other exhibitors; as a result, anyone could now charge a fee to handle a dog. This removed a substantial load from the AKC and the Field Staff.

Through the years, the American Kennel Club had tried to maintain a regular dialogue with the professional handlers, just as it had tried to remain as receptive as possible to input from all segments of the fancy. However, it became apparent very early on that there were many problems inherent in the licensing process. By 1950, Henry Bixby, AKC Executive Vice-President, had advised the Professional Handlers' Association that the AKC could foresee the possibility of discontinuing licensing. Finally, in 1977, the AKC Delegates were advised that the time had come—the American Kennel Club could no longer adequately oversee the licensing of professional handlers.

At the July 1977 meeting, AKC President John A. Lafore, Jr., explained: "We have been receiving applications from a large number of people with limited experience in one or two breeds who are not pursuing handling on a full-time basis, but simply want to supplement their regular source of income or to help defray expenses of showing their own dogs. Since AKC licenses all professional handlers, many feel that AKC has conferred its unqualified stamp of approval on the professional competence of each handler it licenses. Unfortunately, such is not the case, as in the majority of cases, there is no definitive practical means by which such large numbers of applicants can be properly tested and screened."

There was a great deal of debate and controversy concerning this proposal. There was also a great deal of lobbying done by the Professional Handlers' Association and the Dog Handlers Guild. In response to the lobbying that was being done, John A. Lafore, Jr., directed a memorandum to all Delegates in August 1977, emphasizing again that the current rule requiring the licensing of any individual who handled a dog for pay was virtually unenforceable. He also explained that the discontinuation of licensing would not lead to a loss of control over the activities of handlers, as the Constitution and Bylaws of the American Kennel Club, as well as the rules, provided that charges had to be preferred against "any person" for conduct alleged to be prejudicial to the welfare of the sport.

The matter was presented to the Delegates for a vote at its September 1977 meeting. There were 265 Delegates present and voting at this meeting, which was an all-time record at that point, exceeding the previous total of 209. William F. Stifel, AKC Executive Vice-President, reiterated the American Kennel Club's arguments with regard to the discontinuation of licensing. He also addressed the proposals submitted by the Professional Handlers' Association, which would have enacted stricter policies for the licensing of handlers but did not address the fact that it was virtually impossible to control the handling of dogs for pay by

Top Ten Breeds of the 1980s

Cocker Spaniels

Poodles

Labrador Retrievers

German Shepherd Dogs

Golden Retrievers

The number-one breed of the 1940s, the Cocker Spaniel, enjoyed a renaissance in the 1980s, climbing to the number-one position. The breed was the most popular dog in the nation from 1983—1990, giving it the distinction of holding the number-one spot for twenty-three years, tying with the Poodle. After two decades as the country's number-one breed, the Poodle slipped into the number-two position and would continue falling for subsequent decades. The Labrador Retriever bettered its number-nine position in the 1970s by leaping to the number-three spot in the 1980s, and the Golden Retriever broke into the top ten for the first time at number five.

Doberman Pinschers

Beagles

Miniature Schnauzers

Dachshunds

Chow Chows

Standards for Handlers

In 2000, the American Kennel Club began the planning stages for the Registered Handlers Program and registered its first members in 2001. The program establishes criteria and standards for responsible, knowledgeable professional handlers. All handlers enrolled in the program have made the commitment to follow the guidelines and Code of Ethics as set forth by the American Kennel Club.

Judge and former professional Boxer handler Jane Forsyth reviewing her lineup of Boxers; professional handler Kimberly Pastella (Calvacca) presenting to the judge.

CODE OF ETHICS FOR REGISTERED HANDLERS

I agree to:
- Ensure that the welfare of the dogs in my care is a priority, not only at dog shows but at home and on the road.
- Their well-being, security, and safety is to be placed above all other business considerations. The ultimate responsibility for the dogs cannot be transferred to assistants, or others.
- Conduct myself in a sportsmanlike manner at all times in my relationships with fellow handlers, assistants, exhibitors, judges, and clients, which includes courteous verbal interchanges and a professional appearance.
- Abide by all published AKC rules applying to registration and dog shows.
- Conduct my business relationships with clients in a fair and honest manner, based on a published rate schedule and handler/client agreement.
- Provide my clients with their ribbons, trophies, and information about their dogs' placements at each show in a timely manner.

Professional handler Bill McFadden, presenting Kerry Blue Terrier Ch. Torum's Scarf Michael.

- Provide my clients with itemized monthly billing statements.
- Ensure that my clients thoroughly understand payment and release terms.
- Avail myself of educational opportunities as may be established by the American Kennel Club.
- Inform the Handlers Department (AKC) of any change in home address, telephone number, kennel facilities, or travel vehicles.

individuals not licensed by the American Kennel Club. The rule changes that were necessary to eliminate the licensing of handlers were adopted by the Delegates with 228 votes for the motion and 37 votes against the motion.

In 1983, a landmark change took place. The number of Groups was increased from six to seven, a change approved by the Delegates in March 1982. This was the first change in the number of Groups since the 1930s. This was accomplished by splitting the very large Working Group into two Groups: the Working Group and the Herding Group.

Despite fuel shortages and other problems, the 1970s and 1980s were years of continuous success for purebred dogs, as evidenced in part by the registration figures. Registrations exceeded one million dogs in twelve of the fourteen years from 1970 to 1983. These statistics demonstrated that interest in purebred dogs had risen dramatically in the past hundred years. Through the guidance of the American Kennel Club, this interest has grown in a way that the purebred dog, regardless of breed, has continued to improve in conformity and ability throughout the years.

The Standard Poodle, historically, has been a working bird dog and water retriever, as this proficient hunter demonstrates.

The Newfoundland, a versatile companion and working dog, can be trained to adapt and work in the country or the big city.

John Sargent Noble's *On the Scent*, given to The AKC Museum of the Dog by Robert V. and Nancy D. Lindsay, depicts a pair of Bloodhounds giving voice in search of a lost victim.

OBEDIENCE FROM THE BEGINNING

By the 1920s and early 1930s, the concept of dog training was already known in the United States. There were professional trainers who would board and train a dog for the owner or who would give private lessons to overcome special behavior problems. Some of these trainers were Josef Weber (author of *The Dog in Training,* 1939), Carl Spitz (of Hollywood fame—trainer of "Buck" in *Call of the Wild* and Cairn Terrier "Toto" in *The Wizard of Oz*), and Hans Tossutti (author of *Companion Dog Training,* 1946).

Long before 1933, owners trained in groups, gave Obedience exhibitions, and competed in Trials. But these get-togethers were confined to the Working Breeds such as the German Shepherd Dog and the Doberman Pinscher.

HELENE WHITEHOUSE WALKER

Obedience as we know it in America owes its very being to Helene Whitehouse Walker. In 1933, the Standard Poodles of her Carillon Kennels were fast gaining recognition as dogs of outstanding quality and character. But her friends often badgered her by calling her Poodles "sissy dogs." She decided to convince everyone that despite

Judge Blanche Saunders awarding the Utility Class trophy to Mrs. Fred Otte, Jr., with Bedlington Terrier Ch. Rock Ridge Rocket, UD, in 1949.

their seemingly fancy clips, Poodles were as intelligent as any other breed. To do this, she would have them perform in a series of Obedience exercises.

What Mrs. Walker had in mind were tests patterned after those held in England under the sponsorship of the Associated Sheep, Police, and Army Dog Society. This English society had modified the requirements of its Field Trials, making it possible to hold competitions both indoors and outdoors and opening up the tests in England to all breeds.

Helene Whitehouse Walker approached dog clubs and private kennel owners with her idea of competitive tests held in connection with dog shows here in the United States and received a small but "most enthusiastic" response. The first Obedience Test in the United States for all breeds was held in October 1933 in Mount Kisco, New York. There were eight entries—two Labradors, three Poodles, two English Springer Spaniels, and a German Shepherd Dog.

In an Obedience Test, a dog was required to walk at the handler's side without leash, retrieve a dumbbell both on the flat and over an obstacle, remain in the Sit and Down positions with the handler out of sight; come when called; and leap over a Long Jump on command. The judge of this first competition was Robert Carr, a Field Trial enthusiast, and the winner was a Labrador Retriever owned by William F. Hutchinson of Far Hills, New Jersey. The competitors were cheered on by a gallery of more than 150 people.

That first all-breed Obedience Test in Mount Kisco showed that no matter the breed and no matter whether the owners were

Helene Whitehouse Walker with Standard Poodle Berkham Augusta.

Henry Whitehouse with Standard Poodle Nunsoe Skagin of Carillon, winner of the Obedience test in Mt. Kisco, October 1934.

amateurs, here was the opportunity to demonstrate what could be done in training. "Train your own dog!" became a popular slogan, and dog owners from all parts of the country were quick to respond. The widening enthusiasm spurred Mrs. Walker to greater goals, and she began aiming toward the introduction of Obedience at the next all-breed Conformation event, which would be the North Westchester Kennel Club show in June 1934. With little time left, Mrs. Walker sent a letter to *Pure-Bred Dogs/ American Kennel Gazette:* "Test classes could become popular—not only to prove the value of developing a dog's brain, but in interesting the…visiting public at a show. Judging dogs in the breed classes is a mystery to many, but a series of tests displaying the dog's brain is something they can actually see."

Pomeranian Georgian's Betty, UDT, was the first Toy Dog to earn all titles then available (mid-1940s). Owner and trainer, Agnes Niven.

In 1934, Mrs. Walker persuaded the Somerset Hills Kennel Club to follow the North Westchester Kennel Club's lead in holding Obedience Tests. This event took place in September, 1934, in Far Hills, New Jersey. Somerset Hills thus became the second club to hold Obedience Tests in conjunction with its all-breed show.

Mrs. Walker then staged a second private event, held in Mount Kisco in October 1935. For the first time, Tracking Tests were also included. There were eight entries in Obedience and six in Tracking. About 500 spectators watched the Tracking Test on the hill and crowded around a large ring for the Obedience Test.

OBEDIENCE RULES ARE WRITTEN

Obedience rules in 1933–1934 were much more lenient than they are today. For example:

Historic First Obedience Test Exercises

This historic first Obedience Test at an all-breed show consisted of just one class.

(1) Heel on Leash (including figure eight)	—10 points
(2) Heel Free (off-lead)	—30 points
(3) Sit (two minutes, handler out of sight)	—20 points
(4) Recall to Handler (including a Drop, Sit Front, and going to Heel position)	—25 points
(5) Retrieve a two-pound dumbbell on the flat	—20 points
(6) Retrieve an eight- to ten-ounce dumbbell and jump a three-and-a-half-foot obstacle (both going and returning)	—50 points
(7) Long Jump (six feet)	—30 points
(8) Down (five minutes, handlers out of sight, all dogs in ring together)	—65 points

Blanche Saunders, called the "Trainer of Trainers," working with two of her Standard Poodles.

- Commands and hand motions automatically went *together*.

Ch. Nero's Anthony, the first Great Dane to earn a CDX. Owner and trainer, Rose Sabetti.

- The dog's name was used with signals as well as with commands.
- If the dog did not obey the first time, there was always a second chance, although with a penalty.
- If an owner wished to take part in an Obedience Test, it was mostly a matter of obtaining a list of the exercises and then using whatever method was needed to get the dog to obey.
- Performances in the ring varied, but there was little emphasis on handling.

From the sport's point of view, it was fortunate that early rules were less demanding, as it encouraged the amateur. Test simplicity also retained the enthusiasm that brought Obedience to a high degree of performance quality, reflected in accuracy and precision as well as in the dog's happiness and willingness.

The four Obedience Tests in 1933 and 1934 created great interest among spectators, kennel owners, pet owners, and dog clubs. People wanted information on training, what the dogs were required to do, and

Left to right: Blanche Saunders, Helene Whitehouse Walker, and
Catharine (Cae) Reilly with Ch. Carillon Dilemma, UD, Kaeley
Audacious Coquette, UD, and Robin Hill of Carillon, UDT.

Irish Terrier Ch. No Retreat, CDX, owned by Frances Thord-Gray, Glen Antrim Kennels.

how one went about arranging similar tests. Mrs. Walker contacted Charles T. Inglee, Executive Vice-President of the American Kennel Club. She showed him many newspaper clippings and vast amounts of correspondence in evidence of the interest in training, and she stressed that Obedience was not a passing fad, but was destined to become an integral part of future dog activity. Mr. Inglee was interested.

Six Obedience Tests were held in 1935 in conjunction with all-breed dog shows. The sponsoring clubs were North Westchester Kennel Club, Lenox Kennel Club, North Shore Kennel Club, Westchester Kennel Club, Somerset Hills Kennel Club, and the Kennel Club of Philadelphia.

The first Ch./UD Norwegian Elkhound, Ch. Torvald That's All, UD, working with owner-trainer Kathleen Prince.

At the same time, dog journalists wrote of the growing enthusiasm for dog training that was spreading across the country. In May 1935, the *Chicago Tribune* carried a column about the Amateur Training Club of Chicago, "one of the few schools in the country where the owner of a working dog can go to school and learn how to train his own canine." Six months later, the *New York Times* gave a full-page banner headline to a story recounting the intelligence and skill displayed by a Champion Miniature Schnauzer in performing the Novice Obedience exercises at the Kennel Club of Philadelphia's annual exhibition.

Two other events were to have a strong influence on the development of Obedience in the United States. First, in 1935, Grace L. Boyd visited, with three of her Obedience-trained Standard Poodles who were winning against all breeds in England. She later wrote a Tracking booklet for beginners that was widely distributed in the United States. Second, Mrs. Walker wrote a booklet called *Obedience Tests: Procedures for Judge, Handler, and Show Giving Club*. This was the first attempt to standardize the sport for this country.

In addition to setting forth procedures, the booklet discussed both professionalism and irresponsible judging. Mrs. Walker felt strongly that Obedience must appeal to the amateur, the one-dog owner who would bring a dog to the show and handle that dog in the ring. She recommended that professional handlers and trainers be barred from the Novice Class so that the amateurs would not become discouraged and drop out.

Helene Whitehouse Walker submitted this booklet to the American Kennel Club in December 1935. In March 1936, the AKC Board of Directors approved the procedures, and one month later

Left to right: Members of the Metropolitan Boxer Training Club: Judson Streicher, Gus Schneider, Laura Dale, and Henry Hollitscher with Chardythe's Pacemaker, UD; Imperial of Hinshenfelde, CDX; Mozart Sonatina, UD; and Huck Hills Joe Gander, UD.

the first official *Regulations and Standards for Obedience Test Field Trials* was published in the *Gazette*. The regulations were eight pages long and adhered quite closely to Mrs. Walker's procedures.

A NEW CLASS

One difference between Mrs. Walker's procedures and those of the AKC was that a Utility Class (or, as some say, "*fu*tility" class) was added. This class alone was open to professional handlers as well as amateurs. A dog was expected to qualify *twice* in each class to earn a title. The following was required to qualify:

A dog had to have 80 percent of the available points in Novice and Open and 70 percent in Utility.

- The dog had to pass a Tracking Test. Over half of the points in the Utility class were based on Tracking.
- A passing score in a class would count toward a title only if there was competition in the class: six dogs were needed in Novice, four in Open, and three in Utility.

A Norwich Terrier adroitly clears a jump on the Obedience course.

First Obedience Regulation Point Values

Novice (Companion Dog [CD])

1. Heel on Leash	20
2. Heel Free	25
3. Come When Called	20
4. Sit—one minute	15
5. Down—three minutes	20

Total points 100

Open (Companion Dog Excellent [CDX])

1. Heel on Leash	40
2. Heel Free	50
3. Come When Called (including a "drop" on command)	25
4. Retrieve Dumbbell on the Flat (dumbbell in proportion to dog)	25
5. Speak on Command	20
6. Long Jump	30
7. Sit—three minutes (handler out of sight)	25
8. Down—five minutes (handler out of sight)	35

Total points 250

Utility (Utility Dog [UD])

1. Tracking (quarter-mile track, aged for half an hour)	225
2. Scent Discrimination (3 articles, including one metal)	75
3. Seek Back (find inconspicuous article dropped by handler)	60
4. Retrieve Dumbbell over an Obstacle (dog jumps both going and coming; jump height in proportion to size of dog with a maximum height of 3' 6")	40

Total points 400

The first licensed Test held with these regulations took place in June 1936 at the North Westchester Kennel Club all-breed show in Mount Kisco, New York. It consisted of only a Novice Class. All dogs, whether they had competed in Open previously, had to enter Novice until they won more than 80 of the possible 100 points. Under the new regulations, they had to qualify twice. There were twelve entries, and eight qualified. The next day, eight of the sixteen entered qualified. The first six CD titles were earned. New titleholders were five Standard Poodles and one Miniature Schnauzer.

FINE-TUNING

After a six-month trial period, the American Kennel Club issued the revised *Regulations and Standards for Obedience Test Trials*, approved November 1936. The rules had been expanded so that Novice and Open Classes were now divided into A and B divisions—A was for amateurs only and B was for professionals and amateurs alike. There were other changes, too. The Speaking on Command exercise was moved from the Open Class to the Utility Class. A Stand for Examination exercise was added to Utility. The Retrieve over the Hurdle, which had been in Utility, was moved to Open, making the CDX requirements the same as at present, although with different scoring.

The next time that the Obedience rules were amended by the AKC was in June 1938, when sample judging sheets were added. These broke the exercises into parts and showed the number

A Norwegian Elkhound intently demonstrates scent discrimination.

The Port Chester Obedience Training Club (above) and the AKC/USA World Agility Team (below) pose for the camera.

An American Eskimo Dog clears a trial jump with ease.

of points to be awarded for each part, but they proved to be too complicated and were dropped in the 1939 revision.

Beginning in 1938, dogs were required to clear rather than climb the jumps, and exceptions were made in the jump heights for certain breeds. In 1939 as well, the word *Test* was eliminated and the new title became *Regulations and Standards for Obedience Trials.* They have been called Obedience Trials ever since.

EARLY GROWTH AND EARLY CLUBS

In the first year of AKC-recognized Obedience, 1936, eighteen tests were held. Thirty-three CDs were earned by nine different breeds: thirteen Standard Poodles, seven German Shepherd Dogs, six Doberman Pinschers, two Wire Fox Terriers, and one each to a Great Dane, a Newfoundland, an Irish Terrier, a Miniature Schnauzer, and a Keeshond. Three Standard Poodles earned CDX titles that first year.

In response to a suggestion made by Mrs. Walker, the October 1937 *Gazette* began to list all Obedience winners along with their scores, the numbers of competitors, and the names of the judges. Until that time, only the dogs' names were published, and the extra details helped to spark more interest in the sport.

In 1937, eighty-two dogs won CD titles, twenty earned CDX titles, and four won UD titles. In this second year of AKC Obedience, a number of new breeds joined the ranks of titleholders. By the end of 1937, twenty-five different breeds had earned at least one CD and eight breeds had made it to the CDX level. The first four Utility Dogs (with the Tracking requirement) were finished in 1937—two German Shepherd Dogs and two Standard Poodles. One of these Poodles was Carillon Epreuve, who passed the Tracking Test on the same day that one of the German Shepherd Dogs did, but had completed the UD work a month earlier than the Shepherd. Therefore, this Poodle was credited as the first dog of any breed to earn all Obedience degrees. Carillon Epreuve was owned by Helene Whitehouse Walker.

Early in 1938, Henry R. Ilsley wrote in the *New York Times*, "The growth experienced by Obedience Tests during the last two years in the United States has been unprecedented in dog show history."

With Obedience growing by leaps and bounds and interest increasing with each event, the Obedience Test Club of New York was founded. This club was actually an outgrowth of the Bedford Hills Training Class, formed by Mrs. Walker in December 1935. Since the intent was to establish a national all-breed Obedience organization, the members chose to call this

Bulldogs can take to Obedience and are guaranteed crowd-pleasers.

club the Obedience Test Club of America. However, the American Kennel Club advised that it could not approve "of America" in the club's name, as this covered too much territory. The name was thus changed to the Obedience Test Club (OTC) of New York. This club unquestionably was *the* dominant influence in the sport during the first four years of AKC jurisdiction, yet it was never recognized as a Parent Club by the AKC, because its activities involved all breeds.

In addition to an annual Obedience Test, the OTC conducted all-breed training classes and widely distributed information on training and handling. They also established a list of approved judges, which started with five in 1936: Josef Weber, E. D. Knight, Mrs. Wheeler H. Page, W. C. Green, and Helene Whitehouse Walker. By 1938, the list had expanded to fifteen judges, including Major Bryant Godsol, the first "all-rounder" licensed for Obedience. The club supplemented the roster of approved judges with a list of recommended judges, those who were anxious to learn Obedience and then be approved for judging. Some of these were Charles LeBoutillier, Jr., Rose Sabetti, Benno Stein, and Madeleine Baiter. The Obedience Test Club of New York helped to standardize judging by establishing classes for judges.

No breed should be excluded from the fun and excitement of competitive Obedience.

In spite of its prominent role in developing Obedience, the OTC was dissolved in May 1940. It had never become a Member Club of the AKC, as its members voted to operate independently. At the time of dissolution, the OTC had fifteen affiliated clubs with a combined total of more than 500 members.

Established in October 1936, the New England Dog Training Club (NEDTC), Inc., became the first Obedience club to become an AKC Member Club, this occurring in June 1941. Their first Obedience Trial was held in February 1937, with the Eastern Dog Club show in Boston, at which twenty-four dogs competed in the five regular classes. The NEDTC still exists and continues to hold Obedience Trials with the Eastern Dog Club shows.

The Third Leg

From the beginning, and to this day, when a third "leg" is won for a particular class, AKC awards a title certificate. (It should be noted that in the first two years, only two legs were required for a title, and from 1938 to 1949, "at least two different judges" was the rule.) From 1950 on, regulatons required three legs under three different judges.

MOVING FORWARD

Very little change was seen in Obedience Trials during the next few years. Obedience was growing, and the AKC kept watch on the sport's progress. In 1941, a Hurdle and Bar Jump exercise was added to the Utility level. Initially, this exercise was performed with the dog in the Heel position while holding a dumbbell and then jumping on command. In 1947, regulations were changed so that the exercise was performed the same way that the Broad Jump was. The handler placed the dumbbell in the dog's mouth, left the dog in a Sit-Stay in front of the jumps, and stood midway between the jumps. Then, on command, the dog jumped and delivered the dumbbell to the handler as in the Retrieving exercises. In 1950, the Hurdle and Bar Jump exercise was replaced by Directed Jumping.

In 1947, a qualifying score for a title required that the dog earn more than 50 percent of the available points for each exercise as well as a minimum total of 170 points, with a required number of dogs competing. The total number of points for a perfect score was 200 for all three levels. Tracking was dropped as a requirement for Utility and became a separate title, although a CD was required to enter a Tracking Test.

The Speak on Command exercise had been part of the Utility Class almost from the beginning, until 1947. In this exercise, the dog was required to *bark* continuously on *command* from the Sit, Down, and Stand positions and to stop on command. The rationale for the exercise was explained by Josef Weber in his 1939 book, *The Dog in Training*:

> "In Europe this feat is of use in guide dogs for the blind, especially in dense and excited traffic in which the blind man may not be noticed…In police work, speaking on command is used first to make the dog bark to attract the officer's attention when the dog has found his quarry or something of a suspicious nature." [p. 160]

In spite of this, many exhibitors did not like the exercise. Field Trial competitors objected to it on the grounds that a dog giving voice was undesirable in the field. Many exhibitors who live in densely populated cities or apartments did not want to teach their dogs to bark because of urban pressures and therefore did not enter Utility Classes because of this exercise. The 1946 Advisory Committee recommended eliminating the Speak on Command and replaced it in the 1947 *Regulations* with the Signal Exercise.

THE OBEDIENCE ADVISORY COMMITTEE— CHANGES TO UTILITY AND TRACKING

Four evenly matched Collie braces in a Long Sit are an impressive sight.

The AKC convened an Obedience Advisory Committee in 1946 (the first such committee met in 1939) to consider changes to the regulations.

This committee helped standardize judging. For the first time, the 1947 *Obedience Regulations* contained a section called Standard for Obedience Trial Judging (previously called Suggestions for Obedience Trial Judges). The principal part of each exercise was clearly defined in this new section, and the rules spelled out what constituted minor or substantial deductions.

A Pembroke Welsh Corgi retrieves his dumbbell with determination.

Until 1947, the Utility exhibitor had to bring only three articles to the Trial for the Scent Discrimination exercise. Only one had to be metal; none could be a handkerchief. The judge provided the remaining several articles (five of each type for a total of fifteen). The Obedience Advisory Committee made numerous attempts to standardize the Scent Discrimination exercise so that all handlers had the same kinds of articles, recommending that the handler bring all fifteen articles to the Trial, five each of wood, metal, and leather.

Warm debate followed. Many exhibitors did not like the idea of providing fifteen articles, arguing that either the judge or the hosting club should provide anything required beyond the three articles that exhibitors had been bringing. One suggestion was that, if there had to be a change, the show-giving club could send three articles to each handler a few days before the show or could have each handler purchase three standard articles on the day of the test, with the club providing the balance of twelve.

The Obedience Advisory Committee prevailed, and the AKC did approve that the handler should provide the three groups of "absolutely identical" articles, five each of metal, wood, and leather. A later advisory committee discontinued the wooden articles, but the other requirements remain the same today.

A German Shepherd Dog working with conviction on a Tracking course.

Another Obedience Advisory Committee met in 1949 and primarily recommended changes for the Utility Class. Directed Jumping would replace the Hurdle and Bar Jump. Instead of the handler leaving the dog as in the Hurdle and Bar, the dog was to leave the handler on command, without a dumbbell, and go out "at a smart pace" to the other end of the ring, turn, and sit on command. The dog would then take the jump as directed. The exercise was repeated for the other jump.

Many felt that this exercise was too difficult to train for. John Brownell, a member of the Obedience Advisory Committee and later of the Executive Staff of the AKC with responsibility for Obedience, wrote to the AKC in support of this exercise:

> I discussed that part of the proposed exercise which involves sending the dog away in a straight line and making it sit at a distance, with our training director and our head trainer. They worked out a training method and tried it out on two or three of our advanced dogs.... [T]hey were able to get the better dogs to do it in a reasonably short time, and while they think it will be quite difficult for some dogs, they both feel, as I believe all of your committee felt, that we need something more difficult in Utility.

Some trainers and clubs wrote to the AKC objecting to this exercise. They felt that people did Obedience training to teach their dogs to come when called and could see no practical reason to teach dogs to go away from their owners. This argument notwithstanding, the Directed Jumping exercise was instituted in 1950.

More was at issue here than just changing an exercise. The committee decided that the Utility Class should present a significant challenge to both handler and dog. Although the committee knew that the new exercise might put the Utility title beyond the reach of some, it did not compromise.

The year 1950 also saw the new stipulation that "there shall be no penalty of less than ½ point or multiple of ½ point." Previously, judges had sometimes scored in fifths or even tenths of points. The new rule brought more uniformity to judging. In 1964, the rule book title was shortened from *Regulations and Standards for Obedience Trials* to the present-day *Obedience Regulations*.

As mentioned earlier, Tracking originally was part of the Utility Class, and a dog had to pass a separate Tracking Test to earn a UD title. For roughly the first ten years, Tracking received one paragraph of description in the regulations, giving the bare basics for the length and age of the track. On the day of the Test, the tracklayers were to walk to track, deposit the article, and retrace their steps to remove all but the two starting flags. By 1938, the regulations stated that the tracklayer could not wear rubber-soled shoes and that the dog had to

With long ears and furrowed brows that trap scent, the Bloodhound is an accomplished search dog.

Although training techniques may differ, all breeds will enjoy the challenge and satisfaction of Tracking. Above, a Sussex Spaniel, and below, a Standard Poodle, pursue a trail.

be on a 30- to 40-foot leash and work without help from the handler. By 1943, the tracklayers were required to follow the track, deposit the article, and walk directly off the course.

In 1947, Tracking became a separate class. Other details appeared in the Regulations:

- A tracklayer was required to wear leather-soled shoes until he deposited the article. After depositing the article, the tracklayer was required to put on a pair of rubber galoshes over his shoes and walk off the course at a right angle.
- The article was to be a leather glove or leather wallet.
- Dogs were permitted a second chance to take the scent between the starting flags, provided they had not passed the second flag.

It is obvious from these changes that there had been considerable discussion about the proper way in which the tracklayer should lay the track. Tracking and Advanced Tracking regulations grew from a single paragraph in 1936 to some eight pages in 1947—the entire length of the 1936 rule book! Today's *Tracking Regulations* totals forty-nine pages.

In December 1966, another AKC Obedience Advisory Committee recommended the following:

- that qualifying scores be required for prizes in the four official placings
- that the fencing used for Obedience rings be the same as for the Breed rings
- that no tags or ornaments be hanging from the dogs' collars

At this point, the wooden articles were eliminated from the Scent Discrimination exercise. The reasoning was that the dog had already retrieved a wooden article, the dumbbell in the Open Class.

The Seek Back exercise had been in the Utility Class from the very beginning, but had come under attack over the years. It was argued that this was not really a scenting exercise because of the limits imposed by ring size. The 1966 committee recommended that the Seek Back be eliminated in favor of the Directed Retrieve. This exercise involved having three gloves placed across the far end of the ring, and the dog would retrieve one of the three gloves as chosen by the judge. Directed

Tracking Today

Today, all recognized, Miscellaneous, and approved Foundation Stock Service (FSS) breeds are eligible to compete for AKC Tracking titles.

Tracking was first offered as a separate event in 1947, when the first Tracking Dog (TD) titles were awarded. Tracking was originally part of the Utility Class and was therefore part of an Obedience title.

The Tracking Dog Excellent (TDX) title was first offered on March 1, 1980, and was first achieved by Dachshund Gretel Von Bupp Murr, UD, two weeks later on March 15.

The Variable Surface Tracking (VST) title was introduced in 1995 to evaluate tracking ability in an urban setting. The first qualifier was German Shepherd Dog Sealair's Raggedy Ann, UD, TDX. She simultaneously earned the first AKC Champion Tracker (CT) title

awarded to dogs earning TD, TDX, and VST titles.

Since 1995, 191 dogs have earned VST titles and 185 dogs have earned the Champion Tracker titles.

The AKC also encourages excellence in Tracking through the National Tracking Invitational an annual event since 2003.

Since 2001, tracking dogs of all breeds can also earn Versatile Companion Dog (VCD) titles by competing in Obedience, Agility, and Tracking events.

The Versatile Companion Champion (VCCH) title is awarded to dogs earning an Obedience Trial Champion (OTCH), a Master Agility Champion (MACH), and a Champion Tracker (CT). The title was first awarded on February 15, 2009, to VCCH Jakki, UDX, a Golden Retriever.

Regulations

In 2007, there were more than 2,500 Trials. The Obedience Regulations have grown from eight pages in 1936 to sixty, but the basic structure of the sport and many of the exercises remain the same as when they were first approved.

Retrieve was approved, and it first appeared in the 1969 Obedience Regulations, although to this day the Seek Back is advocated as valuable training for Tracking.

Until this time, if a dog maintained the Long Sit or Long Down position for three-quarters of the time allotted, a qualifying score would be earned, but with a penalty. The 1966 committee strongly recommended that in order to qualify, the dog should maintain the position for the full duration of the required time. This change was approved in 1969.

Other changes included clarifications in the working and scoring of dogs and clear distinctions between commands and signals. The 1966 committee also recommended that the Scent Discrimination exercise be moved to follow the Signal exercise; this was approved in January 1975. In addition, the committee recommended revising the testing prodecure for judging applicants and closer observation of judges. It was suggested that a judges' handbook be provided, and in 1972 the first *Guidelines for Obedience Judges* was issued.

A young handler in the field with her Golden Retriever and scenting articles.

Education, Accomplishment, and Growth

The Advisory Committee saw a need for clinics or classes to educate judges, but these did not come about until 1975, when the Obedience Department inaugurated judges' educational seminars.

An Obedience Trial Championship title had been long recommended by Obedience enthusiasts in the hope that this would showcase the exceptional competitor. In July 1977, such a Championship program was inaugurated. Just twenty-three days later, a Golden Retriever, Moreland's Golden Tonka UD, earned her Obedience Trial Championship (OTCh.). The first OTCh, she was owned, trained, and handled by Russell H. Klipple of Pennsylvania.

Moreland's Golden Tonka, winner of the first OTCh., with proud owner-handler Russell Klipple.

As early as 1947, encouraged by Obedience Advisory Committees, the Tracking fraternity lobbied for a more advanced Tracking Test, one that would assess a dog's ability to track a person for about twice the distance required by the Tracking Test and over a course aged for at least three hours. Called Tracking Dog Excellent (TDX), this was approved in 1979 and became effective in March 1980. The first TDX dog was a Dachshund, Gretel Von Bupp Murr, UD, TDX, who passed the Tracking Dog Excellent Test on March 15, 1980. This dog was owner-handled by George Richards of Florida.

Growth in the sport of Obedience since its AKC inception was phenomenal. In 1936, perhaps 200 dogs were entered in 18 licensed Tests, with a total of 33 CDs and 3

CDXs awarded in 9 different breeds. In 1983, there were more than 1,400 Trials, with roughly 104,000 dogs competing. More than 11,000 titles were earned by dogs in 121 different breeds.

Obedience demonstration at Rockefeller Center in conjunction with National Dog Week in 1945. Note the great variety of breeds participating.

In September 1983, on the occasion of the fiftieth anniversary of Obedience in America, the AKC Board of Directors adopted a resolution of gratitude and appreciation to Helene Whitehouse Walker, who was still residing in Mount Kisco, New York.

Donalds

American artist John Donaldson's *Ch. Rapide*, 1980, given to The AKC Museum of the Dog in 2004 by Ray and Lucille Myrick. Ch. Rapide was the winner of the 1980 United States Quail Shooting Dog Futurity. In 1991 an exhibit called "John Donaldson Sporting Dog Paintings: A Twenty Year Retrospective" was the first one-man show presented at The Dog Museum.

FIELD TRIALS IN AMERICA

Tests for field dogs were developed for the purpose of encouraging hunting dogs to compete, thereby improving their performances in the field. It is generally agreed that these tests originated in England in 1866.

THE SPORT IN THE UNITED STATES— THE BEGINNING

A wounded Civil War soldier named P. H. Bryson from Memphis, Tennessee, was released from the hospital after the war ended and permitted to go home to die and have a decent burial. When he reached home, his physician advised him to buy a shotgun and a bird dog and get as much exercise as possible. In time he recovered, became a dedicated sportsman, and through the sporting journals at that time, began to advocate the holding of dog shows in the United States.

Bryson formed the Tennessee Sportsmen's Association and organized a combined Conformation Show and Field Trial in October 1874. The only breeds represented at the show on the first day were Pointers and Setters, with ninety-five entries. The soldier's Setter, "Maud," was awarded Best in Show!

Intensity in a gundog is well illustrated by this Weimaraner pointing in the water, not a muscle twitching, fixing his gaze on his quarry.

Fourteen Pointers and Setters competed in the Field Trial on the second day. The winner was an all-black Setter. The results are recorded in Volume 1 of *The National American Kennel Club Stud Book*.

The forerunner of the American Kennel Club, the National American Kennel Club, supported both Bench and Field activities, although the majority of its members were mainly Field Trial oriented. The club also sponsored a stud record, compiled by Dr. Nicholas Rowe, a strong supporter of all efforts to bring the purebred dog into greater prominence. The initial volume of this stud book, appearing in 1878, reported Shows and Trials from 1876.

Not until 1884 did Dr. Rowe produce Volumes 2 and 3 at his own expense, immediately giving them to the fledgling American Kennel Club. Following these volumes, the AKC published subsequent volumes, containing fifty million registrations that follow the previously mentioned dog Number One, the English Setter Adonis.

Volume 1 of *The National American Kennel Club Stud Book,* by virtue of Dr. Rowe's generosity, also became Volume 1 of *The American Kennel Club Stud Book* and contains records from 1876, eight years before the AKC's founding in 1884, to 1878. A second edition published in 1885 contained records through 1884.

In order to follow the development of the sport of Field Trials, we must separate the sport into its four component parts, each based on the hunting characteristics of the breeds involved:

- Pointing Breeds—which include Brittanys, Pointers, German Shorthaired Pointers, German Wirehaired Pointers, English Setters, Gordon Setters, Irish Setters, Spinoni Italiani, Vizslas, Weimaraners, and Wirehaired Pointing Griffons—assist the hunter by stopping or pointing the very moment they scent the presence of a game bird. This permits hunters to walk past their dogs on point and flush the birds into the air.
- Flushing dogs such as Clumber Spaniels, Cocker Spaniels, English Cocker

A Golden Retriever appears airborne, diving into the water to retrieve game shot by the hunter.

Spaniels, English Springer Spaniels, Field Spaniels, Sussex Spaniels, and Welsh Springer Spaniels are expected to search for feathered game within gunshot range of the hunter. When game is located, dogs must flush the bird into the air. They must also retrieve the bird on command if it is shot.

- Retrievers do just what their name implies, that is, fetch or retrieve all game shot by the hunter, from both land and water. These breeds include Chesapeake Bay Retrievers, Curly-Coated Retrievers, Flat-Coated Retrievers, Golden Retrievers, Irish Water Spaniels, and Labrador Retrievers.

- Scenting or Trailing Hounds such as Beagles, Bassets, and Dachshunds pursue the cottontail rabbit or hare either in Packs or Braces (pairs) at Trials.

A Chesapeake Bay Retriever enthusiastically returns with his quarry. FACING PAGE: An Irish Setter assumes the classic pose as he stops at the presence of a game bird.

A dog can be awarded the title of Dual Champion only in AKC-licensed competition. In order to achieve this title, the dog must complete the requirements for both a Field Championship and a Show Championship. The Dual Champion title serves as great incentive to breed dogs that do equally well on the bench and in the field.

POINTING-BREED FIELD TRIALS

The first Field Trial for any breed in America belonged to the Pointing breeds. In 1884, eight years after the British held their first Field Trial, the first recorded Trial in America was held near Memphis, Tennessee. H. C. Pritchard's Setter "Knight" was the immortalized first winner.

Dr. Nicholas Rowe, the same nineteenth-century sportsman who played such a vital role in the founding of the American Kennel Club, maintains a place of honor in the history of Pointing Breed Trials (then only for Setters and Pointers). In 1876, Dr. Rowe bought the *Chicago Field,* changing it to the *American Field* some five years later.

Irish Setter Dual Ch. Tyrone's Mahogany Mike, CDX.

It is still published today and is America's oldest continuous sporting journal.

German Shorthaired Pointer Dual and National Fld. Ch. Ehrlicher's Abe, owned by L. and L. Cross, handled by D. McGinnis.

Trials for Setters and Pointers grew rapidly under the aegis of the *American Field,* particularly in the southern states, where these breeds still are referred to as "bird dogs." It was not until 1924 that there was a written record of a Pointing Breed Trial under AKC license. This event was held by the English Setter Club of America on their Medford, New Jersey, grounds, which they owned and used for Trials.

Seven years elapsed before the AKC recorded another Pointing Breed Trial, when a joint Trial was held by the Gordon Setter Club of America and the Irish Setter Club of America in October 1931, at the Owen Winston estate in Gladstone, New Jersey.

Coming out of the Depression in the 1930s and through the years of World War II, the number of AKC Trials for Pointing Breeds never exceeded ten in any year, and in several years only two were held.

The end of World War II, however, brought a dramatic upsurge in the number of Pointing Breed Trials. The American servicemen had been

Fld. Ch. County Clare's Jiggs, an Irish Setter owned by Kathleen and Sean Byrne.

to Europe, and the hunters among them had seen firsthand the efficiency of the "Continental" breeds, which included Brittanys, German Shorthaired and Wirehaired Pointers, Vizslas, Weimaraners, and Wirehaired Pointing Griffons. These were all marvelous utilitarian breeds that put game on the tables of American hunters fortunate enough to own one of these dogs.

The competitive American spirit brought the Continental breeds into popularity at American Field Trials. However, these Trials were

nowhere near the developed level of competition seen in the previous Pointer/Setter Trials held under the so-called minimum requirements of the *American Field.* In the 1950s, the presence of professional trainers handling Pointing dogs at AKC Trials marked a major turning point in the quality of performance required to win.

AKC Trials did not permit the handling of dogs from

Dual Ch. Frei of Klarbruk, UDT, a German Shorthaired Pointer owned by Joseph France.

Fld. Ch. Johnny Crockett, an orange belton English Setter, and winner of the Purina award for Top Field Trial Bird Dog in the US for the 1969-70 season.

horseback, unlike the *American Field's* Trials for Setters and Pointers. Professional trainers, many of whom had experience in Trials held by the *American Field,* felt that this was highly detrimental to improving their dogs' performance, and they campaigned actively against the restriction. In 1966, the *AKC Standard Procedure for Pointing Breed Trials* was changed to include horseback. Having overcome that alleged restrictive barrier, the popularity of competing in AKC Trials for Pointing breeds doubled in the next 20 years to more than 450 Trials per year, with more than 35,000 dogs competing annually at that time.

In 1965, taking a cue from the successful Beagle Trials, the first of four Pointing Breed Advisory Committee meetings was held at the AKC offices to recommend rule and procedure amendments to the AKC Board. A representative from each of the nine Pointing Breed Parent Clubs made up the committee, which was chaired by an AKC Field Staff Member.

Problems encountered with AKC Pointing Trials were the same as those encountered with Beagle and Retriever Trials. The sophisticated modernized Trial format created a void for the many hunters who did not have the time or money to be successful in such competition. As the AKC moved into its second century, it was predictable that a program would soon be developed to allow Pointing breed dogs to be tested

ABOVE: German Shorthaired Pointer, "Charger," Gilman's Black Diamond on a hunt. FACING PAGE, top: A Pointer in the field. FACING PAGE, bottom: A German Wirehaired Pointer watches waterfowl.

A yellow Labrador Retriever watches over his fallen waterfowl.

under standards of performance that were truly characteristic of hunting on foot.

In addition to the two AKC-licensed Pointing Breed Trials mentioned above, the American Brittany Club and the German Shorthaired Pointer Club of America held Trials in 1943 and 1944, respectively. In 1953, the American Pointer Club held its first Trial, with the Weimaraner Club of America following suit in 1955. The 1960s saw the first Viszla Club of America Trial in 1962, followed closely by the German Wirehaired Pointer Club of America in 1963.

Pointing Breed Field Trials continued to gain momentum.

RETRIEVER FIELD TRIALS

The organization of Retriever Field Trials did not follow the AKC's traditional single-breed competition concept. All-Retriever (multi-breed) clubs were allowed to foster competition for all Retriever breeds. The *AKC Rules for Retriever Trials* state that the word *Retriever* includes the several breeds of Retrievers and/or Irish Water Spaniels and says that Field Trial clubs formed to improve any one of the Retriever breeds may hold Field Trial stakes in which *one or more* Retriever breeds may compete.

Chesapeake Bay Retriever Dual and Fld. Ch. Baron's Tule Tiger, CD, owned by Eloise Heller (Cherry).

In 1983, 119 clubs held 201

licensed Trials for all Retriever breeds across the United States. In addition, the American Chesapeake Club and the Golden Retriever Club of America each held a National Trial for their respective breed. National and National Amateur Championship Stakes were held by two National Clubs formed to sponsor these annual events for a few qualified Retrievers.

Golden Retriever Bonnie Island Ladd, UDT, delivering the bird to hand at a practice trial with owner John Anderson. Ladd also was awarded a Golden Retriever Club of America working certificate.

Considering that the first Chesapeake Bay Retriever was registered in 1878, six years before the AKC's founding, it is hard to believe that the still-burgeoning popularity in Retrievers began only some fifty years ago in America. Labradors and Goldens were not accepted into the *Stud Book* until 1917 and 1925, respectively. It is also startling to note that only sixty-four Retrievers of all kinds were registered in 1926. In 1983, this figure was 124,785, with 67,389 of these Labrador Retrievers, placing Labradors third in the registration rankings.

The Chesapeake Bay Retriever is a strong gundog that's happy to work all day.

The fortunes of the Retriever breeds in America, and the Labrador in particular, were tied to the fortunes of wealthy estate owners in the East. They were accustomed to shooting in Scotland and began to import Labradors from the British Isles in the late 1920s and early 1930s. *Since these imports were strictly hunting dogs, the owners saw no reason to register these imports with the AKC.* Scottish gamekeepers and kennel men accompanied the dogs to America as trainers.

Noted American Retriever owners of the late 1920s and early 1930s and their trainers included:

Owner(s)	Trainer(s)
Hon. W. Averell Harriman	Tom Briggs & Jim Cowie
Jay F. Carlisle	Dave Elliot
Mr. & Mrs. Marshall Field	Douglas Marshall
Robert Goelet	Colin MacFarlane & Jock Munro
Dr. Samuel Milbank	Lionel Bond

The Labrador Retriever Club, organized in 1931, elected Mrs. Marshall Field as its first President. In December of that year, the club held the first Retriever Field Trial in America on Robert Goelet's 8,000-acre estate in Chester, New York. The Trial was deliberately held on a Monday so it would not attract a gallery.

The George Foley Dog Show Organization of Philadelphia managed this event for the few dozen wealthy competitors. Although the program stated that it was held under AKC and Labrador Retriever Club rules, the accounts of the Trial indicate that it was clearly run under British rules. Mr. and Mrs. Field took First and Second, respectively, in the Open All-Age Stake. W. Averell Harriman won the American-Bred Stake.

The Trials that followed continued through the 1930s with British rules. Increased numbers of entries and sophisticated training methods made British Trialing procedure impractical in America. Controlling the dogs by whistle, voice, and hand signals (handling) revolutionized the sport, starting in the 1940s. The competition at Retriever Trials in the new milennium has pushed the dogs to performance levels never imagined when the Field Trial program began. Today, extremely difficult retrieves are often required to identify the most highly skilled competitors.

The Chesapeake Bay Retriever can be relentless when working birds.

This Labrador Retriever's body language conveys a dog absolutely
riveted on doing his job.

The Retriever breeds remained popular as superb hunting companions, both in duck marsh and on upland game. **A trusty retriever is a hunter's best friend.**

A large group of non-Trialers wanted to have an organized activity in which their Retrievers could be tested under simulated hunting situations. In 1983, the North American Hunting Retriever Association (NAHRA) developed the necessary **The Labrador is renowned as a tireless gundog.** regulations and field procedures, and these received AKC Board approval.

The Flat-Coated Retriever's prowess on land and in water has earned him a host of admirers.

The NAHRA became the Parent association for this new sport, and the first AKC-sanctioned Hunting Retriever Field Test was held in Richmond, Virginia, in February 1984. The test drew an entry of more than 200 Retrievers.

A talented Pointer enjoys his day out with hunters.

This new Field Test for Hunting Retrievers and the ever-expanding sport of Retriever Field Trials were both vibrantly popular, predicting dramatically increased participation in these two AKC Field activities.

SPANIEL FIELD TRIALS

Spaniels were used for hunting game birds and waterfowl in America long before Spaniel Field Trials. The Cocker Spaniel, recognized by The Kennel Club (England) in 1892, had no trouble gaining stature in the United States as a hunting dog. The breed even had a sponsoring club early in the game; this was the American Spaniel Club, a strong organization founded in 1881. This club eventually accepted all hunting Spaniels—American Water, Clumber, Field, Irish Water, Springer (both English and Welsh), and Sussex.

English Springer Spaniel Fld. Ch. Stubblefield Ace High competed past age ten and figured prominently in many pedigrees.

ABOVE: English Springer Spaniel Fld. Ch. Rivington Countryman pictured with Dr. Samuel Milbank and Henry P. Davis, writer and Field Trial judge. BELOW: Cocker Spaniel Dungarvan Ready Teddy displaying the form that won the Open Class at the Connecticut Spaniel Field Trial Ass'n. event in the 1950s along with many other awards. Dungarvan Cockers have been a prominent influence in Field Cockers for decades.

The first Stakes for Cocker Spaniels were held in Verbank, New York, in 1924 by the Hunting Cocker Spaniel Field Trial Club of America, a club largely the creation of Ella B. Moffit, a well-known sportswoman from Poughkeepsie, New York.

Cocker Spaniel Merribarks Michelle closing in on the bird for owner Elaine Poole.

The name of the Hunting Cocker Club was changed to Cocker Spaniel Field Trial Club of America. The catalog of its Trial held in October 1931 shows that the judges were David Wagstaff and Captain Paul A. Curtis. Other luminaries of the Spaniel world who officiated as gunners or stewards included Ralph C. Craig, Henry Ferguson, Elias Vail, Dr. Samuel Milbank, and H. E. Mellenthin, breeder of the first Dual Champion—Dual Ch. My Own High Time—and the famous Ch. My Own Brucie, the Wesminster Best in Show winner in both 1940 and 1941.

FORM TRUMPS FUNCTION

The Depression and World War II caused an alarming decline in Spaniel Trials between 1934 and 1945, but rekindled interest in Field Trials for Cocker Spaniels during the late 1940s and 1950s led the way to increased activity in Spaniel Trials. For nine years, there was an annual National Championship for Cocker Spaniels, the last one in 1962 in Amwell, New Jersey. The last Field Trial stake for Cocker Spaniels was held in 1965. The game little Cocker Spaniel had become the darling of the Conformation world, where, in misguided innocence, the natural hunting instincts of some Sporting breeds are bred out on the notion that function follows form. With few, if any, Cockers in America having hunting genes available for breeding, the Cocker may have become a modern-day Field Trial dinosaur.

The English Springer Spaniel, which became eligible for AKC registration in 1910, gained popularity as an effective hunting dog in the early 1920s. Freeman Lloyd, a respected gundog journalist, wrote glowingly in the field press of that time about this new breed's ability as a hunter and a retriever.

There was never any conflict between the Cocker people and the Springer people. From the beginning, Trials held by the Cocker clubs included stakes for Springers. Likewise, Springer clubs throughout the country held Cocker Stakes. Interestingly, American and English Cockers competed in the same Stakes without breed distinction.

Field Trials were the perfect showcase for the Springer. The first Field Trial for Spaniels in the United States took place late in 1924 at Fishers Island, New York. Fishers always held Conformation competition in conjunction with the early Trials, and it was judged by a Conformation judge. Conformation was later dropped, but the Horsford Dual Challenge Cup still exists. It was originally presented in 1926 by William Humphrey of Shrewsbury,

Spaniels can be tenacious in the field.

England, for the Best Looking/Best Working Dog in the Trial. The Trial judges now select the winner.

The Springer's Parent Club, the English Springer Spaniel Field Trial Association, was founded in 1926, a direct outgrowth of the popularity of Springers competing in Spaniel Trials. It is the only AKC Breed Parent Club to still carry a Field Trial reference in its name.

The Brittany is among the most versatile of gundogs. It is a credit to breeders that so many Brittanys have both Conformation and Field titles.

FORM AND FUNCTION

Fortunately, the English Springer Spaniel did not suffer the same fate as the Cocker did, as the basic Springer gene pool remained intact in England. Nevertheless, breeding for form in the American show ring produced an entirely different dog from those on the modern English Springer Spaniel Field Trial circuit.

BASSET HOUND FIELD TRIALS

It is generally acknowledged that the first Basset Hounds came to America from France. George Washington's friend Lafayette sent him hounds for pack hunting in America, and these hounds were probably the so-called Old Virginia Bench-Legged Beagles.

Basset Hounds finding the scent in this training session in preparation for a Field Trial.

Other imports in the early nineteenth century were obtained from France, but some also came from British Packs, especially the Walhampton Pack. Gerald Livingston imported from the Walhampton Pack in the 1920s and formed his well-known Kilsyth Pack. Loren Free of Ohio also imported from the Walhampton Pack to form his Shellbark Pack, and during the 1930s, Carl Smith acquired the Starridge Pack.

The American Kennel Club began to register Basset Hounds in 1885 and recognized them as a breed in 1916. After AKC recognition of the Basset Hound Club of America in 1937, Conformation and Field Trial activities grew and spread rapidly.

The first Basset Field Trial was an AKC-sanctioned Trial held in Michigan in October 1937 by the newly formed Basset

The Basset Hound's ears pick up and help carry the scent.

Hound Club of America. It attracted seven Bassets. The hounds were run in Braces under AKC rules and procedures in use for Beagle Trials.

Soon after, each year two AKC-licensed Basset Field Trials were held in Michigan, Ohio, or Pennsylvania, with growth to about thirty to forty entries per Trial. By 1964, ninety-seven Bas-

The Basset Hound's short legs allow hunters to travel by foot.

sets had fulfilled the requirements for the Field Champion title. The sport spread rapidly to New

York, Massachusetts, New Jersey, Maryland, Kentucky, Illinois, California, and Texas, with many Trials attracting more than 100 entries. Today some twenty-four Basset Hound clubs hold Trials each year, and the Basset Hound Club of America gets the best of the Bassets together each spring and fall for national events.

There have been approximately twenty-two Dual Champion Bassets over the years. The first, Dual Ch. Kazoo's Moses the Great, became a Dual Champion in 1964.

Although not an AKC-recognized sport, Basset Hounds hunting in Formal Packs remains an interest in America, encouraged by the Basset Hound Club of America. Eleven Packs active into the 1980s included the Ashland, Sandanona, Tewksbury Foot, Three Creeks, Winward, Boniwell, Skycastle French, South Illinois, Wayne DuPage, Tantivy, and Timber Ridge Packs. Early Packs that no longer exist include the Kilsyth, Starridge, Shellbark, Brandywine, Stockford, and Coldstream Packs.

BEAGLE FIELD TRIALS

Beagle Field Trials, found only in the United States and Canada, started with this announcement in the Sunday *Boston Herald* in October 1890: "A group of Beagle owners would hold a Beagle Field Trial in Hyannis, Massachusetts, in a fortnight." This group called themselves the National Beagle Club of America, and the advertised Trial was held in November 1890, with eighteen entries (including Braces) made up of fifteen dogs and three bitches.

The Beagle's white tail tip is often all a hunter can see.

The Buckram Beagles of Dr. and Mrs. Joseph Connelly, ready for the day's hunt.

Shortly thereafter, they applied for AKC membership, but they were denied because a group of Conformation enthusiasts, known as the American English Beagle Club, already held membership. The men in the National Beagle Club of America refused to give up. Finally, in May 1891, the American

Beagles are stubborn, steady hunters.

An energetic group of Beagles competing in a Small Pack Trial.

Beagle Club (formerly the American English Beagle Club) merged with the National Beagle Club of America. The new group called itself the National Beagle Club, and it became the Parent Club for the breed.

Beagles make enthusiastic and hardy field dogs.

At that time, the AKC was completely Conformation oriented. An interesting note regarding the club's admission to AKC membership was the AKC's strong objections to the Parent Club's involvement in both Field Trials and Conformation. National Beagle Club President and AKC Delegate at the time, H. F. Schellhass, told the AKC: "This club was formed for improvement in the field and on the bench of the Beagle hound in America, and will enter the AKC with its constitution unchanged, if it enters at all." The AKC dutifully backed off.

HUNTING IN PACKS AND SINGLES

The sport of AKC Beagle Field Trials has something to offer any Beagle owner. Dogs can compete in any of five Trial formats or hunting styles. The oldest Trial format is that in which the Beagles compete in pairs, or Braces (divided by sex), today often called Traditional Brace. These Braces compete in pursuit of the cottontail rabbit. When this type of hound is run in a pack, it is called a Small Pack Trial, with between four and seven dogs to a pack. Another Beagle hunting style is called Gundog. When these dogs compete in groups of two, it is known as

A group of Small Pack Option Beagles ready for the hunt. The Small Pack Option still enjoys some loyal followers today.

a Gundog Brace Trial. The American Kennel Club began offering Gundog Brace Trials in 2002. When this type of Beagle runs in a pack, as opposed to a brace, it is known as a Small Pack Option Trial. In the northern states, where the snowshoe hare is found, Beagles may be trialed in Large Packs, where having twenty to forty hounds or more in a single class is not uncommon. Lastly, there is the non-AKC hunting format called Formal Packs, which are either privately owned or supported by subscription from local Beagle devotees. These events are run by the National Beagle Club, the AKC Parent Club for Beagles.

Three Formal Packs were entered at the National Beagle Club's meet in 1896. Today, twenty-eight such Packs are registered with that club. They are hunted as Three-Couple (six), Four-Couple (eight), and Eight-Couple (sixteen) Packs. At a Formal Pack Field Trial, each Pack is judged as a unit or team, and its performance is measured against that of other Packs in the Trial. The Packs are foot handled, with the Huntsman and his/her assistants, called Whippers-in. Packs are identified by the unique colored piping on the Huntsman's jacket.

In the United States, the traditional method of evaluating working dogs, sporting dogs, and hounds was in competition. In fact, the *AKC Beagle Field Trial Rules and Standard Procedures* states: "The holding of Field Trials at which pure-bred dogs may be run in competition . . . has been found to be the best method by which the progress which has been made in breeding can be shown."

CONSERVATION AND THE HUNT

Early Beaglers became aware that business and residential development was reducing the availability of hunting and training grounds. The purchase of land by Beagle clubs was encouraged and even mandated by the AKC. Beagle Field Trials are limited to the pursuit of quarry that is acclimated to the terrain, so Beaglers became ardent conservationists. Natural food and cover on Beagle club grounds became increasingly necessary to maintain a natural supply of rabbits for training and trialing. Clubs reclaimed marginal land, soil fertility was measured and improved, and the term *rabbit farming* became the byword at any progressive Beagle club. Today more than 400 Beagle clubs either own or lease land in excess of 150 acres each.

The building boom that followed World War II introduced hazards to hunting Beagles. Too often the rabbit would take the dogs across a new road or superhighway. For the hounds' safety, clubs were forced to fence their land. This also enclosed the rabbits, which then developed running styles unlike their cousins outside the enclosures.

Every Man's Dog

Participation in the sport of Formal Pack Beagling had always been limited to people with means. Beagle popularity inspired a new concept in the early 1900s. Middle-class Americans became interested in the development of an individual hound that could trail the hare or rabbit effectively and efficiently without the assistance of pack-mates. Beagles selectively bred with this concept in mind were referred to as "singles." It is not unusual to hear this term on the running grounds of the National Beagle Club when reference is made to Beagles in Braces.

BREEDING FOR STYLE—HUNTING, THAT IS

As a result, Beaglers bred for a slower, more precise working dog. Beagles, when run in Braces, were faster and less precise. The old one-on-one competition was replaced by an appreciation for the style in which the Field Trial Beagle tracked a rabbit. This was significant because nearly 90 percent of the 400 clubs holding AKC-licensed Trials ran Brace events.

At these Trials the Hounds with the "tracking style" that most impressed the judges won the ribbons. Through selective breeding, Beagles used at Field Trials and run in Braces became slow and extremely accurate when following a rabbit.

Rabbit hunters, the largest segment of game hunters in the United States, found that the slow, "stylish" Field Trial Beagle was totally undesirable as a hunting dog. By the early 1970s, there was a need for a real gundog or hunting Beagle. This movement gathered momentum, and breeding programs reflected the trend back to the early days.

The situation was different for northern clubs that ran their Large Pack Hounds on hare. They justifiably prided themselves on producing hunting Beagles and believed their Trials showed the Beagle to such an advantage.

The fans of the gundog or hunting Beagle did not believe that the Large Pack was the most acceptable method by which to pursue the cottontail rabbit. In the late 1970s, the *Small Pack Option* (SPO) became the fourth and newest type of competition for Beagles. As mentioned, in this format, gundog Beagles are run in packs of four to seven. This format called for testing the hounds for gunshyness and searching ability to prove beyond a doubt that they were competing with "hunting Beagles."

Judges then select the outstanding performers to run in a second series, a Winners Pack. The fifth and most recent AKC Beagle Field Trial format is *Gundog Brace*. These dogs hunt in a manner similar to SPO dogs, but run in groups of two.

KEEPING IT ALL ON TRACK

The sport of Beagle Field Trials was very diversified and yet had traditions dating back nearly 100 years. How could the AKC cope with the administration of five distinctive competitive standards for Beagle Trials, recognizing that purebred Beagles are competing in all five standards?

An AKC Member Parent Club, such as the National Beagle Club, was responsible for approving dates for local breed club events, as well as proposing the Standards by which the breed is judged in both Conformation and Performance Events.

In 1936, the National Beagle Club voted to abrogate part of its responsibilities as a Parent Club and ceased granting consent for Field Trial dates. Instead, they recommended that the AKC appoint a ten-member Advisory Committee from among the Delegates of the Beagle AKC Member Clubs. The purpose of this committee would be to advise the AKC Board of

Directors on the matter of granting licenses for Beagle Field Trials and propose changes to the Performance Standards. An AKC staff member would chair this Advisory Committee.

And so for over seventy years, a Beagle Advisory Committee (BAC) has been responsible for advising the AKC Board of Directors on the administration of Beagle Field Trials. Evolution played its part, and there have been some significant changes in the BAC structure. Since 1962 it has been a committee of twelve, eleven of whom each represent some forty Beagle clubs. The twelfth person belongs to the National Beagle Club of America. An AKC staff member still chairs the meeting, for a total of thirteen. The system has worked well.

DACHSHUND FIELD TRIALS

In the early 1930s, the short-lived United States Dachshund Field Trial Club held the first organized Field Trial for Dachshunds. The Hounds were put to ground in artificial rabbit burrows and judged by rules that originated in Germany.

In 1935, the Dachshund Club of America, Parent Club for the breed, held its first Trial in Lamington, New Jersey,

All Dachshunds, including these Wirehairs, can show their scenthound ability in Dachshund Field Trials.

under revised rules for American competition. This was under the leadership of the renowned Dachshund fancier Laurence A. Horswell. The Parent Club remained the only Dachshund club holding Field Trials until the Dachshund Club of New Jersey held its first Trial in 1966. Thus, with only one Trial each year, the greatest challenge for all Dachshund owners was to keep the Field Trial prospects alive long enough to earn the twenty-five points required for the Field Champion title. Today, thirty-two clubs hold Trials each year.

AKC rules for Dachshunds specify that judging be based on the following Standard of performance:

> In all Stakes the principal qualifications to be considered by the Judges are good noses, courage in facing punishing coverts, keenness, perseverance, obedience, and willingness to go to earth. Should a rabbit lodge in any earth, or run through any drain large enough for the Dachshund to enter, the dogs should, of course, be expected to enter without hesitation; and failure to do so should automatically render them ineligible for first award, even though their performance was in all other respects outstanding.

Since Dachshund Trials must use live rabbits or hares, they are always held on the grounds of a Beagle club, where game is plentiful. Like Beagles, Dachshunds compete in Braces, and the dogs both seek and pursue their game with obvious delight. However, unless the scent is particularly "hot" or the quarry is in sight, most Dachshunds run mute.

All varieties (Longhaired, Wirehaired, and Smooth) and sizes (Standard and Miniature) of Dachshunds compete in the field on an equal basis. At a Trial, a Dachshund is a Dachshund regardless of coat type or size, and all varieties have done their share of winning over the years.

The AKC record books also show that 313 Dachshunds have achieved the title of Dual Champion, thereby proving that function can definitely follow form.

PRESERVING INSTINCT

In the mid-1980s, the AKC created Hunting Test Programs for Pointing Breeds, Retrievers and Flushing Breeds.

These tests are *noncompetitive*. In a Hunt Test, dogs are judged against a standard of performance, and each performance is judged on

Earthdog Trials for Dachshunds and short-legged Terriers allow breeders and trainers to evaluate hunting instinct in today's dogs.

Real working Terriers were tethered while one was chosen for a particular task. At the time, the dogs shown here were called Jack Russell Terriers.

its own merit. Everyone could pass or everyone could fail. Without the pressure of competition, a dog's performance is not pushed to extremes in order to stand out from the rest of the class. Many dog owners prefer this type of event.

The three Hunting Test programs were each established with three levels of skill—Junior Hunter (JH), Senior Hunter (SH), and Master Hunter (MH). A dog can enter at the appropriate skill level. This approach allows owners to continue to participate as their dog gains experience and maturity. Over time they can progress toward a more complete and skillful performance.

The present-day Earthdog Program has its roots in the beginnings of small-game hunting. Farmers and hunters used the small Terriers and Dachshunds to pursue vermin to their lairs and then follow the game into the ground. These dogs had to possess not only the physical attributes that would allow them to descend into the animal's den and battle the animal on its own terms but also the needed courage and mental ability to accept the challenge of underground pursuit. The AKC's first licensed Earthdog Test was held on October 1, 1994.

Herding Breeds have been used since the 1800s for livestock control in many parts of the world. The AKC Herding Program was designed to

preserve the instinct and trainability of the dogs in the Herding Group. Today, with twenty-six AKC fully recognized breeds and eleven Foundation Stock Service breeds, the program includes breeds from many countries of origin.

A Samoyed demonstrates his natural skill at herding ducks.

Breeders want to ensure that, from generation to generation, our dogs retain the instincts for which they were originally bred. Below, a Bearded Collie, and at right, Pembroke Welsh Corgi pups get their first experience with sheep.

These Bloodhounds give voice as they utilize their training and genetic heritage on the trail.

Tracking and Trailing is an activity that grew in the mid-twentieth century. Some Bloodhound/Coonhound crosses were developed to lend the best native abilities of both breeds. However, dogs used for man-tracking were usually Bloodhounds, although they might have only a slight resemblance to the dogs of the latter

The Bloodhound is considered such a reliable tracker that its evidence has been accepted in a court of law.

twentieth century bred for the conformation ring.

The American Sighthound Field Association was founded in 1974 to keep all sighthounds in top running shape for Open Field Coursing. In 1974, there was no Lure Coursing as it exists today, although Whippets had been running 200-yard straight races as far back as 1964, and some individual breeds had competitions that would help Coursing Trials evolve. At that time, there were no machines to run a lure, so a bicycle's rear wheel rim with the tire removed was used as a take-up reel. The AKC Lure Coursing program began in 1991. Lure Coursing enthusiasts now have the ability to fashion a course up to 1,200 yards long in any configuration.

Salukis Srinagar Shaheen of Ellora and Celerity Jadid Sahib Kaaba show great enthusiasm at a Lure Coursing Field Trial in 1975. Shaheen (left) won the Trial for owner Ann Mary Pine.

It is evident that there has long been an effort to preserve many breeds' original functions, whether within the breeds themselves or through a collective, organized, and Trial-oriented plan.

Sighthounds such as this Scottish Deerhound show their skill on the Lure Coursing field.

James Ward's *Salukis*, circa 1807, given to The AKC Museum of the Dog by the estate of Cynthia S. Wood.

EDUCATION AND OUTREACH

n 1953, the progressive thinking of AKC Executive Vice-President John Neff led to the production of the first AKC film. This developed into an ongoing program of audiovisual educational materials for the fancy.

AKC's first film was titled *221*—the then street address of AKC headquarters on Fourth Avenue in New York. The 16-millimeter color film, intended for dog clubs, was an account of what happens inside the American Kennel Club—and why. The film's success prompted the AKC to produce its second film, *The Dog Show and You,* released in 1954. This film featured a Bench Show hearing, with the message that the sport of dogs is built on mutual respect and sportsmanlike conduct. By the time these films were retired in the 1960s, *221* and *The Dog Show and You* had been seen by hundreds of clubs in every region of the country.

In 1973, the American Kennel Club began another series of films, producing eleven between 1973 and 1980. The first film in this series was titled *Inside AKC*. Like its predecessor *221*, *Inside AKC* was intended to give the fancy a tour of the American Kennel Club and was an instant hit with dog clubs.

By the mid 1970s, the sport of dogs in the United States was experiencing a gigantic growth spurt. The number of dog clubs had climbed into the thousands, all eagerly seeking informative material for their meetings. The AKC's films were filling an increasing demand.

AKC Gazette's Annual Photo Contest, Honorable Mention, 2002, photographer Connie Whitmer.

AKC's most notable and successful film was *Gait: Observing Dogs in Motion,* which premiered at the "Day with AKC" symposium on November 9, 1974. The subject of how dogs move is of critical interest to fanciers, and this film employs special techniques that are very useful in fully analyzing movement, notably super-slow motion and stop-action photography.

Rachel Page Elliott, the noted authority on canine movement, served as a special consultant for *Gait.* This film won numerous awards, including the Silver Screen Award from the United States Industrial Film Festival. *Gait* has been viewed by thousands of dog clubs and purchased by more than forty other kennel clubs around the world. The film continues to be as useful as when it first appeared.

AKC Gazette's Annual Photo Contest, First Place Color, 2001, photographer Rebecca Ford.

Another film, *Dogsteps*, was based on Rachel Page Elliott's bestselling book of the same name. First published in 1973, this book enjoyed such popularity and acclaim that a second edition, *The New Dogsteps*, was introduced in 1983. The film was converted to a DVD and, along with the book, enjoyed active circulation into the new millennium.

AKC *Gazette*'s Annual Photo Contest, First Place Color, 2006, photographer Charles Guthrie III.

In the Ring with Mr. Wrong and *The Quest for a Quality Dog Show* highlighted Conformation. *In the Ring* is a humorous look at what can go wrong in the judging process, and *The Quest* is a visual checklist of what goes into staging a successful show.

Two of the AKC's films were devoted to Obedience. *200?*, which is the perfect score in Obedience competition, is a look at what goes into a truly outstanding Obedience performance. *Exercise Finished, A Day with an Obedience Judge* is a judge's eye view of Obedience competition with an emphasis on ring procedure as well as the judge's responsibilities.

Two films are devoted to Field Trial activities. *Carrying the Line* is all about Beagle Field Trials, and *With Courage and Style: The Field Trial Retriever* is a comprehensive look at the world of Retriever Trials.

AKC and the Sport of Dogs was the one film intended for general nondog audiences. The film opens with a two-minute history of purebred dogs and follows with a look at Field Trials, Obedience, and Conformation. Each year, thousands of different schools and other groups request this film, distributed for the AKC by Modern Talking Pictures.

Three films were produced in cooperation with breed Parent Clubs. These films were *The Irish Setter, The Doberman Pinscher,* and *The Shetland Sheepdog.* They were precursors to the American Kennel Club's joint Parent Club sound/slide show program, which began in the early 1980s with *The Dalmatian* and *The Basset Hound.* The program has expanded into a comprehensive effort to provide judges and everyone else seriously interested in any AKC breed with a quality educational audiovisual aid.

In August 1982, all Parent Clubs were contacted and invited to participate in the sound/slide show program, and the response was overwhelming. Within just a few years, programs for twenty-seven breeds were completed and sixty more were in some stage of development. The rapid growth of the home videotape industry at that time meant that breed audiovisuals could be produced as videocassettes for convenient home study.

One unique educational activity of the American Kennel Club should be noted. Between December 1, 1973, and May 24, 1975, the American Kennel Club hosted four all-day symposia about various aspects of the AKC. Called "A Day with AKC," these symposia were held in December 1973 in New Jersey, March 1974 in California, November 1974 in Illinois, and May 1975 in Texas. Collectively, more than 5,000 fanciers attended these symposia, which were intended to bring the American Kennel Club to dog people throughout the country.

Few subjects are as appealing as the dog. The American Kennel Club remains committed to educational activities about dogs and to providing the fancy with quality audiovisual projects about purebred dogs through breed DVDs and other educational materials.

THE COMPLETE DOG BOOK

The American Kennel Club is the author of the most successful dog book of all time. Continuously in print since 1929, *The Complete Dog Book* has sold well over 2,000,000 copies. The twentieth edition was released in 2006.

The first edition of the book was titled *Pure-Bred Dogs, The Breeds and Standards as Recognized by the American Kennel Club*. The main purpose of the book was to offer the public a single source containing all official Breed Standards. Accordingly, of the book's 315 pages, all but the final 15 pages of glossary were devoted to the Standards of the 79 breeds then recognized. In this first edition, each Standard was introduced by a single paragraph that summarized the breed's personality. A photograph of a typical representative of the breed accompanied the Standard. The majority of these photographs were taken by the celebrated dog photographer Rudolf W. Tauskey.

The cover for the 1943 edition of *The Complete Dog Book*.

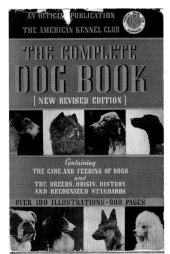

Through the years, *The Complete Dog Book* has grown, but its essential purpose has remained the same. The 1929 total of 79 breeds would be 128 by 1984, and then 158 by 2008. Two breeds, the Collie and the Poodle, were four breeds in

The best-selling dog book of all time, *The Complete Dog Book*: covers from the 1964, 1968, 1979, and 1985 editions.

1929: the Collie was divided into Collies, Smooth and Collies, Rough, and the Poodle was divided into Toy and Non-Sporting. Today these different types are recognized as Varieties, but in 1929, they were treated as separate breeds. Two breeds recognized in 1929 were no longer with us in 1985 —the Eskimo and the Mexican Hairless. Today, the American Eskimo Dog, virtually no relation to the Eskimo from 1929, is a member of the Non-Sporting Group, and the Xoloitzcuintli (formerly known as the Mexican Hairless) entered the AKC Miscellaneous Class on January 1, 2009.

The seventeenth edition of *The Complete Dog Book,* popular in the 1980s, contained the Standards of the 129 breeds then recognized—almost

50 percent more breeds than when the book was first published. In 1929, the eighty-nine breeds were divided into six Groups: Sporting, Hound, Working, Terrier, Toy, and Non-Sporting. The 1985 edition of the book was the first to incorporate the Herding Group, which began in January 1983 and included breeds that had previously been part of the Working Group.

The first two editions of the book, published in 1929 and 1935, were produced for the American Kennel Club by G. H. Watt Publishers. Subsequent editions were published by Halcyon House, NY, Garden City Publishing, and Doubleday, NY, respectively. Howell Book House began to publish the book beginning in 1972 with the fourteenth edition of the book. In 2006, the twentieth edition was published by Ballantine Books, a division of Random House.

The Complete Dog Book acquired its name when the third edition of the book appeared in 1938, which was also the first time that the book contained a section on dog care. Although vastly expanded since 1938, the book's basic contents today are similar to those of the third edition. The official Standard for each recognized breed appears with a brief history of the breed given by the Parent Club, along with a high-quality photograph depicting an excellent representative of that breed. There is an explanation of how AKC registration services work, an extensive section on care, advice on selecting a breed, and a description of the dog sports—Field Trials, Obedience Trials, Conformation, and Junior Showmanship—as well as a glossary. There are also anatomical drawings of the dogs and pages of color plates, full-color pictures of purebred dogs in all their diversity—one of the finest collections of dog photography ever assembled. The color sections were added to the Golden Anniversary edition of the book, which appeared in 1979

The twentieth edition of *The Complete Dog Book* (2006) contains 858 pages, 543 more than the first edition, an increase of 172 percent. More than ever, *The Complete Dog Book* remains dogdom's most sought-after volume and the only book containing the official Breed Standards of all AKC-recognized breeds. It is the essential source for everyone entering the world of purebred dogs.

The Complete Dog Book has long been the AKC's largest-selling publishing endeavor, joining the *Gazette*, the AKC's monthly magazine, and *Family Dog,* a bimonthly. Each year the American Kennel Club also publishes tens of thousands of pamphlets, booklets, rule books, and other specialty publications associated with the administration of the sport of purebred dogs in the United States.

THE GAZETTE

A period of four years elapsed between the founding of the American Kennel Club and the acknowledgment of a real need for this new "Club of clubs" to have a voice throughout the sporting world. What better way to communicate the decisions of this organization, its rules and regulations relating to Conformation and Trials, and its newly acquired registry than a journal, or, as it is known, the *Gazette*.

The November 1984 issue of the *American Kennel Gazette*, marking the one hundredth anniversary of the AKC.

In 1889, the AKC President, August Belmont, Jr., was one of the foremost Smooth Fox Terrier breeder/exhibitors in America and a prominent, somewhat colorful, judge. He was also one of the most innovative guiding spirits in the dog world. A gentleman of great vision and even greater wealth, Belmont put the wheels in motion to produce a "gazette" by guaranteeing $5,000 per year of his own money against any losses for five years. In January 1889, the *Gazette* made its first appearance. It not only survived those first five years without any blemish on its financial record but also has been published without interruption for more than a century, making it the oldest dog magazine in existence and possibly one of the oldest continuously published magazines anywhere.

FIRST ISSUE

The first issue of the *Gazette* was truly a collector's item. The cover, by today's standards, was an artist's nightmare and an advertiser's dream. It featured a lengthy advertisement for "Spratt's Patent Meat Fibrine Vegetable Dog Cakes with Beefroot and Cod Liver Oil." Visually, it left a lot to be desired. The inside front cover of the premiere issue announced the thirteenth annual Westminster event, and the masthead listed AKC officers, thirty-six active Member Clubs, applications for five new Member Clubs, and the resignation of the Western Pennsylvania Poultry Society of Pittsburgh.

Wasting no time with editorial frivolities, page 2 plunged into "Champions of Record"—ninety-four dogs in fifteen breeds. The show date section, called "Fixtures," listed eleven upcoming venues. A "Greeting" from the American Kennel Club stated its editorial policy, and from its tone was more likely to reassure the competition than to garner subscriptions:

Cover of a 1915 American Kennel Gazette. Note the accompanying ad for Spratt's Dog Cakes.

> The American Kennel Club…will endeavor, as much as lies in their power, to meet what they feel the Kennel World requires in the shape of an official organ; taking as their guide the expres-

The *Gazette's* Annual Photo Contest

A gallery of winners from the *AKC Gazette's* Annual Photo Contest, Black and White. Clockwise from left: Third Place, 1998, photographer September B. Morn; Third Place, 2006, photographer Chet Jezierski; First Place, 1993, photographer Eric Albrecht. FACING PAGE, clockwise from left: First Place winners from 2001, photographer Mary Ludington; 2002, photographer Jeff Zucker; 2009, photographer Debby Palleschi; 2005, photographer Cheryl Snyder; 2006, photographer Diane Lewis; 2000, photographer Doris Ratzlaff.

3rd
1998

3rd
2006

1st
1993

1st
2001

1st
2000

1st
2006

1st
2002

1st
2005

1st
2009

Samples covers from the *AKC Gazette* from October 2006, featuring a brindle Basenji (right), and April 2007, featuring a black Portuguese Water Dog (left).

sions of opinion on the subject from breeders and exhibitors, both in the past and since the adoption of the plan of publishing this *Gazette.*

It is proposed to afford the Kennel Club and its individual members an official medium for the publications of all proceedings and announcements bearing upon any subject embraced by the interests of the Kennel World, and to keep and publish a complete and official record of all that transpires during the year, either in connection with shows, Field Trials or matters affecting the breeding, kennel, or field management of any known breed of dog. It will be the policy of the *Gazette* to infringe in no way upon the province or enter into the field of the regular sporting journals. Having received the most flattering assurances of friendly feeling and professional co-operation from such sound and powerful sporting authorities as the *American Field,* the *Turf, Field and Farm,* and other journalistic friends, any fears respecting the advisability of the movement may be dismissed.

That first issue was a brisk twenty pages and contained one particularly intriguing entry—"Stud Visits" —with information concerning two

Collie stud dogs belonging to W. Atlee Burpee of flower and vegetable fame. This item was no doubt a forerunner of the breed club department's publications, coyly titled "Litterally Speaking," or "From the Litter Box."

No death notices of judges or other mere mortal humans appeared, but a discreet canine obituary column was found on the last page.

Advertising was accepted, and the rates would make present-day advertisers wild: the cover sold by inches, at two dollars per inch, and the inside pages could be bought on a descending scale. A twelve-time, one-inch insertion cost seventy-five cents.

Covers continued to be ads until 1924, and Spratt's Dog Cakes hung in there to the bitter end. Finally, photographs and fine artwork made their appearance on the covers. The January 1924 cover featured a pen-and-ink drawing of a Boston Terrier titled "An American Gentleman," by famous illustrator Carl Anderson. The inside pages featured drawings by Gustav Muss-Arnolt and S. Edwin Megargee that are museum collectibles today.

By June of that momentous first year, official Breed Standards were published, and show reports detailed the judges' findings with finely honed criticism.

More than a hundred years later, many of the same concepts still guide the magazine's editorial policy. The monthly "Secretary's Page" and quarterly Delegates' Meeting minutes keep the fancy informed of the American Kennel Club's business and are true records of all that transpires during the year. Feature articles on individual breeds, breeding, and related subjects bring the most up-to-date information available to subscribers.

The Early Years

In the *Gazette's* early years, the weighty matters rested on the shoulders of James Watson, an AKC Founder, Delegate from the Collie Club of America, and a newspaper man of some renown. He was officially appointed Editor in 1898; in 1900, he founded *Field and Fancy,* which in 1928 became the great and then greatly lamented *Popular Dogs*, a truly unique dog magazine in its time.

After Watson's resignation, there is no doubt that A. P. Vredenburgh, then Secretary-Treasurer of the AKC, who held that office for more than thirty-five years, had a hand in things. Finally, in 1924, Louis de Casanova was identified as Editor in Chief, ably assisted by a young man whose presence would have a profound effect on the magazine for more than forty years. That was Arthur Frederick Jones, an editor with unerr-

ing good taste and longevity. His continuing series, "Great Kennels of the Past," written in conjunction with Freeman Lloyd, provoked an acerbic reporter for the *New Yorker* to make this comment in his two-part dissection of the AKC: "[Jones' series is] the work of a single, appallingly persevering author." The "Great Kennels" series may well have set the world's record for number of articles on one theme; Jones wrote 365 and Lloyd produced 220. They appeared in the *Gazette* for more than seventeen years. Some even were reprinted in later issues.

The April 2008 cover of the AKC Gazette featured a Brussels Griffon as its cover dog.

Jones became Editor in Chief in 1942, holding the position until his retirement in 1968. His was a distinguished career indeed. He drew many top dog writers to the *Gazette* and wrote volumes himself under the monthly deadlines. His account of the Sesquicentennial Show bears careful reading to capture the true flavor of this unique and exciting dog event.

No mention of the *Gazette's* editorial pages would be complete without singling out Freeman Lloyd, one of the most knowledgeable dog writers of his day. John Marvin, another longtime contributor to the *Gazette*, wrote of Lloyd: "[His] knowledge of dogs, art pertaining to dogs, and general activities involving them has never been equaled…he was truly 'one of a kind.'"

Inflation took its toll over the decades. From twenty cents per copy and two issues per year in 1889, it grew to three dollars per copy and eighteen dollars per year for a subscription in 1985. Today the price of a single copy as measured against other long-running publications is probably still the best buy for the money among specialized publications. In January 1981, the Show Awards section became a separate publication called *The American Kennel Club Show, Obedience, and Field Trial Awards.*

The *Gazette* also went through various name changes. It started out as a publication called the *American Kennel Gazette.* In 1918, when it annexed the Stud Book, it was known as the *American Kennel Gazette and Stud Book.* When the *Stud Book* went off on its own, the *Gazette* went back to its original name. In March 1943, it became *Pure-Bred Dogs American*

Gazette Features

The *Gazette* highlights the following areas of interest, in addition to the "Secretary's Page" and quarterly Delegates' reports:

- quarterly breed columns written by a member of the breed's Parent Club
- veterinary news
- grooming, nutrition, and general health
- show dates and judging panels as they are approved by Event Plans
- statistics relating to all aspects of registration, all-breed and Specialty Shows, Obedience Trials, and Field Trials
- geographic lists of clubs
- breeding and puppy raising
- dog legislation and society's concern with the role of dogs in our lives
- therapy and assistance dogs
- Junior Showmanship
- book reviews
- Annual Photo Contest, initiated in 1979, with entries of over a thousand from both amateur and professional photographers
- an increasingly popular fiction contest that draws entries in the hundreds

Kennel Gazette (with the masthead emphasis on the word *Dogs*). In 1985, it was officially known as the *American Kennel Club Gazette*.

MOVING ON

What is the *Gazette* today? Over the years it has changed a lot, at least in physical characteristics. and stands firmly planted in a media-oriented society. In philosophy, however, it has changed very little. It is still the official publication of the American Kennel Club and, as such, tries to meet what the AKC requires of an official voice for the governing body of the sport of purebred dogs.

"KC," a resident cartoon dog, continued into the new millennium, passing judgment on a variety of subjects each month. In 2007, a new series, "Dog People," began a monthly look into contemporary ring personalties through the medium of affectionate caricatures.

The *Gazette* also attempts to bring educational material to all facets of the dog fancy through in-depth articles on interpretation and understanding Breed Standards. In summary, the *Gazette* has covered all aspects of the human-animal bond.

OTHER AKC PUBLICATIONS

Topping the list of other in-house publications before the mid-1980s is the *Obedience Regulations*, with well over 60,000 copies printed each year. The *Obedience Regulations* are followed by the *General Information* booklet and the *Rules*, with 43,000 and 32,000 copies printed, respectively.

One of the American Kennel Club's charter responsibilities involves issuing a monthly publication titled the *Stud Book Register*. One of the principal responsibilities of all agencies involved with the improvement of animals through selective breeding is the maintenance of pedigree information or a stud book. Until 1925, the AKC *Stud Book* registrations were published as part of the *Gazette*. From 1925 to 1952, a separate publication covered all *Stud Book* registrations. Since 1952, only dogs or bitches producing a litter for the first time have been published in the *Stud Book Register*. A dog's *Stud Book Register* publication date is always indicated in parentheses after the dog's name and becomes part of that dog's ongoing vital statistics in AKC records. The dog's entire pedigree can be traced by referring to the issues of the *Register* in which preceding generations of sires and dams appeared.

Even though any dog or bitch will appear only once in the *Register*, following the registration of the first litter produced by that dog (or bitch), the *Register* annually contains the names of several hundred thousand *new* sires and dams.

As part of its hundredth anniversary celebration in 1984, the American Kennel Club prepared and published a very special commemorative book titled *The AKC's World of the Pure-Bred Dog: A Celebration of the Pure-Bred Dog in America*. This was a handsome pictorial that touched on all facets of the dog sport. The book is a delight to leaf through, with a full-color insert featuring the dog in art from the collections of the AKC and the Dog Museum of America.

THE LIBRARY

At its April 10, 1934, meeting, the AKC Board of Directors appointed a committee to establish a library in its then headquarters at 221 Fourth Avenue in New York City. The committee was chaired by Hubert H. Brown, AKC Director and Delegate from the Irish Terrier Club of America, a publisher by profession. The other members were Louis de Casanova, editor of the *Gazette*; William Cary Duncan, AKC Director and Delegate from the Irish Setter Club of America; S. Edwin Megargee,

AKC Director and Delegate of the Los Angeles Kennel Club (and later of the Louisiana Kennel Club), a professional artist; and James W. Spring, Counsel for the American Kennel Club. In 1936, when Hubert Brown died, Edwin Megargee became the Committee Chair and held that position until his own death in 1958.

In November 1934, a report from Mr. Brown was published in the *Gazette* informing readers that the American Kennel Club Library was a reality. He stated, "It is the aim of the American Kennel Club to compile a great reference library of books treating all recognized breeds, and everything in which the dog is concerned."

In 1936, Edwin Megargee, a well-known artist, designed a special library letterhead and a bookplate that was placed in the 1,125 books in the collection at that time. The design featured three breeds native to North America: the American Foxhound, the Newfoundland, and the Chesapeake Bay Retriever. The Statue of Liberty appears in the background. The original drawing still hangs in the library. A special bookplate was used in commemorative gifts and featured the name of the donor and the date of the gift.

A primary activity of the library is answering requests for information that cannot be handled by other AKC departments. Thousands of visitors come into the library each year. People want to find out what breed of dog to choose, what to feed, and how to train. Some people come to trace pedigrees. Many of the well-known dog writers have also done much of their research in the AKC library.

THE COLLECTIONS

The heart of any library is its collections. The AKC book collection is one of the largest and best collections of canine literature anywhere in the world. In 1984, the collection was estimated to hold about 15,000 volumes, including bound periodicals as well as foreign and domestic stud books. The volumes cover many categories, such as individual breeds, art, literature, history, nutrition, breeding, training, disease, care, kennel management, showing, judging, and dog sports. Publications on other related subjects, such as works on wolves and animal behavior, also have their place on the shelves. Today, approximately 18,000 volumes fill the AKC Library's collection.

The library owns many of the major rare books about dogs. Among these treasures is *De Canibus Britannicis* (1570), the first book devoted to dogs. It was written in Latin by Johannes Caius, physician to Queen Elizabeth I and founder of Caius College, Cambridge, England. A translation into English was done in 1576 by Abraham Fleming, and the library has the 1881 reprint, itself a rare work, acquired in 1983. The significance of the book lies in the system of classification of dogs developed by Dr.

A Commemorative Stamp Issue

On October 6, 1982, the United States Postal Service advised the American Kennel Club of plans to do a block of four dog stamps to honor 100 years of purebred dogs in the United States. Dennis J. Holm called from Washington, DC, to say that Roy H. Andersen would be the designer of this commemorative issue. Mr. Holm said that the stamps would be ready for distribution in October 1984.

As it developed, the commemorative block of canine stamps was ready for release in September 1984. There was a strong possibility that the stamps could be released on September 17, 1984, which would have been a marvelous coincidence, as September 17,

1884, was the date of the American Kennel Club's founding. However, given many conflicting release dates, the official release date was set for September 7, 1984.

The American Kennel Club was chosen to host the first-day issue ceremony for the block of four twenty-cent stamps. New York Life, the owner of 51 Madison Avenue, graciously offered the use of its auditorium for this function. Approximately 250 guests attended the ceremony. Immediately following the ceremony, the speakers, the West Point Color Guard, musicians from the Juilliard School, and honored guests adjourned to the 200 Club for a social hour and luncheon.

Caius. Another important work is *The Master of Game,* written between 1406 and 1413 by Edward of Norwich, second Duke of York, although it was not published until 1904. The library's copy is one of the first 600 issued and has a foreword by Theodore Roosevelt.

Space does not permit more than a brief mention of the library's outstanding books. There is the 1881 facsimile of Dame Juliana Berner's *The Boke of St. Albans,* written about 1480, which was the first English-language book to discuss dogs. The author describes the British dogs as she knew them.

Sydenham Edward's fascinating book *Cynographia Britanica* was the first illustrated dog book and was published in 1800. The library obtained a copy with most of the pictures in 1983. In 1803, William Taplin wrote a two-volume work called *The Sportsman's Cabinet,* which discussed various dogs used in sports. The oldest breed book in the collection is *A Treatise on Greyhounds,* written by Sir William Clayton in 1819.

There are books in other languages, including French, German, Italian, Spanish, and Russian. Special collections of prominent dog people such as John Cross, the Shearer sisters, Alva Rosenberg, Robert Wiel, Dorothy Howe, and Major and Beatrice Godsol are shelved separately.

Each year the library receives and files periodicals and newspapers from all over the world. Among these are foreign magazines covering Sporting, Hound, Working, Terrier, Toy, Non-Sporting, and Herding Breeds. There are veterinary journals, rare-breed publications, and publications relating to humane societies and pet owners in general.

Our library is unique in that it is available to the public for research. A complete set of bound copies of the *Gazette* from 1889 to date and all AKC *Stud Books* are available for researchers. There is a large clipping file, and *Gazette* tear sheets are filed along with historical and archival matters, such as materials dealing with Breed Standards and breed recognition. The library maintains files and records for the AKC's extensive art collection, much of which is on display in the halls and offices. There is a large photographic archive and bookplate, medal, and stamp collections, all of which are housed in the AKC's corporate headquarters in New York.

The AKC library initiated its stamp collection in 1980. There are nearly a thousand stamps from all over the world, depicting dogs either as primary subjects or as part of larger scenes. The oldest is an American stamp from 1898 depicting a small dog seated on a plow in a wheat field. Many people and clubs from around the world have contributed stamps to the AKC collection, which can be viewed by the public with the assistance of an AKC staff member.

THE AKC MUSEUM OF THE DOG

Virtually every culture has cherished the special relationship between people and dogs. Cave paintings are alive with dogs and dog-like creatures, and that tradition has continued throughout the history of art, which has depicted canines in their many roles—as allies to hunters, farmers, and sportsmen and, in more recent centuries, as companions and honored pets.

Major museums around the world have collected works of art depicting the dog. Other such works are in private collections, not available to the general public. Indeed, the dispersion of one major art collection related to the dog dramatically illustrated the need for a museum dedicated to the dog and the dog in art.

In June 1980, the American Kennel Club responded to that need, creating

A gift to The AKC Museum of the Dog from the estate of Nancy-Carroll Draper, an exquisite blue leather chair with carved wood Dachshund arm rests.

the American Kennel Club Foundation, with the primary goal of setting up a national repository for works of art, books, and artifacts related to the dog. The Foundation moved quickly toward the establishment of the Dog Museum of America, the first repository for the display and study of canine art. The museum formally opened in September 1982 in space provided on the main floor of the AKC headquarters at 51 Madison Avenue in New York City.

The premiere exhibit at the Dog Museum of America, "Best of Friends," courtesy of the gallery's original director, William Secord.

From the beginning, the museum's exhibitions, publications, and educational programs were designed to illuminate the extraordinary part that dogs have played in our lives. The premier exhibit, "Best of Friends: The Dog in Art," revealed this rich heritage. The show featured artwork and artifacts spanning twenty-seven centuries, from the dog's earliest appearance in prehistoric cave drawings to twentieth-century artworks, including Alberto Giacometti's attenuated sculpture, *Dog*. In photographs, paintings, sculptures, lithographs, and watercolors, humankind's high regard and love for the dog have been profusely illustrated.

Gift from Frank T. Sabella of June Harrah's bronze, *Ch. Duc de la Terrace of Blakeen*, dated 1936. Duc was the 1935 Westminster Best in Show winner.

Matilda Lotz's *At the Garden Gate*, a gift to The AKC Museum of the Dog from Ronald H. and Kathleen S. Menaker.

Other exhibitions have been of a more documentary nature. "Show Dog!" was a visual history of showing dogs in England and America, and "The Dog World—How the Dog Made Man More Human," was a sweeping survey of organizations and institutions that have nurtured, studied, and honored our canine companions.

Of course, the dog has also been featured as a pet. Two very different exhibitions have highlighted the unique bond that exists between people and dogs. "Pampered Pets" traced the care and attention lavished on the dog from 350 BC, represented by an Egyptian mummified dog, to the twentieth century, represented by clothing, collars, and furnishings. A media extravaganza was staged during this show. An exhibition called "Canine Couture" was a fashion showing of more than twenty-five contemporary and vintage outfits for dogs.

"Era of the Pet: Four Centuries of People and Their Dogs" at the University Museum in Philadelphia honored the centennial of the American Kennel Club. Paintings, drawings, etchings, and sculptures recorded the evolution of today's concept of the pet from its earliest stages under

the reign of Louis XIV in the seventeenth century. This show also traveled, as the museum continued to reach out to people across the country—educating, enthralling, and exciting the enormous numbers of people who love the dog.

Special exhibitions for youngsters have been presented annually. Designed to create and develop an understanding between children and pets, programs have been given on the care of animals, and numerous films with canine stars have been shown. More than 10,000 New York City schoolchildren visited the museum in its first three years, enjoying the imagery of "Color Me Dog," "D is for Dog," and, in 1984, "Presidential Pets: Finny, Furry, and Feathered Friends in the White House." Coloring books, posters, and games accompanied these educational and entertaining shows.

In-depth art history shows have also been presented. "Fidos and

ABOVE: This nineteenth-century English inkwell of a reclining Mastiff was donated to the AKC by Marie A. Moore in 1972. BELOW: George Earl's *Bob*, 1871, a gift to The AKC Museum of the Dog from Frank T. Sabella.

ABOVE: *Setter in a Field*, by American painter Percival Leonard Rosseau, 1900, a gift to The AKC Museum of the Dog from The Westminster Kennel Club Foundation. LEFT: Rosseau's *Head Studies of Borzois*, 1911, a gift from Mr. and Mrs. Lawrence Kalstone, which was used as artwork for the poster announcing the creation of the Dog Museum.

Heroes in Bronze" was a landmark exhibition, depicting dogs in bronze sculptures from prehistoric Greece to the present day. Images ranged from faithful companion, guardian, hunter, and shepherd to religious symbol, mythological beast, and fantasy creature, all reflecting the changing attitudes of civilization.

In 1983, the museum mounted "The Dog Observed: Photographs 1843–1983." The exhibition was extremely well received by the press, earning writeups in *Newsweek*, the *New York Times,* and *Smithsonian* magazine. In 1985 and 1986, it trav-

eled under the auspices of the Smithsonian Institution Traveling Exhibition Service to cultural institutions in the United States and Canada, accompanied by a lavishly illustrated book published by Alfred A. Knopf. Works in the exhibition were drawn from the museum's expanding collections and from major private and public collections around the world, bringing into public view treasures that in many cases had been hidden for years.

A gift to The AKC Museum of the Dog from Katherine S. Finch, Frederick Thomas Daws's Afghan Hound painting from 1933, *Ch. Asri Havid of Ghazni, Ch. Sirdar of Ghazni, Ch. West Mill Omar of Prides Hill* and *Ch. Badshah of Ainsdart.*

Geraldine Rockefeller Dodge, a woman many call the greatest dog fancier ever, along with being a well-known philanthropist and art collector, was the subject of a major exhibition in 1985 and a book. Her extensive art collection, the basis for this exhibition, included thousands of works depicting animals and was dispersed by auction in the late 1970s, along with family photos, scrapbooks, and memorabilia. This, too, was an exhibition that appealed to dog fanciers and art and history lovers alike.

AKC exhibitions are diverse, designed to attract people of all ages, with a wide variety of interests, highlighting the importance of the dog in history, art, and contemporary life.

Through its exhibitions, publications, and educational programs, along with the research library, oral-history program, film archives, and lectures on dogs and the dog in art, the AKC Museum will continue to expand its ever-widening national audience.

CANINE HEALTH

The title of this section is also currently the name of one of the standing Delegate Committees. Before the creation of the Canine Health Foundation (CHF), this was a Board Committee, and one that had existed longer than all other Board Committees.

Early on, the Board of Directors of the American Kennel Club recognized the need to assist in solving canine health problems by supporting worthy research projects. Even today, the American Kennel Club encourages advances in canine health research through the Canine Health Foundation. Funding today is large compared with that of the early years, but the need for support is ever-growing.

Canine health research has always been a top priority with the American Kennel Club Board of Directors. One must remember that the American Kennel Club went through a dynamic growth period following World War II, when funds for canine health grants were not as readily available.

On December 29, 1952, the American Kennel Club's Board of Directors made the first formal appropriation of funds to an account known as Reserve for Educational Purposes and Research on Dog Health. The initial appropriation was $15,000. It was stipulated that these funds be used for the calendar year 1953. This was a landmark departure from the AKC's previous practice. In prior years, the sporadic gifts from the American Kennel Club for canine health and research were not only considerably lower in dollar amount but also earmarked for a particular problem.

The $15,000 appropriated for 1953 was awarded to fund a project titled Research on Canine Diseases. Cornell University College of Veterinary Medicine, Ithaca, New York, was the recipient of this landmark grant for canine health research.

The first fellowship sponsored by the American Kennel Club was in 1961. The fellowship went to the Animal Medical Center (NYC) for a study of comparative radiology. This first fellowship with specific focus was for $5,000. The second American Kennel Club fellowship followed in 1963 and was again awarded to the Animal Medical Center, this time for a study in cardiology. This fellowship was also for $5,000. The year 1963 also saw the American Kennel Club's funding of the American Veterinary Medical

AKC Gazette's Annual Photo Contest, First Place Color, 1994, photographer Carolyn Bolt.

Association (AVMA) symposium on hip dysplasia. This AVMA project was awarded a $4,000 grant to help defray costs.

In 1983, the Board of Directors of the American Kennel Club set up two postdoctoral fellowships for research in canine health. These were to be awarded to outstanding postgraduate students who wished to pursue a canine health research project.

Appropriations for canine health, research, and education given by the American Kennel Club Board of Directors from December 29, 1952, to December 11, 1984, totaled $2,313,161.08. This figure includes all research grants, fellowships, postdoctoral fellowships, educational films, slide projects, American Kennel Club symposiums, and related legal and public affairs budgets.

Canine Health Research Grants, Fellowships, and Postdoctoral Fellowships Before the Mid-1980s

Cornell University Baker Institute	$ 570,000.00
University of Missouri	207,364.00
Frozen Canine Semen (various research projects)	187,777.00
Morris Animal Foundation	186,148.28
University of Pennsylvania Veterinary School and Veterinary Hospital	151,200.00
Postdoctoral Fellowships, 1984	30,000.00
Health Research Inc., Albany, New York	29,735.00
American Veterinary Medical Association	25,758.61
Orthopedic Foundation for Animals	17,000.00
Dr. Priscilla Stockner, Project Monitor	16,146.15
University of South Carolina	15,000.00
Animal Medical Center, New York	10,000.00
All Other Projects	24,714.33
Total	$1,470, 843.37

AKC efforts to work with researchers in the field of canine health and research units in the United States are well documented. It should be noted that the dog is an excellent model for the study of human disease. Because of the parallels between canine and human disease, most fields of canine research also benefit humans. It is hoped that the American Kennel Club's canine health, research, and education efforts will repay, in some small way, the friendship and devotion of our canine friends.

The AKC Commitment to Canine Health

The AKC Canine Health Foundation (CHF) was founded in 1995 with the mission "to develop significant resources for basic and applied health programs with emphasis on canine genetics to improve the quality of life for dogs and their owners."

Since its creation, $22 million has been donated to fund more than five hundred research projects at seventy-four vet schools and research institutes worldwide. The AKC has been the largest contributor to date, donating more than $18.5 million. Parent Club Health Committees also facilitate Donor Advised Funds through the AKC CHF for research on breed-specific genetic diseases.

CHF-funded research in areas such as canine cardiology, critical care, dermatology, behavior disorders, and infectious diseases results in health-care improvements that benefit all dogs. To date, more than a dozen genetic tests have been developed to identify widespread diseases such as progressive retinal atrophy (PRA), hypothyroidism, and Fanconi syndrome.

A number of the resulting advances in canine research have also proven valuable to human researchers, particularly in the area of genetics. The AKC CHF has also donated $2.2 million to canine genome-mapping research projects, which contributed to the complete genome sequence performed by the National Institutes of Health.

Specific information on numerous ongoing CHF research studies is available on the CHF Web site: www.AKCCHF.org.

The AKC CHF also offers educational programs for breeders and Parent Clubs each year to present new information on canine health, genetics, reproduction, and nutrition.

The Canine Health Resource Center, on the Web at www.akcdoghealth.com, is the AKC's newest online resource for comprehensive information on current canine health research, available tests, links to health registries, informative articles, and educational podcasts. The site contains information for major canine health registries, parent clubs, tests, and results available from the Canine Health Information Center (CHIC), as well as resources to help potential puppy buyers find a well-bred healthy dog.

Maud Earl's *Great Dane*, given to The AKC Museum of the Dog by the estate of Nancy-Carroll Draper, a well-known Great Dane breeder of the Danelagh Kennels, whose contributions to the breed spanned fifty years.

THE AKC CENTENNIAL

Most appropriately, the American Kennel Club marked its 100th birthday with a truly spectacular Conformation Event and Obedience Trial. It was only the second show that the AKC had ever staged, the first one being the Sesquicentennial in 1926. Since many of the AKC-registered dogs are at least part-time show dogs, it was a proper way to mark the occasion. Such was the concept created by then AKC Executive Vice-President Charles A.T. O'Neill.

ANOTHER WORLD

The show, held on November 17 and 18, 1984, at the massive Philadelphia Civic Center, was officially labeled the AKC Centennial Dog Show and Obedience Trial. More than 8,000 dogs were entered, making it the largest dog show ever recorded in the United States. When combined with numerous Specialty Shows on Friday, and the Philadelphia Kennel Club Show the following Monday, it became the largest canine weekend in the world, with 14,000–15,000 entries. Getting a hotel room anywhere near the Civic Center that weekend was about as tough as getting a seat in the United States Senate.

Anyone entering the arena on the upper level from Civic Center Boulevard could only describe the experience as mind-boggling. Straight ahead was a handsome AKC display, and to the left was a post office offering first-day cachets and special commemorative sheets. Below, in some kind of self-contained chaos, were people and dogs by the thousands. It was like entering another world—an ultimate world of dogs.

Thousands of local dog lovers and just plain curious spectators joined exhibitors, handlers, and well-wishers who had come in throngs to the Civic Center to see the impossible come true. What was impossible? The very idea that any kind of order could emerge from that many participants, spectators, animals, vendors, officials, and security

Highest Scoring Dog in Obedience: English Springer Spaniel Donahan's Whimsy, CDX; Open B, 199. Owner, Martha S. Leonard; breeders, Donald and Carol Callahan.

HIGHEST SCORING DOG IN OBEDIENCE

THE WHITE HOUSE

WASHINGTON

November 13, 1984

I am delighted to send my warm greetings to all those gathered to celebrate the 100th anniversary of the American Kennel Club.

Helping dog lovers throughout the nation to organize shows and trials guided by uniform standards of breeding and registration, your fine organization has a reputation as being a dog's best friend. I commend you for your devoted efforts to promote proper pet care and a better appreciation of our canine companions.

Nancy joins me in congratulating you on this important milestone, and we send you our best wishes for continued success in the years ahead.

Ronald Reagan

Terrier Group First, Irish Terrier Ch. Tralee's Rowdy Red. Owner, Edward B. Jenner; breeders, Mary Roberts and Cary Klemperer; judge, Michele L. Billings; handler, Robert A. Fisher.

personnel. It wasn't that this show differed so drastically from any other dog show; it was just that it was four to five times larger than any dog show ever seen in the Western Hemisphere. And it worked. On two consecutive days, from 8 a.m. until 11 p.m., it worked.

If you assemble approximately 8,075 dogs from all over North America, it stands to reason that many good dogs will show up—and they did. Exhibitors and handlers came with the best they had, to face the toughest roster of judges that could be assembled, 121 in all. The people who help give the fancy its dignity and quality came from all over the continent to appraise dogs that completed the equation. It was quality against quality being judged by the best.

ON WITH THE SHOW

Saturday morning, the show began at 8 a.m. With resounding support from the Obedience community, there were 574 Obedience entries ready to compete. This size of this entry necessitated dividing each of the six Classes into two parts. Kent Delaney, Don Young, Louis Garfield Menninger, Mary Lee Whiting, Samuel Gardner, Charles LeBoutillier, Irma Dixon, and Melinda Giles were the judges.

The Obedience competition began when the show opened, and some remarkable performances were recorded. The Novice A Class was won by a Labrador Retriever bitch, Whitehead's Ms. Mocha, with a score of 195. Novice B honors went to a Border Collie dog, Wayside Catch the Spirit, who earned a score of 199. Open A was captured by a Shetland Sheepdog bitch, Karenwoods Sheza Joy, who scored 197-½ and won a runoff to take First Place. In Open B, an English Springer Spaniel bitch, Donahan's Whimsey, CDX, triumphed with 199 points. Utility A was won by a Pembroke Welsh Corgi dog, Larklain Lees Honeybear, CDX, who earned the Class win with 198 points. The Utility B Class was won by a Golden Retriever bitch, OTCh. Richess Merri Mindi of Shy-Yo, TD, with a score of 198.

At the end of the two-day Trial, the coveted High in Trial honor was won in a runoff by the English Springer Spaniel from Open B. It is interesting to note

Working Group First, Doberman Pinscher Ch. Brierpatch's Christmas Dream. Owner, Tonja Chiles; breeders, Tonja Chiles and Ruth Kearney; judge, Mrs. Augustus Riggs IV; handler, Vicki Fillinger (Seiler).

Toy Group First, Maltese Ch. Keoli's Small Kraft Warning. Owner, Carol Andersen; breeder, Jeff and Molly Sunde; judge, Melbourne T. Downing; handler, Jackie Liddle (Stacy).

that in this, some of the toughest competition waged to date, the six Classes were won by six different breeds! The dog sport begun in America by Helene Whitehouse Walker was continuing to evolve.

At 9 a.m., Conformation judging commenced with the Toy, Working, Non-Sporting, and Herding Breeds. This was not a show where a hair could be out of place or a misstep taken. It was the best against the best under the eyes of the most discerning. Just to add a little extra pressure, the crowds around every ring included some of the most knowledgeable dog fanciers from the United States and around the world.

It was not long before the Best of Breed winners began to emerge, forming the Groups that would be judged that evening. By evening, all of the breeds in Saturday's four Groups had been judged. Out of 674 Non-Sporting Dogs, only the 13 Best of Breed winners remained. The 546 Herding Dogs were narrowed to 15, and out of 1,117 Working Dogs, 19 would go on to face Group competition. Nineteen Best of Breed winners would represent the 799 Toy entries that night. An incredible 3,136 dogs had been meticulously evaluated by 59 judges. The judges, in turn, were equally scrutinized by thousands of spectators, some of whom had never been to a dog show. It was, by anyone's standards, a remarkable mix.

On Saturday evening, following an excellent Field Trial Demonstration Program, Group judging began. Mrs. Augustus Riggs IV examined the Working Group and began her final selection process. The field was distinguished and the task a difficult one, but Working Group First went to a Doberman Pinscher, Ch. Brierpatch's Christmas Dream, a five-year-old dog who had bested 177 entries in the breed. The Toy Group was next, with Melbourne T. L. Downing presiding. Maltese Ch. Keoli's Small Craft Warning, one of thirty-two judged in the breed that day, won the Group and became part of the elite lineup for Best in Show the next evening.

Henry H. Stoecker judged the third of Saturday's Groups, Non-Sporting; after careful consideration of the field of thirteen, he awarded the Group to a Bichon Frise, Ch. Camelot's Brassy Nickel. The little champion had a lot of fans in the audience and seemed to know it. The last Group of the evening was Herding. Langdon L. Skarda had fifteen outstanding dogs. As is generally the case, the Group attracted a great deal of attention, virtually all of it partisan in one way or another. The spectacular German Shepherd Dog Ch. Covy Tucker Hills Manhattan won the Group, an honor that was a fitting addition to his already distinguished career.

Non-Sporting Group First, Bichon Frise Ch. Camelot's Brassy Nickel. Owner, Pam Goldman; judge, Henry H. Stoecker; handler, Clifford Steele.

World Congress of Kennel Clubs

The third World Congress of Kennel Clubs was held in Philadelphia, Pennsylvania, on November 12–14, 1984, in conjunction with the AKC's 100th anniversary celebration. The chairman of the congress was Mr. William F. Stifel, President of the American Kennel Club. Forty-five Delegates from eighteen countries and six continents attended the Congress to discuss topics as wide ranging as international breed standards and judging to genetic and infectious canine diseases and restrictive canine legislation.

The Delegates visited the University of Pennsylvania University Museum for an exhibition on domesticated animals created by the School of Veterinary Medicine, as well as an exhibit of canine art produced under the auspices of the Dog Museum of America. Other activities for the Delegates included a Dog Judges Association presentation on numerous breeds, which was followed by twenty-seven Specialty shows. This culminated with the Delegates attending the AKC Centennial Dog Show and Obedience Trial as AKC guests.

Of the 2,998 dogs assembled on Sunday, only 3 would face the 4 survivors from the preceding day. Everyone involved in the show anticipated another exciting event, as thousands of spectators began streaming into the aisles and benching areas to view the contenders.

"What kind of dog is that?" was asked a thousand times by people new to the dog world. The newest of the recognized breeds at that time, the Ibizan Hound and the Pharaoh Hound, were represented by a remarkable showing of eighteen and sixteen entries, respectively. For many, it was their first chance to observe these ancient breeds, at least in numbers that would allow comparisons to be made. The Otterhound, so often unseen at shows, had sixteen breed representatives on hand for competition.

Junior Showmanship finals were judged by Robert S. Forsyth and preceded the evening's Group judging. The winner was Penelope A. Bender, showing a 15-inch Beagle.

The Hound, Terrier, and Sporting Breeds were judged on this day, with Group judging to follow. The Sporting Breeds in general constituted one of the most distinguished Groups ever assembled in this country. Even more than usual, the Terriers were exciting, and the Hound Group featured some of the most venerable breeds in the history of humankind.

In each breed/variety, and in each of Sunday's three Groups, judging moved forward with excitement. The show was heading toward the culmination of this unprecedented event, and the anticipation was certainly building. A win of any kind at this landmark show was important not only to one dog or bitch but also to their offspring and kennel name. The fact that a ribbon or trophy earned at this show would be a part of dog-show history was not far from anyone's mind, certainly not anyone in the sport of dogs.

By late evening, out of Sunday's 2,998 entries, 3 dogs remained: an Irish Terrier, a Bloodhound, and a Golden Retriever. The Group judges were E.W. Tipton, Jr., Sporting; Maxwell Riddle, Hound; and Michele L. Billings, Terrier. The Irish Terrier, Ch. Tralee's Rowdy Red, had been a popular choice for his breed win earlier that day. The Golden Retriever, Ch. Libra Malagold Coriander, triumphed over 136 entries in the breed. Ch. Baskerville's Sole Heir, the Blood-

Sporting Group First, Golden Retriever Ch. Libra Malagold Coriander. Owners, Carole Lazor, Diane Pavella and Connie Gerstner; breeder, Cheryl Blair; judge, E.W. Tipton, Jr.; handler, Connie Gerstner (Miller).

Hound Group First, Bloodhound Ch. Baskerville's Sole Heir. Owners, Drs. Stephen and Susan Harper; breeders, Bill and Sandy Barber; judge, Maxwell Riddle; handler, Thomas A. Glassford.

hound Best of Breed winner, sang to the audience in return for their applause.

And then there were seven. The Best in Show lineup would include a Golden Retriever, a Bloodhound, a Doberman Pinscher, an Irish Terrier, a Maltese, a Bichon Frise, and a German Shepherd Dog. One of them would go on to become the winner of the biggest and one of the most distinguished dog shows recorded by the fancy in North America to that time. Other dogs were already homeward bound, traveling on airplanes or headed out in vans to almost every state and province. But the mighty seven remained.

As is the custom, Best in Show judge William L. Kendrick had been waiting in his hotel room and would not come to the Civic Center. He would not see a catalog until the show was over and did not know what dogs or even what breeds he would be seeing, as no news had been allowed to pass his way.

There wasn't a dog in the final lineup that did not have many fans in the audience. Even people whose interests were in breeds other than the seven represented had enthusiasm for their Group winner. The atmosphere was electric, as expected.

William L. Kendrick was the only person who could make the decision. As experienced with dog shows and judging as he was, he no doubt still felt special pressure. After thoroughly examining each Group winner and allowing the anticipation to build, he made his choice. The German Shepherd Dog, Ch. Covy Tucker Hills Manhattan, took the rosette and silver trophies. "Hatter," as he was called by those who knew him, was one of the most distinguished representatives of the newly formed Herding Group as had ever been seen.

EPILOGUE

The AKC Centennial turned out to be not only the dog show of the century but also a major spectator attraction in a city thoroughly conditioned to superlatives.

Dogs, the first domesticated animals, and perhaps for two hundred centuries the favorite companion animal, were given their day in November 1984 in Philadelphia. In fact, two very exciting days will always be remembered by all who were there and will be recounted repeatedly to those who were not.

Best in Show, German Shepherd Dog Ch. Covy Tucker Hills Manhattan. Owners, Shirlee Braunstein and Jane Firestone; breeders, Cappy Pottle and Gloria Birch; judge, William L. Kendrick; handler, James A. Moses.

Arthur Wardle's *Rabbiting* (undated), given to The AKC Museum of the Dog by the estate of Cynthia S. Wood.

THE AKC
AT HOME

On September 17, 1884, the meeting that resulted in the organization of the American Kennel Club was held in the Philadelphia Kennel Club office. During the next several years, the American Kennel Club did not have an official office. Meetings were held in various cities: Baltimore, Cincinnati, Boston, Newark, and New York. In New York City, meetings were held at the Downtown Association on Pine Street, the Hoffman House, the old Madison Square Garden, and the New York Life Building.

AKC OFFICES

The American Kennel Club's offices were in the Wall Street district of Manhattan and in different spaces on Liberty Street in Manhattan. By 1909, the American Kennel Club had outgrown its offices and relocated to 1 Liberty Street for a ten-year stay. In 1919, the AKC moved to what was to be its longest occupancy, a little more than forty-four years, 221 Fourth Avenue, later renamed Park Avenue South. Starting out on the building's fifth floor, the offices moved in 1928 to the twelfth floor of the same building. In January 1964, with more than 300 employees and the largest canine library in the world,

Reception area of the AKC's headquarters at 260 Madison Avenue, adorned with beautiful artwork on the walls.

the American Kennel Club moved to the New York Life Building at 51 Madison Avenue, New York, New York. The AKC stayed at that address until November 1998, when it moved to 260 Madison Avenue, where the New York headquarters remains at the time of this writing.

ORGANIZATION AND STRUCTURE

From its inception, the American Kennel Club has been a "Club of clubs." Although during the early years of the American Kennel Club's existence there was a provision for individual Associate Members (later called Associate Subscribers), this practice ended in 1924. Ever since that time, only dog clubs have been allowed to become AKC Members.

The organizational structure of the American Kennel Club has been adjusted over the years as the interest in purebred dogs has grown. Before the establishment of the Board of Directors in 1906, an Advisory Committee, and then an Executive Board consisting of Delegates, handled the affairs of the club between quarterly Delegates' meetings. The actual guardianship of the AKC office was in the hands of the Secretary, who operated with a very small staff. After 1906, the AKC bylaws stipulated that the Secretary could not serve as a Delegate.

In 1906, when the AKC began to actively pursue incorporation, the club created the Board of Directors, consisting of thirty members, made up of five classes with six members each. The Delegates from all of the Member Clubs elect the Board of Directors from the Delegate body and vote on any amendments to the AKC bylaws or rules. The size of the Board was reduced in 1931 so that it subsequently consisted of twelve members (four classes with three members each).

The front foyer, appointed with sculptures gifted to the AKC, of the current Madison Avenue headquarters.

Seated Whippet bookends from the Shearer Collection, a gift to the AKC from the Shearer sisters, on display at the AKC's headquarters in New York.

In 2001, the number on the Board was expanded to thirteen (one class to include four members) to avoid future tie votes on issues. At that same time, going forward, the President would be designated as an ex officio member of the Board. This was a substantial change, as throughout most of the American Kennel Club's history, the Board had been chaired by the President of the American Kennel Club, who was an amateur sportsman. In 1913, Dr. John E. De Mund was briefly designated as Chairman of the Board. However, it was specified that the Chairman was only to preside at the Board meetings in the absence of the President and Vice-President, who were also members of the Board. The actual running of the AKC on a day-to-day basis was variously in the hands of the Secretary, the Executive Vice-President, or the Executive Secretary, who were full-time employees.

GROWTH AND REORGANIZATION

The greatest growth at the AKC took place in the years following World War II. In 1946, there were 206,978 registered dogs and a total of 806 AKC-approved dog events. There were 179,967 dogs in competition, and a staff of 149 employees at the AKC handled this volume. In 1984, the American Kennel Club registered 1,071,299 dogs and held 9,926 dog events. There were 1,352,099 dogs in competition, and 409 employees handled this volume. The number of AKC employees reached a peak in 1971 with a total of 724. The reduction in employees from 1971 to 1984 was made possible with the advent of system design and computerization. To illustrate the growth of the American Kennel Club since World War II, comparisons are given among registrations, dog events, dogs in competition, and number of employees:

Year	Registrations	Dog Events*	Dogs in Competition	Employees
1946	206,978	806	179,967	149
1950	251,812	2,878	190,188	188
1960	442,875	5,364	359,552	242
1970	1,056,225	7,063	758,261	636
1980	1,011,799	8,885	1,153,347	422
1984	1,071,299	9,926	1,352,099	409
2008	716,195	22,630	3,043,672	378

* Sanctioned and Licensed Events

In 1968, Alfred M. Dick was named President, and he was the first who would function as the Chief Operating Officer on a full-time basis. Simultaneously, a provision was added to the bylaws that enabled the Board to appoint one or more Vice-Presidents, who also were to devote their full-time efforts to the AKC. The bylaws in effect prior to 1969 only provided for a President, an Executive Vice-President, an Executive Secretary, a Treasurer, and a Secretary.

In 1972, then AKC President John A. Lafore, Jr. proposed an amendment to the bylaws—"In order to blend the advantages of a professional President, and at the same time, have an amateur officer in the top position in the same tradition as our policy for more than 80 years…"—that would create the position of Chairman of the Board.

Many of the changes that came about in the organization of the American Kennel Club resulted from the increasing volume of work associated with the sport of purebred dogs. Over the years, both registrations and dog show activities steadily increased. This necessitated a larger office force and a more complicated management structure to supervise that staff.

DELEGATES' MEETINGS

During the American Kennel Club's early years, Delegates' meetings were held in hotels. However, while the AKC offices were at 221 Fourth Avenue, the quarterly Delegates' meetings were held at that address, a practice that continued until September 1946.

After the September 1946 meeting, the quarterly Delegates' meetings, which had grown considerably in size, were again relocated to hotels. The December 1946 Delegates' meeting, at the Hotel Commodore in New York City, was the site of the Delegates' quarterly meetings until March 1954. The June 1954 Delegates' meeting found the American Kennel Club at the Roosevelt Hotel, where the meetings remained until December 1956. In March 1957, the meeting moved to the Hotel Biltmore, where the quarterly meetings remained until June 1981. From September 1981 until June 1988, meetings were again held at the Roosevelt Hotel. In September 1988, meetings were moved to the Marriott Marquis, and then were held variously at the Hyatt, Sheraton, and Crown Plaza, all in New York City. In recent years, meetings have been held in New Jersey and in various cities around the country.

The original publication *The American Kennel Club 1884–1984: A Source Book,* edited by Charles A. T. O'Neill, covered the high points, historical facts, and significant landmarks in the American Kennel Club's first century of growth. We are certain that many of the recorded changes relating to the early days of the American Kennel Club were accompanied by debate, argument, and resistance. Dog fanciers and breeders of past eras probably were just as divided on Breed Standards, Conformation, and Field Trial rules and procedures as we are today. The important point is that the American Kennel Club was responsive to the need for change. Had it not been, the club's growth would have slowed and stopped.

The American Kennel Club's record of positive change throughout its first century is a marvelous heritage. We cherish it and have looked forward to greater growth and achievements in our second century. Read on.

AKC Gazette's **Annual Photo Contest, First Place Color, 2004, photographer Carol Beuchat.**

American artist Roy Andersen's *Ch. Ginjim's Royal Acres*, 1986, given to The AKC Museum of the Dog in 1997 by the Janet A. Hooker Charitable Trust and Gilbert S. Kahn.

THE AKC'S
SECOND CENTURY

Throughout the decade of the 1980s, the American Kennel Club continued its longstanding commitment to ensuring the integrity of the registry and promoting responsible dog ownership. As a result, the AKC collaborated with the Delegate body, breeders, various organizations, government agencies, and countless volunteers to launch new programs and services and to work for fair and uniform dog laws across the country.

FIRSTS

The first AKC program open to all dogs was the Canine Good Citizen® (CGC) program. Approved by the Board of Directors in June 1989, the AKC's Canine Good Citizen Test was designed to create better dog manners and encourage responsible dog ownership.

This program was created in part in response to increasing anti-dog sentiment in the country, as evidenced by an increase in breed-specific legislation. The choice to make the program open to all dogs emphasized the AKC's commitment to responsible dog ownership. The Canine Good Citizen Program was designed as a two-part program that stresses responsible pet ownership for owners and basic

Canine Good Citizen test underway with this Bullmastiff and his owner.

good manners for dogs. CGC was developed by the AKC and under the direction of then AKC Secretary James E. Dearinger, but was administered by individual clubs and certified trainers. This program achieved national recognition. By the end of 1989, over 5,000 Canine Good Citizen certificates had been awarded.

The first full year of the AKC's CGC program was 1990, and by the end of that year, it was estimated that over 1,000 dogs per month had been tested. During May of 1994, the program was heavily promoted through "National AKC CGC Month." More than 450 communities participated, and the CGC message reached more than 22.3 million households.

Canine Good Citizen

AKC's Canine Good Citizen (CGC) Program was introduced in 1989 to encourage and acknowledge responsible ownership. All dogs are welcome in CGC, including purebreds and mixed breeds. The CGC Program has become recognized as a stepping stone to AKC Companion and Performance Events, therapy dog work, and various dog sports. Its success has also led to the development of similar programs in other countries.

With the tagline of "Responsible Owners, Well-Mannered Dogs," the CCG program consists of two parts: The first involves the owner's signing the Respon-

sible Dog Owner pledge, thereby agreeing to conscientiously supervise the dog's behavior, health care, safety, exercise, training, and quality of life. The second part is the CGC test itself, which consists of ten exercises. The CGC test is designed to demonstrate good manners, social skills, and comprehension of basic commands.

Dogs passing the test receive the attractive AKC CGC certificate with the CGC logo embossed in gold at the bottom. CGC evaluators and upcoming tests throughout the country can be located through the AKC Web site. Today, there are nearly ten thousand CGC evaluators in the United States.

These are the ten exercises

1. Accepting a friendly stranger
2. Sitting politely when petted
3. Appearing healthy and accepting grooming
4. Walking on a loose lead
5. Walking through a crowd
6. *Sit*, *Down*, and *Stay* on command
7. Coming when called
8. Behaving appropriately toward another dog
9. Reacting appropriately when faced with common distractions
10. Behaving acceptably when left on leash with a trusted person for three minutes.

AKC MUSEUM OF THE DOG

On September 15, 1982, the Dog Museum of America, as it was originally named, unveiled its first exhibition: "Best of Friends: The Dog and Art." It was the AKC's intention to "improve the life of the dog through humane education, to gather and add knowledge on the care and history of the dog, and to develop and support a museum of art and books focusing on the dog."

By 1985 it was apparent that the museum was outgrowing its loaned space at 51 Madison Avenue. The Dog Museum Board of Directors, then chaired by Nancy D. Lindsay and the Museum President, Dorothy Welsh, voted to move the museum to St. Louis in September of 1986. By November 1987 the move had been made to Jarville House, a charming Monsanto Greek Revival house in the 570-acre Queeny Park outside St. Louis. An addition increased the space to 14,000 square feet, and the museum was opened in spring 1991. The carriage house adjacent to Jarville House was transformed into a museum shop that overlooks the Charing Cross Courtyard, the gift of Gilbert S. Kahn.

It was clear to the museum's Board of Directors that while the art collection was increasing in both volume and value, the finan-

AKC S.T.A.R. Puppy

The new puppy level of Canine Good Citizen, the AKC S.T.A.R. Puppy program, is an exciting new AKC program designed to

get dog owners and their puppies off to a great start. Launched in November 2008, AKC S.T.A.R. Puppy is an incentive program for loving dog owners who have taken the time to take their puppies through a basic training class lasting at least six weeks. S.T.A.R. is an acronym for Socialization, Training, Activity, and a Responsible owner, all of the things every puppy needs to have a good life. AKC S.T.A.R. puppies receive the coveted gold Olympics-style STAR Puppy medal. AKC S.T.A.R. Puppy training and testing is administered by AKC CGC evaluators.

cial support was not keeping pace. A reaffiliation with the AKC was completed in October of 1995, and the official name of the museum became the American Kennel Club Museum of the Dog.

REVIEWS AND REVISIONS

ANTI-DOG LEGISLATION

In 1989, the AKC took an unprecedented role in fighting anti-dog legislation, particularly breed-specific dangerous-dog legislation. For the first time, the AKC participated in a vicious-dog court case, successfully contributing to winning a temporary restraining order against the New York City Health Department's proposed "pit bull" legislation. The AKC told its story through widespread media coverage, including a press conference on the steps of New York's City Hall.

Limited Registration

AKC created Limited Registration status to provide the benefits of AKC registration for puppies that breeders deemed to be pet quality. Litter owners can make this designation simply by checking the appropriate box on the registration application.

Limited Registration status bars participation in AKC conformation events, and any offspring produced by the dog are ineligible for AKC registration.

Limited Registration dogs are eligible for Junior Showmanship competition, and they can earn Companion Dog and some Performance Dog titles. Limited Registration status can be revised at the litter owner's request.

Be a PAL

The AKC Indefinite Listing Privilege/Purebred Alternative Listing (ILP/PAL) program registers approximately three thousand purebreds every year from undocumented backgrounds, such as rescue programs and animal shelters.

For decades, the ILP registration number was used to enter AKC Companion and Performance Events, AKC Juniors competition, and Miscellaneous Class prior to 1995.

ILP registration was expanded and renamed PAL in 2008 with a few added perks. PAL registration includes access to AKC educational resources; a copy of *Family Dog Magazine;* a subscription to AKC's e-newsletter, "Your AKC"; information from the breed's Parent Club; and details on AKC Pet Healthcare and AKC Companion Animal Recovery programs.

ILP/PAL applications must be accompanied by veterinary certification proving that the dog is neutered as well as two recent front- and side-view color photographs showing that it possesses recognizable breed traits.

BYLAWS CHANGES

AKC continued to revise its bylaws, based on recommendations from a Board Committee. The key to this process came in 1988 when a bylaws change eliminated the requirement that a Delegate could vote on bylaws revisions only at each year's March meeting. Since that time, such votes can be taken at any quarterly meeting.

NEW REGISTRATION OPTION

The AKC implemented the Limited Registration option for breeders who wanted to sell their dogs with AKC registration, but not for breeding purposes. A dog with AKC Limited Registration is registered, but no off-spring produced by that dog are eligible for registration. Such a dog is also ineligible for Conformation competition but may participate in any other Licensed or Member Event, including Obedience, Tracking, Field Trials, Hunting Tests, Herding, Lure Coursing, Earthdog, and Agility.

DOG SHOW RULES—REVISIONS

A number of dog show rules and regulations were amended during 1989. The 12- to 18-Month Class could now be given at Specialty Shows held in conjunction with all-breed shows even if the all-breed show did not

Responsible dog care glistens in the eyes of this handsome West Highland White Terrier.

Ins and Outs of Miscellaneous Class

Since 1995, the AKC Foundation Stock Service (FSS) program has streamlined the recognition process, and breeds move through the Miscellaneous Class at a steady pace. This was not always the case.

Xoloitzcuintli ARBA Ch. Xcel's Nuez Taboo, CGC, CD, NAJP, winning Best of Breed in the Miscellaneous Class.

The Austrailan Kelpie remained in Miscellaneous for forty years before being dropped. The Cavalier King Charles Spaniel lingered from 1962 to 1996 before entering the Toy Group. The Chinese Crested was ejected from Miscellaneous in 1965 and forced to repeat the process. The Shih Tzu was admitted in Miscellaneous in 1955, where it remained for fourteen years as a result of questions about the *Stud Book*.

Today, breeds must meet eligibility requirements to enter FSS. These include registration with an AKC-acceptable foreign or domestic regis-

try, the existence of an active national breed club, and an AKC-acceptable breed standard. After entering FSS, breeds are monitored by AKC Special Services to evaluate gene pool viability, registration growth, and activities of the national club.

When 150 dogs with acceptable three-generation pedigrees are recorded by FSS, the breed becomes eligible for AKC Companion Events and Performance Events, if applicable.

When three hundred to four hundred dogs with complete three-generation pedigrees are FSS-registered and the Parent Club includes one hundred active households nationwide, the breed becomes eligible to enter the Miscellaneous Class. Today, breeds generally remain in Miscellaneous for one to three years. Those with a thousand or more dogs enrolled in FSS may be evaluated after six months. Breeds with fewer than a thousand dogs are evaluated at the end of each year in Miscellaneous.

During the breed's stint in Miscellaneous, the Parent Club works with multiple AKC departments preparing to close the stud book and transition to full recognition. This includes encouraging fanciers to register dogs and participate in AKC activities, educating judges about the breed, and revising the standard and Parent Club's bylaws if necessary. When these criteria are met, the information is presented to the AKC Board for approval to move the breed to full AKC recognition.

offer the class. In the past, it could only be given at Independent Specialty Shows. Also in 1989, a longstanding policy was modified, allowing clubs to schedule multiple-entry Non-Regular Classes (Stud Dog, Brood Bitch, Brace, and Team) before, rather than after, Best of Breed.

AKC Gazette's **Annual Photo Contest, First Place, 1998, photographer Nanette Phipps.**

These changes also provided that the Miscellaneous Class could be divided by breed as well as by sex. Previously, all breeds in this competition had to be shown in the ring together, the only Miscellaneous Class division being by sex.

In May of that year, the new nationwide alignment and point schedule went into effect. The revised plan divided the country into twelve divisions instead of the previous seven.

The AKC looked ahead to the new decade with goals of maintaining the integrity of its registry through the expansion of its inspections program as well as the use of new technologies. These included DNA testing for proof of parentage and the use of microchips for permanent identification. The club would increasingly have to focus on dangerous-dog legislation and anti-breeding laws, at the same time keeping the sport vital and relevant for future generations.

American artist Christine Merrill's *Millie on the South Lawn*, 1990, given to The AKC Museum of the Dog by the William Secord Gallery, Inc., New York. President George H. W. Bush's First Dog was English Springer Spaniel "Millie," who "co-wrote" a book with the First Lady on life in the White House as a fund-raiser for the Barbara Bush Foundation for Family Literacy.

THE
1990s

The 1990s became one of the most interesting decades in American Kennel Club history. It was marked by external relocation, expansion, and innovation, as well as internal turmoil and, at times, good luck.

During this time, steps were taken to strengthen the integrity of the AKC's registry. In August 1990, a new and completely automated registration system was activated. In 1996, a Care and Conditions Policy was adopted, followed in 1998 by a DNA Certification Program and a DNA Compliance Audit Program. These two new initiatives verified and underscored accurate parentage.

To say that the 1990s were accompanied by some internal turmoil would be an understatement. Between 1990 and 1999, there were six AKC Chief Executive Officers and five AKC Board Chairmen. For a short period in 1991, Louis Auslander held both positions. Because AKC Presidents had previously received three-year contracts, there were two time periods when the AKC was paying two Presidents' salaries. In 1995–1996, there was a period when the Board was split into two factions of six members each. This created a paralytic situation, resulting in lack of action in several instances. The 1995 election of the Board Chairman took several hours and numerous ballots before one side finally gave in. In 1996, just prior to the March Board election, there was a boycott of a Board meeting to prevent a quorum from being attained. The stalemate was broken when one side attained a clear majority. Despite this, the decade of the 1990s saw noticeable progress and innovation.

GROWTH AND INCLUSION

From 1884 until 1936, the AKC offered only Conformation and Field competitions. In 1936, Obedience (including Tracking) was added. While Hunting Tests were added in the 1980s, the real explosion of activities began with the addition of Herding Tests and Trials in January 1990. That was followed by Lure Coursing in 1991, then Agility and Earthdog in 1994. Agility quickly became one of the AKC's strongest activities in terms of events and entries. That popularity continues to this day.

Organizational changes were needed to accommodate the different types of competition that continued to grow under the AKC umbrella during the 1990s. By 1998, the events open to all breeds, such as Agility, Obedience, and Tracking, became the Companion Events department. The Canine Good Citizen Test®, begun in 1989, was later added to this division.

All of the breed-specific Performance Events, e.g., Field Trials, Hunting Tests, Herding, Lure Coursing, and Earthdog, became part of the newly created Performance Events Department. The AKC also initiated a Field Championship for all Pointing Breeds.

In August 1990, a Judges' Training Institute was initiated by then Vice-President of Dog Events Terry Stacy. The week-long program was designed to provide judges with exposure to every facet of judging, from the application process to managing a ring. The first institutes were held at Cal Poly Pomona and Indiana University of Pennsylvania. Both institutes reached the limit of sixty participants within a month of being announced.

New Breeds for the 1990s

American Eskimo Dog	Cavalier King Charles	Havanese
Anatolian Shepherd	Spaniel	Löwchen
Australian Shepherd	Chinese Crested	Miniature Bull Terrier
Border Collie	Chinese Shar-Pei	Parson Russell Terrier
Canaan Dog	Finnish Spitz	Petit Basset Griffon
	Greater Swiss Mountain	Vendéen
	Dog	Shiba Inu

Comprehensive, informative, and entertaining, the AKC Web site offers a wealth of resources for novice owners, breeders, and expert competitors on health, training, nutrition, and grooming, as well as registration and event information.

For prospective owners, the Web site is an excellent starting point to research the responsibilities of dog care and to select the right breed. Since its formation, the AKC has consistently promoted the advantages of owning responsibly bred dogs.

In coordination with national and local clubs, the AKC developed a proactive nationwide Breeder Referral Program in 1992. Multiple pages on the AKC Web site assist potential dog owners in their search for reputable breeders. By utilizing information and contacts on the AKC Web site, potential owners can find a comprehensive presentation of each AKC-recognized, Miscellaneous, and FFS breed. Information provided on each breed includes drawings, photos, videos, the Breed Standard, fun facts, breed history, and

contact links for national breed club, breeder referral, breed rescue, and online classified listings from breeders with AKC-registered litters.

Breeders of AKC-registerable dogs can also be located through links to specialty, all-breed, and training clubs.

Web site resources for new owners include online registration services for both dogs and litters, a link for subscription services for *AKC Family Dog* and the *AKC Gazette*, search tools to locate training resources, local clubs, and upcoming AKC events as well as the results of all AKC events.

For every dog owner, the Web site offers worldwide news updates, AKC surveys, legislative alerts, and several free e-newsletters such as Your AKC, featuring monthly articles and news; AKC Breeder; AKC Jr. News; Public Education; Companion Events Updates on Rally, Tracking, Obedience, and Agility; and Taking Command for updates on canine legislation.

AKC's comprehensive herding program was implemented in 1989, and its consistent growth attests to its success. Between 1997 and 2002, the number of tests and trials grew by 30 percent. In 2007, 2,628 dogs competed at 250 AKC Herding Tests, 9,403 competed at 369 AKC Herding Trials, and a total of 1,923 AKC titles were awarded.

Dogs from eligible breeds—all Herding Group breeds plus several other breeds—nine months of age or older, including those with FSS, ILP/PAL, and Conditional registration, can compete in AKC Herding events.

In Noncompetitive Herding Instinct Tests, dogs are evaluated on trainability and instinctive ability to move and control livestock. Dogs must pass two tests under two different judges to earn Herding Tested (HT) and Pre-Trial Tested (PT) certification.

Competitive herding trials are designed to preserve inherent herding skills and demonstrate traditional working function in arenas and simulated pastoral situations. Three qualifying scores from three different judges are required to earn each of three levels of competitive Herding titles:

Herding Started (HS)
Herding Intermediate (HI)
Herding Excellent (HX)

HX-titled dogs are eligible to compete for the AKC's Herding Champion (HC) title, for which fifteen championship points are required.

LEFT: Border Collie moving young lambs in a Herding Test. BELOW: Pembroke Welsh Corgi Ch. Sippiwisseset Helmsman passing his Herding Test.

TOP: Shetland Sheepdog moving sheep at a Herding Trial. MIDDLE LEFT: Border Collie staring down a stubborn goat. MIDDLE RIGHT: Bouvier des Flandres herding bovine charges. BELOW LEFT: Border Collie with sheep. BELOW RIGHT: German Shepherd Dog working a small flock.

Shetland Sheepdog in a demonstration at the Herding Judges Institute in 1999.

In 1999, the approval process for prospective provisional judges was modified to include counting a Sweepstakes or Futurity as two matches.

In 1995, the AKC established the Foundation Stock Service (FSS) to facilitate bringing new breeds into the registry, breeds that are well established in many other parts of the world. This service enables the AKC to maintain accurate pedigree and ownership records for purebred breeds not currently eligible for AKC recognition. While in the FSS, breeds become eligible to compete in Companion Events and in applicable Performance Events.

ON THE MOVE–TIMES TWO

Between fall 1990 and spring 1991, AKC moved all of the registration-related services to Raleigh, North Carolina, leaving the remainder of departments in New York City. In 1998, all Operations services were relocated to 5580 Centerview Drive in Raleigh, with AKC headquarters remaining in New York. The New York offices moved "up the street," from 51 Madison Avenue (AKC's home for thirty-four years) to 260 Madison Avenue. The construction and organization of this new space was accomplished under the supervision of then Vice-President Dennis Sprung.

In 2008, the AKC offices in Raleigh were moved to a newly designed and constructed space to better facilitate the services for the club's constituents under the leadership of Chief Operating Officer John Lyons.

Earthdog Tests

Dachshunds and many Terriers were traditionally bred to rout vermin from underground tunnels. This work, greatly diminished today, has been replaced by Earthdog Tests as a way to preserve essential working traits in these breeds.

In 1994, AKC approved three levels of Earthdog Tests for Dachshunds and Terriers. Earthdog Tests are open to dogs of eligible breeds, six months of age or older, including those with PAL/ILP, Conditional, and FSS registration.

These standardized, noncompetitive tests are designed to evaluate working instinct (gameness) and trained hunting behaviors in a simulated underground hunting situation.

Dogs are expected to willingly enter the tunnel, actively seek prey (safely caged rats), and work the quarry by digging and barking. Each level of the test pres-

Australian Terrier entering a hole at an Earthdog Test.

ents additional challenges. Dens become progressively longer with more turns and distractions, and time allowances to find and work the quarry become stricter.

Dogs earning Junior Earthdog titles (JE) may go on to compete for Senior Earthdog titles (SE). In 1995, the first Senior Earthdog title was awarded to Border Terrier Lady Wheaton.

The Master Earthdog (ME) Test most closely simulates an actual working situation. Dogs must investigate an empty den on command, willingly work with another dog to find and enter an active den, navigate multiple underground obstacles, locate quarry in ninety seconds, cooperate when removed from the den by a handler, and patiently wait as another dog works the quarry. In 1996, the first Master Earthdog title was earned by Beejay's Chocolate Smoke CD, ME, a longhaired Miniature Dachshund.

Since its inception, the AKC has approved 1,220 Earthdog events, with 54,507 entries, and issued 4,765 Earthdog titles.

West Highland White Terrier returning through the tunnel at a test.

New office building in Raleigh, North Carolina, officially opened in 2009.

EXPANSION AND DIVERSIFICATION

Two nonprofit AKC affiliates were established in 1995. The first was the AKC Canine Health Foundation (CHF), which was initially funded by a one-million-dollar grant from the AKC. To further the goal of developing resources for basic and applied health programs, the AKC has contributed over a million dollars to the Foundation every year since its inception. The goal of these contributions has had an emphasis on canine genetics and improving quality-of-life issues for dogs and their owners. As of this writing, the AKC has donated $18,500,000 to the Foundation.

AKC Companion Animal Recovery (CAR) was the second affiliate formed in 1995. Its goal is to reunite lost pets with their owners. AKC/CAR provides 24-hour/365-day recovery service for all enrolled animals. By 2008, there were nearly 4 million animals enrolled in the program, and there have been more than 260,000 recoveries.

SUPPORTING FAIR AND JUST LEGISLATION

Throughout the 1990s, communication strategies included messages surrounding the AKC's being the authority on all things canine and at the heart of the purebred dog world. As such, it was only natural that the club began to establish a leadership role in the legislative arena.

AKC Companion Animal Recovery

The AKC/CAR program was founded in 1995 to help reunite lost pets with their owners. Based in Raleigh, North Carolina, the CAR database provides recovery services 24 hours a day, 7 days a week, 365 days a year for pets identified with a microchip, tattoo, or AKC/CAR collar tag.

CAR has become the nation's largest nonprofit recovery service. All species of pets are eligible for enrollment regardless of the identification brand or type of microchip or tattoo. The AKC/CAR database of more than 3.9 million enrollment records has been used in 340,000 recoveries. The Labrador Retriever is the most recovered breed, with more than 10,000 pets successfully recovered through the CAR program.

The one-time enrollment fee includes unlimited updates, and the AKC/CAR database safeguards personal data through sophisticated multilayered security methods.

CAR also offers discounts on CAR microchips and enrollment fees to shelters, humane societies, and rescue groups

The AKC/CAR Canine Support and Relief Fund was established as a permanent charitable fund to provide resources, support, and grants up to $10,000 to not-for-profit canine search-and-rescue organizations, veterinary units providing support to the canine rescue teams, and animal shelters and similar organizations providing care for domestic animals orphaned or displaced during natural or civil disasters. In 2008, AKC/CAR grants were awarded to twenty-nine worthy groups.

A new position was created in early 1991 for an AKC Government Relations Representative to support the AKC's goals for fair and just legislation in Washington, DC. Former AKC Board Member Dr. James Holt helped create and ultimately filled this crucial position.

During the 1990s, the AKC continued to speak out against breed-specific legislation. Although two dozen additional breed-specific dog laws were enacted in 1990, there were also strong signs that the campaign in favor of generic dog laws enforcing responsible ownership was gaining ground. Five states adopted AKC-supported *generic* vicious-dog laws in 1990, and fifty-five generic ordinances were passed across the country from 1987 through the 1990s. This brought the total to 285. This immediately shows the effect of the legislative efforts. In this same time span, five breed-specific ordinances were repealed and thirty failed to pass.

Another victory came early in 1991. After three long years of hard work, determination, and court action on the part of the AKC, New York City Mayor David Dinkins signed a reasonable, enforceable, nondiscriminatory vicious-dog ordinance into law, focusing on the behavior of the specific dog, rather than on the breed.

In April 1991, the Florida House of Representatives unanimously adopted a resolution endorsing the AKC's Canine Good Citizen Test® (CGC program) *"as a means of teaching owners responsible pet owner-ship, and as a means of teaching dogs canine good citizen behaviors for the community."* To date, thirty-five states have adopted similar resolu-tions. There were 35,000 CGC certificates issued by end of 1991. Over 600,000 were issued by the end of 2008. Currently there are over 9,500 approved CGC evalutators. The CGC program has played a significant role in enacting fair and just canine legislation.

PUBLIC OUTREACH

A new quarterly magazine, *AKC Puppies*, was launched in 1992. Pub-lished quarterly, it was distributed to all new AKC puppy registrants. This publication was geared toward the new puppy owner, while emphasizing responsible dog ownership and the benefits of participa-tion in AKC events. The magazine evolved into the *AKC New Puppy Handbook*, which is mailed to every new registrant.

The AKC produced two videos for major television audiences. One of them, a five-minute video called *Best Friends,* depicted the

---

Top Ten Breeds of the 1990s

Labrador Retrievers	The country's top breed of the 1990s con-tinues to enjoy the number-one position to this day. The Rottweiler, accepted by AKC in 1931, makes its first appearance in the decade's top ten as the number-two breed, the highest ranking of any first-timer on the list (since the Boston Terrier in the 1900s). The 1990s also marked the first appear-ances of the Yorkshire Terrier in the top ten of the decade. The Pomeranian returns to the top-ten list for the first time since the 1930s.	Poodles
Rottweilers		Beagles
German Shepherd Dogs		Dachshunds
Golden Retrievers		Yorkshire Terriers
Cocker Spaniels		Pomeranians

---

valuable work of dogs in society. A six-minute version was widely shown during in-flight presentations on Trans World Airlines and Continental Airlines.

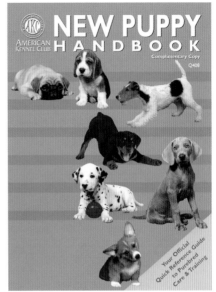

AKC New Puppy Handbook

The Communications Department introduced a program to teach responsible dog ownership at the elementary-school level. Developed by the Public Education Division with input from an educational consultant and educators including those in the fancy, the kit for teachers was based on the 1991 Best Friends video.

Initiated in the fall of 1994, the AKC Web site, www.akc.org, underwent a total redesign in 1999. For the first time, the AKC offered various e-commerce canine information products, goods, and services online. This was a premier AKC initiative, reaching out to both the fancy and the public at large. Launched in September 1999, the new Web site tripled its traffic nearly overnight. As of October 2008, the site attracts 1.6 million individual users monthly.

By the end of the 1990s, the AKC's communication strategy included the goal of becoming the premier information source for all purebred dog enthusiasts.

A SPECIAL EVENT

The first AKC National Invitational Dog Championship was held in April 1992 at the Baltimore Arena in Maryland. The event was nationally televised and gave Americans a real look at the excitement of our sport. The primary goals were to offer the national television audience a positive perception of dogs and give the AKC a platform to promote responsible dog ownership. It was watched by more than 3 million Americans.

This event marked only the third time in the company's then 108-year history that the AKC had sponsored a dog show. *Sports Illustrated* magazine cited the event as one of the top twelve sporting events to watch for in 1992. (See the AKC/Eukanuba National Championship section in the next chapter.)

Lure Coursing

Lure Coursing was originally based on a combination of live game coursing and dog racing. In the early 1970s, sighthound breeder Lyle Gillette perfected a system of mechanized lures and pulleys to simulate the unpredictability of chasing live prey. The advent of artificial lures greatly expanded the sport.

In 1991, Lure Coursing was approved as an AKC Performance Event. Dogs of eligible breeds are evaluated for follow, speed, agility, endurance, and overall ability as they pursue an artificial lure zigzagging across an open field.

AKC titles offered through achieving a number of qualifying scores

TOP: Greyhound and owner, entrants in the 1997 AKC National Coursing Championships. MIDDLE: Lure Coursing Trials can take place on sand, grass, or snow, as these Greyhounds illustrate. BOTTOM: Scottish Deerhounds, nearly a blur at a Lure Coursing Trial.

ABOVE: Afghan Hound gazing pensively before a competition. BELOW: Salukis being released at the beginning of a race. BELOW RIGHT: Rhodesian Ridgeback moving out on a race.

include Junior Courser (JC), Senior Courser (SC), and Master Courser (MC). Dogs can also obtain Field Championships (FC) through competitive Lure Coursing Trials. Dogs earning FC titles may go on to compete for increasingly higher levels of the Lure Courser Excellent (LCX) title, e.g., LCX II, LCX III, and LCX IV.

The American Kennel Club also encourages Lure Coursing excellence through the National Lure Coursing Championship.

INNOVATIONS AND BYLAWS CHANGES

This was a time that required the Delegate body to become increasingly more active. The Delegates passed several major amendments to rules and bylaws, including changes to the occupational eligibility of Delegates, now indicating that the following individuals could not become or remain Delegates: professional judges, handlers, or trainers; commercial breeders; individuals involved in the manufacture or sale of dog food; and anyone working for a commercial dog publication or dog-show superintendent.

The Delegates voted in favor of another key amendment in 1990, reducing the majority required for amendments to the bylaws from three-fourths to two-thirds. They also voted to permit outgoing Delegates to continue representing their clubs until new Delegates were formally seated. This would eliminate a gap in representation for any club that changed Delegates.

In September 1991, the Delegates amended the bylaws to allow the President to serve without being a voting Board member. The Board elected Robert Maxwell as President immediately after the passage of this amendment.

The Delegates voted to establish several standing Delegate Committees in June 1993, thereby increasing and facilitating their input on the policies and workings of the AKC. These committees originally included Parent Clubs, All-Breed Clubs, Obedience Clubs, Field Trial Clubs, Health Research and Health Education, Constitution and Bylaws, Dog Show Rules, and a Coordinating Committee. Three special committees were also formed: Judges Approval Procedure, Canine Population Issues, and Future Nature and Structure of the Delegate Body. This last committee eventually became a standing committee, first named Strategic Planning and ultimately called the Delegate Advocacy and Advancement Committee.

RECOGNIZING OUR CONSTITUENTS— IN AND OUT OF THE SPORT

Numerous awards of recognition were established in the 1990s. In1996, Dennis Sprung instituted a program to honor our constituents in many different categories. Among these were Delegates, judges, and show chairs who had served in their positions for twenty-five years; breeders who finished dogs' championships entirely from the Bred-by-Exhibitor Class were also recognized. As of this writing,

more than 26,000 medals have been earned in this category.

Five ACE award winners are selected annually to celebrate the strength of the human-canine bond.

In 1998, Sprung's idea for the Lifetime Achievement Award, designed to recognize outstanding members of the fancy in the categories of Conformation, Companion Events, and Performance, was inaugurated. The Award for Canine Excellence (ACE) was established the following year. It is intended to demonstrate the AKC's respect for the extraordinary canine-human bond as well as to celebrate the immeasurable ways in which dogs make meaningful contributions to our lives. Each year, an ACE award is given in each of five categories: Law Enforcement, Search and Rescue, Therapy, Service, and Exemplary Companion Dog.

The American Kennel Club approached the cusp of the new millennium and embarked on the ambitious task of meeting the twenty-first century. The dramatic reengineering of the AKC's computerization continues to move forward as the AKC works to maintain its leadership role as the expert on all matters pertaining to purebred dogs.

Keeshond (above) and Papillon (below) going over the bar jump at an Agility Trial.

Since 1994, when it became an official event, Agility has consistently been the AKC's fastest-growing sport. The AKC offered 23 AKC Agility Trials in 1994. In 2007, 747,715 entries competed in 12,014 trials.

Agility requires control, team-work, physical dexterity, and split-second decisions as dog/handler teams negotiate obstacle courses that change with each event. These challenges produce an event that is equally enjoyable and exciting for dogs, human participants, and spectators.

The AKC offers three competitive Agility classes.

Standard Class courses include contact objects (dog walk, A-frame, and seesaw) with designated safety zones that dogs must touch with at least one paw to complete the obstacle.

Jumpers with Weaves courses dispense with contact objects, having only jumps, tunnels, and weaves poles to provide much faster competition.

FAST (Fifteen and Send Time) courses are specifically designed to test a dog/hander team's strategy, accuracy, speed, and distance handling.

Novice, Open, Excellent, and Master titles are offered in each

Soft Coated Wheaten Terrier clearing the bar jump with ease.

Vizsla sailing effortlessly over a bar jump at an Agility Trial.

class. All breeds run the same course, but classes are divided into height divisions, and times and jump heights are adjusted to accommodate the relative size and jumping ability of various breeds.

In 1999, the AKC began offering Master Agility Championship (MACH) titles for dogs completing both Excellent Standard and Excellent Jumpers titles. Shetland Sheepdog MACH7 Joy's Remar Wild West Wyatt was the first recipient of an AKC MACH title.

All AKC-registerable breeds can compete in Agility, including ILP/PAL and approved FSS breeds meeting eligibility requirements.

Titles have been earned by almost every breed, and 33,259 dogs earned AKC Agility titles in 2007. The top five AKC Agility competitors belong to members of the following five breeds: Papillon, Border Collie, Australian Shepherd, Shetland Sheepdog, and Golden Retriever.

The AKC also encourages Agility excellence through its annual AKC Agility Invitational, in which the top five Agility dogs in each recognized, Miscellaneous, and approved FSS breed compete by invitation.

Russell Terrier moving through a tunnel with enthusiasm.

Clockwise from left, Shiba Inu exiting the tunnel; Bulldog, up and over the bar jump; a senior Golden Retriever on the pause table; Bullmastiff stretching over a bar jump. FACING PAGE: The first winner of the Versatile Companion Champion (VCCH) title was Golden Retriever VCCH Jakki, UDX, shown here going over the bar jump at an Agility Trial. Jakki earned his OTCH, MACH, and CT titles to become the first VCCH in 2009.

Reuben Ward Binks's *Show and Field Trial Ch. Banchory Bolo and Banchory Corbie*, 1924, given to The AKC Museum of the Dog by Grace L. Lambert. Countess Howe's Bolo was the first Labrador Retriever to earn the Dual Champion title.

THE TWENTY-FIRST CENTURY

The twenty-first century saw the role of the American Kennel Club grow and expand in ways that its forefathers could never have imagined. The power of the canine-human bond now came to the forefront of society. The AKC played an important role in the evolution that saw the dog become a respected and valuable member of the American family and remained committed to taking the necessary actions to ensure the continuation of purebred dogs and the sport.

Purebred dogs and AKC events had become a vital part of American culture. There was a consistent and steady increase in the number of events held annually and in the total entries for all of these. By 2007, AKC Member, Licensed, and Sanctioned Clubs held more than 20,000 events per year with more than 3 million entries across the various dog sports. Televised coverage continued to increase as the AKC/Eukanuba National Championship was launched in conjunction with the AKC National Agility Invitational and the AKC Obedience Invitational.

The Long Beach Convention Center in Long Beach, California, to date has housed the National Championship Show more times than any other venue.

ON WITH THE SHOW

The National Championship Show, a unique and historic showcase created by the AKC with the sponsorship of the Iams Company, saw its first annual event held in December 2001. Then called the AKC/Eukanuba American Dog Classic, the show was taped by Animal Planet and held at the TD Waterhouse Center in Orlando, Florida. The event was designed to showcase the AKC and the breeder-enthusiast. The top twenty dogs of each AKC breed (based only on numbers defeated within the breed) were invited to compete for unprecedented cash prizes, including $50,000 for Best in Show and $25,000 to the breeder of the Best in Show winner.

Beginning in 2003, a special Bred-by-Exhibitor event was initiated at this show. This encompassed competition at the Best of Breed, Group, and Best in Show levels exclusively for Bred-by-Exhibitor dogs. The entries for this event have grown to compose 43 percent of the National Championship's total entry.

The heart and soul of the sport, the breeder, received greater central focus through the creation of an AKC Breeders' Department and the annual Breeder of the Year Awards, with in-ring presentations for the Breeder of the Year Awards during the evening Group judging. The Awards for Canine Excellence (ACE) were highlighted in the same manner.

ABOVE: The winner of the first Eukanuba World Challenge in 2007 was Cocker Spaniel Ch. Very Vigie Vamos A La Playa from Switzerland, owned by Laurent Pichard and Joelle Doucet. RIGHT: Best Bred-by-Exhibitor in Show, 2007 Golden Retriever Ch. Easthill Broxden The Fig is Up, "Newton," owned by Sandra Kim Hoffen, A. and J. Ovalle, and Amy Rodriques, with breeder-owner-handler Amy Rodriques.

The Eukanuba World Challenge was begun in 2007 and is the only event of its kind. As such, it attracted entries from fifty-two countries in its first year. Sponsored by Eukanuba, with the cooperation of the Fédération Cynologique Internationale (FCI), each of the participating countries may select their representative based on a rating system of their choice, or they may designate a specific show in which the Best in Show winner will receive the honor of competing at the World Challenge. In the United States, the AKC representative is the previous year's Best in Show winner of the AKC/Eukanuba National Championship.

Obedience and Agility Nationals

The first AKC National Obedience Invitational was held in St. Louis, Missouri, in June 1995.It was a stand-alone event until December 2003 when it joined the AKC/Eukanuba National Championship Show.

In December 1996, the AKC held the first National Agility Championship, which remained a stand-alone event for seven years, through 2002. The event was open to the top scorers overall, which meant that a few competitive breeds dominated this annual competition. The next three annual events were held in conjunction with the AKC/Eukanuba National Championship Show. The first newly developed AKC Agility Invitational took place in conjunction with the December 2006 AKC/Eukanuba National Championship Show and is open for all top-scoring dogs of each breed. The National Agility Championship resumed its stand-alone status in 2007.

Bichon Frise, "JR," Ch. Special Times Just Right, with judge Dorothy D. Nickles, the Top Dog in 2000 and Westminster Best in Show winner for 2001, came out of retirement to win the first National Championship Show in 2001, handled by Scott Sommer.

Kerry Blue Terrier, "Mick," Ch. Torum's Scarf Michael, handled by Bill McFadden in the United States, Top Dog in 2001 and winner of Crufts and the revived Morris & Essex in 2000, was the victor of the National Championship Show in 2002 under judge Mrs. Constance M. Barton.

Norfolk Terrier, "Coco," Ch. Cracknor Cause Celebre, handled by Beth Sweigart, Top Dog in 2003 and winner of Crufts in 2005, was Best in Show at the National Championship Show in 2003 under judge Frank T. Sabella.

Bloodhound, "Knotty," Ch. Heather's Knock On Wood, handled by Ken Griffith, won the National Championship Show in 2005 under judge Michele L. Billings.

Alaskan Malamute, "Costello," Ch. Nanuke's Snoklassic No Boundries, handled by breeder-owner Sandra D'Andrea, won both Best in Show and Best Bred-by-Exhibitor in Show at the National Championship Show in January 2006 under judge Mrs. Robert S. Forsyth.

English Springer Spaniel, "James," Ch. Felicity's Diamond Jim, handled by Kellie FitzGerald, won the National Championship Show in December 2006 under judge Robert S. Forsyth and continued on to win Westminster in 2007.

Sealyham Terrier, "Charmin," Ch. Efbe's Hidalgo at Goodspice, handled by owner Margery Good, won the National Championship Show in December 2007 under Maxine V. Beam and then went on to win the World Dog Show in Stockholm in 2008 and Crufts in 2009.

Pointer, "Holly," Ch. Cookieland Seasyde Hollyberry, handled by Michael Scott, was the winner of the National Championship Show in 2008 under judge Dr. Robert D. Smith.

ABOVE: The Agility Invitational proves to be a highlight for spectators year after year. BELOW: The AKC Agility Invitational, 2007: Five Agility dogs and their owners—one dog/handler team in each of the five height categories was crowned at the event, which brought together 470 dogs from across the country and beyond. Placing first in their height divisions were: 8 inch—Papillon NAC MACH15 Pinpaps Jonquil Of Skipnlena, MXF, owned by Robin Cohen and Robin Kletke. 12 inch—Parson Russell Terrier MACH2 Dashaway Razor Sharp Edge, owned by Suzanne Birdsall. 16 inch—Nova Scotia Duck Tolling Retriever MACH Foxgrove's Electric Slyde, RN, OF, owned by Kim and Terry Simons. 20 inch—Border Collie NAC MACH8 Super Star, XF, owned by Linda Mecklenburg. 24 inch—Weimaraner Ch. Regen's Rocket Launcher, VCD2, TDX, MX, MXJ, owned by Steve and Laurie Jenks.

ABOVE, left: Pug competing in the long jump at the 2007 AKC Obedience Invitational. ABOVE, right: Welsh Springer Spaniel coming through the tunnel at the Agility Invitational. BELOW: The AKC Obedience Invitational 2007 winners. Left to Right: Third Runner Up—Shetland Sheepdog OTCH Highfields Gone Flying, UDX2, RN, NA, NAJ, owned by Mary Jane Kelley. Second Runner Up—Labrador Retriever OTCH Lakebound's Dancin' Poet, VCD1, UDX, RE, JH, owned by Renate Van Allen. First Runner Up—Miniature Poodle OTCH MACH2 Sanew's Abundance Of Energy, UDX, owned by Shirley Barkan. 2007 AKC National Obedience Champion—Golden Retriever NOC OTCH Dd's Dreams Do Come True, UDX4, RE, TDX, JH, owned by Dee Dee and Billy Anderson.

Breeder of the Year

Each year the American Kennel Club recognizes an outstanding purebred dog breeder with the Breeder of the Year Award. The award honors those breeders who have dedicated their lives to improving the health, temperament, and quality of purebred dogs. At a special presentation held during the AKC/Eukanuba National Championship Show, a breeder, or pair of breeders, is recognized in each of the seven Groups. At the conclusion of the presentation, one of the seven Group recipients is chosen as the Breeder of the Year.

2002

Non-Sporting: Wendell Sammet
—Ale Kai Standard Poodles
Sporting: Melissa Johnson Newman
—Setter Ridge English Setters
Hound: Damara Bolte
—Reveille Basenjis
Working: Peggy and Dave Helming
—Pouch Cove Newfoundlands
Terrier: Barbara Miller
—Max-Well Norfolk Terriers
Toy: Linda George
—Ouachitah Chihuahuas
Herding: Janina Laurin
—Chateau Blanc Belgian Tervuren

2003

Working: Mary M. Rodgers
—Marienburg Doberman Pinschers
Sporting: Helen Szostak
—Grousemoor Flat-Coated Retrievers
Hound: Patricia Craige Trotter
—Vin-Melca Norwegian Elkhounds
Terrier: Capt. Jean L. Heath and William H. Cosby, Jr.
—Black Watch Lakeland Terriers
Toy: Thomas O'Neal
—Dreamridge English Toy Spaniels
Non-Sporting: Joseph D. Vergnetti
—Dassin Poodles
Herding: Jere Marder
—Lambluv Old English Sheepdogs

2004

Terrier: Catherine B. Nelson
—Pennywise Dandie Dinmont Terriers
Sporting: Sandra Bell
—San-Jo Cocker Spaniels
Hound: Gayle Bontecou
—Gayleward Scottish Deerhounds
Working: Patricia Turner and Anna M. Quigley
—Lajosmegyi Komondorok
Toy: Dale Adams
—Chindale Japanese Chin
Non-Sporting: Cody T. Sickle
—Cherokee Bulldogs
Herding: Thomas W. and Nioma S. Coen
—Macdega Shetland Sheepdogs

2005

Working: Peggy and Dave Helming
—Pouch Cove Newfoundlands
Sporting: Douglas A. Johnson
—Clussexx Clumber Spaniels
Hound: Karen Staudt-Cartabona
—Majenkir Borzoi
Terrier: William and Rebecca Poole
—Rocky Top Bull Terriers
Toy: Margery A. Shriver
—Sheffield Pugs
Non-Sporting: Roberta Lombardi
—Rufkins Lhasa Apsos
Herding: Michele Ritter
—Britannia Bearded Collies

2006

Herding: Douglas and Michaelanne Johnson
—Bugaboo Old English Sheepdogs
Sporting: Judy Colan
—Colsidex Weimaraners
Hound: Susan LaCroix Hamil
—Quiet Creek Bloodhounds
Working: Sandra D'Andrea
—Nanuke Alaskan Malamutes
Terrier: Beverly J. Verna
—Regency Miniature Schnauzers
Toy: Jose A. Cabrera and Fabian Arienti
—Starfire Pomeranians
Non-Sporting: Kathy and George Beliew
—Imagine Chow Chows

2007

Terrier: Barbara Miller
—Max-Well Norfolk Terriers
Sporting: Beverley and Adrian Wanjon
—Russet Leather Vizslas
Hound: Stanley D. Petter, Jr.
—Hewly Greyhounds
Working: Jean and Wayne Boyd
—Rivergrove Great Pyrenees
Toy: Glynnette Cass
—Wesglyn Maltese
Non-Sporting: Mikki Demers
—KiMik Tibetan Terriers
Herding: Anne Bowes
—Heronsway Pembroke Welsh Corgis

2008

Sporting: Joan Savage
—Stagedoor English Setters
Hound: Kathy and Julie Jones
—Jasiri Sukari Basenjis
Working: Lilian Ostermiller
—De-Li Bernese Mountain Dogs
Terrier: Miriam Stamm
—Anstamm Scottish Terriers
Toy: Luke and Diane Ehricht
—Hallmark Jolei Shih Tzu
Non-Sporting: Eleanor and Bob Candland
—El-Bo Boston Terriers
Herding: James and Sheree Moses
—Kaleef German Shepherd Dogs

Lifetime Achievement Awards

Winners are in bold.

	CONFORMATION	COMPANION	PERFORMANCE
1999	**Rachel Page Elliott** Anna K. Nicholas Patricia C. Trotter	**James E. Dearinger** Dorothy D. Nickles Robert T. Self	**Tom Sorenson** Arthur Rodger Ray Trimble
2000	**Anna K. Nicholas** Dr. M. Josephine Deubler Dorothy D. Nickles	**Robert T. Self** Dorothy M. McCauley Robert J. Squires	**Ray Trimble** Harold Bruninga Arthur E. Slike
2001	**Dorothy D. Nickles** Melbourne T. L. Downing Dorothy M. MacDonald	**John S. Ward** Dorothy M. McCauley Nancy Pollock	**A. Nelson Sills** Jacquelyn Mertens Arthur E. Slike
2002	**Melbourne T.L. Downing** Dr. M. Josephine Deubler Dorothy M. MacDonald	**Kent H. Delaney** Shirlee Jacobson Judson L. Streicher	**Arthur E. Slike** Harold Brunig Kenneth L. Ruff
2003	**Dr. M. Josephine Deubler** Dr. Robert Berndt Michele L. Billings	**Dorothy M. McCauley** Shirlee Jacobson Nancy Pollock	**Kenneth L. Ruff** Dorothy Metcalf Delmar Smith
2004	**Dorothy M. MacDonald** William Bergum Michele L. Billings	**Shirlee Jacobson** David Maurer Helen F. Philips	**Dorothy Metcalf** Arthur Rodger Delmar Smith
2005	**Michele L. Billings** Maxine Beam Dr. Harry Smith	**David Maurer** Rosalie Alvarez Velma Janek	**John Rabidou** Dennis Bath J.J. Sweezey
2006	**Dr. Harry Smith** Marion Mason Hodesson Dorothy Welsh	**Rosalie Alvarez** Bonnie Baker William (Sil) Sanders	**Marshall Simonds** Harold Bruninga Dr. Ray Calkins
2007	**Jane K. Forsyth** Louis Auslander Damara Bolte	**Marion Mason Hodesson** Ferndandeze Cartwright Lynne F. Eggers	**Kenneth A. Marden** Mario Palumbo Carl Ruffalo
2008	**Damara Bolte** Edd E. Bivin Peter J. Green	**Mildred (Mid) Rothrock** Lynne F. Eggers Richard H. Mullen	**Dennis Bath** Mary Jo Trimble Dr. Warren Wunderlich
2009	**Wendell J. Sammet** Constance M. Barton Dr. Robert D. Smith	**Kenneth A. Buxton** Susan B. Bluford Joanne L. Johnson	**Mary Jo Trimble** Jacquelyn Mertens Wayne R. Price

FACING PAGE: The trophy for the National Championship Show, commemorating the past winners of the prize. "James" and "Costello" on top, "Coco" to the left, "Knotty" to the right, and "Mick" on his twos. "JR," on opposite side, not shown to camera.

Responsible Dog Ownership Day

Since its inception in 2002, AKC Responsible Dog Ownership (RDO) Day has grown into a nationwide event. Each September, more than six hundred AKC-affiliated clubs organize local events to educate and entertain current and future dog owners.

Each AKC Responsible Dog Ownership Day event is unique, featuring a mixture of breed clubs, rescue groups, authors, artists, obedience/agility demonstrations, therapy dog/service dog demonstrations, low-cost microchipping clinics, and presentations by veterinarians, trainers, and nutritionists. There are also promotional giveaways, activities for children, and opportunities for dog owners to put their pets through the paces of the AKC Canine Good Citizen certification tests.

Along with educating the general public about the pleasures and responsibilities of dog ownership, RDO Days provide unparalleled opportunities for communication between canine experts and average dog owners. Attendance at the flagship event in Madison Square Park in New York City typically exceeds five thousand dog lovers.

RDO Day brings out the best in canines and humans alike: Dennis Sprung, Karen LeFrak, and NYC Parks Commissioner Adrian Benepe enjoy the event at Madison Square Park with companion dogs, purebred and mixed-breeds, Canine Good Citizens, therapy and assistance dogs and their proud, responsible owners.

Top Ten Breeds of the 2000s
(Through 2008)

Labrador Retrievers

Golden Retrievers

German Shepherd Dogs

Beagles

Dachshunds

Yorkshire Terriers

Poodles

Boxers

Shih Tzu

Chihuahuas

With the first decade of the 21st century nearly complete, the Labrador Retriever enjoys a healthy reign as the country's number-one dog, outnumbering the number-two breed by two or three to one. Labrador Retrievers took over the number-one position in 1991 and have remained there since. The Golden Retriever continues to climb in registrations, secure in the number-two position, the first time since the 1880s that Sporting breeds have held the top two positions. The German Shepherd Dog remains in the number-three position for the second decade in a row. The Boxer's appearance in the Top Ten is the first time since the 1950s, and the Shih Tzu's appearance is its first ever on the list.

Yorkshire Terrier, the most popular Toy Dog in the nation, wondering what it's like to be king. The Labrador Retriever reigning as the most popular dog in the United States for a second consecutive decade.

Parent Clubs were invited to participate in a new public outreach initative, "AKC Meet the Breeds." In conjunction with the National Championship, this popular program introduced the public to each AKC registered breed, with Parent Clubs hosting educational booths decorated to depict historical or functional aspects of their breeds. Experts staff the booths and supply canine representatives to serve as ambassadors so that the general public could get up close and personal with breeds that were old friends and those that soon would be.

The "AKC Meet the Breeds" booths at the National Championship Show remain a popular attraction. The Cairn Terrier Club of America won "Best Booth" at the 2007 show.

BYLAWS CHANGES

As previously mentioned, in 2001, with the help of the Corporation's Executive Secretary James Crowley, the Delegates adopted sweeping changes to the AKC bylaws. Term limits were placed on AKC Board Members, and to avoid paralyzing tie votes, which plagued the Board in the mid-1990s, the number of voting Board members was increased from twelve to thirteen.

The President was made an ex officio non-voting Board Member to ensure that the organization's CEO would be present at all meetings. There had been prior instances where the President had been excluded from Executive Sessions because he was not a Board Member. Prior to 2001, the Board had elected all AKC officers, but an amendment was made so that the Board would elect only the President-CEO, Chief Operating Officer, Chief Financial Officer, and Executive Secretary, with all

Vice-Presidents appointed by the President. To eliminate perceived conflict of interest that evidenced itself in the mid-1990s, a provision was added to preclude any Board Member from receiving remuneration as an AKC employee or consultant for at least a year after leaving the Board.

There were also extensive changes in the disciplinary provisions of the bylaws for numerous reasons. These changes lessened the Board's involvement, making Trial Boards more independent, thereby improving the appeal process and ensuring due process in disciplinary procedures.

FINANCES AND THE FUTURE

The new century saw a shift in the AKC's revenue sources. In the 1980s, core revenue from registrations had made up 90 percent of the operating capital. That number began to decline annually as the general decrease in registrations of litters and dogs continued.

As operating expenses continued to rise, alternative sources of revenue, such as licensing,

A new member of the Sporting Group, the Irish Red and White Setter became the 159th breed accepted into the AKC on January 1, 2009.

The Swedish Vallhund entered the Herding Group on June 27, 2007, after ten years of enrollment in the AKC Foundation Stock Service.

sponsorships, and pet insurance, began to be explored and implemented. These new alternatives would allow the AKC to subsidize its events, club conferences, scholarships, charitable contributions, lobbying efforts, and the many other crucial functions that would support the core fancy and the purebred dog.

Chairman Ron Menaker and President-CEO Dennis B. Sprung took the advice of external auditors and established the goal of having appropriate operating reserves to maintain the future of the sport and ensure its financial future. The goal of having reserves equaling approximately 50 percent of annual expenses was met within three years.

The AKC's principal role as a service organization remained. Changes were made to fee schedules when appropriate. For instance, after reviewing the costs of the Judges Approval system, the Board approved an application fee for judges of twenty-five dollars per breed, effective March 1, 2002.

The Board of Directors Business Committee, under Ron Menaker, continued to accumulate data on the costs and revenues involved in the services that the AKC provides to its customers and constituents. Menaker's committee reviewed a survey of the costs and revenues in the Events Department. The significance of this was underscored when the consultants, PriceWaterhouseCoopers, through their review of the club's pricing and cost structure for Event Services, noted that the fifty-cent recording fee, which had not been raised since 1983, failed to cover any reasonable portion of AKC costs for recording event results. Any inflation index would justify a much higher fee. As a result, the AKC implemented an Event Service fee to help offset these annual losses.

Presently, the AKC and current Chief Financial Officer James Stevens continue to ask the hard questions about how much of the cost of AKC services should be borne by the persons or organizations who receive the services, in light of the constantly changing economy.

IT'S ALL RELATIVE–KEEPING PACE WITH REGISTRATION NEEDS AND TECHNOLOGY

DNA technology continues to affect the American Kennel Club registry. In July 2000, the AKC implemented its Frequently Used Sires Program. Every sire producing seven or more litters in a lifetime or producing more than three litters in a calendar year must be AKC DNA Certified. These DNA profiles are used for genetic identity and parentage verification to maintain the integrity of the registry. In this vein, the AKC launched many registration initiatives as part of the Board's companywide strategic plan to increase registrations and to make the value of AKC registration known not only to those in the sport but also to all pet owners.

A change in registration policies regarding innocent third parties trying to register with AKC became effective January 2002. People who acquired registration by circumventing their suspension might have sold dogs to these third parties who had no knowledge that the seller was suspended. It was decided that the third parties who purchased such dogs would not have the registration of their dogs/litters cancelled if the parentage of their dogs was not in question.

The reengineering of the registration system was not by any means a smooth transition. There were problems with the new system that were not

DNA

The AKC currently maintains the world's largest canine DNA database, containing more than 425,000 DNA profiles from 196 AKC and FSS breeds for parentage verification and genetic identity purposes.

Canine DNA profiles are collected through voluntary as well as mandatory programs, including the Frequently Used Sires Program, the Fresh-extended /Frozen Semen Program, the Multiple-Sired Litter Registration Policy, the Import Breeding Stock Requirement, the Kennel Inspections/Compliance Audit Program, and the AKC DNA Analysis for Parentage Evaluation.

Using the swab provided in the DNA test kit, a sample of cells collected from inside the dog's cheek is submitted for analysis. The AKC issues a DNA profile containing the dog's reg-istration information, genotype, and a DNA profile number, which appears on subsequently issued registration documentation.

A sample of cells swabbed from the inside of a dog's cheek is all that's needed for DNA profiling.

Conditional Registration

The AKC's DNA program is used to evaluate parentage of AKC-registered dogs and litters.

If registered dogs are found to have an unknown ancestor, the AKC cancels the registration. If parentage of a purebred AKC-registered dog is found to be incorrect through DNA testing, the AKC may downgrade the dog's registration to conditional status in order to avoid canceling the registrations of a dog, its littermates, and progeny.

"Unknown" is substituted for the name of the unverified ancestor on pedigree records, and "Conditional" is designated on the registration certificates of related individuals until three verified generations have been established by the AKC.

discovered until after the old system had been completely dismantled. The scanning technology employed was not suitable for the new system, resulting in unacceptably lengthy delays. It took AKC employees as well as outside consultants countless hours to rectify the problems. In the end, the President, the Chief Operating Officer, and the Chief Information Officer left their positions as a result, which threatened the club's core service to dog owners.

The year 2003 saw the unveiling of the Online Litter Registration system, enabling those who registered dogs to quickly and efficiently access and interact with the registration services of the AKC. Within a year of the program's implementation, more than 100,000 litters had been registered online. This accounted for 30 percent of all litters registered. In December 2006, online litter registration reached 60 percent of total litters registered. In 2008, that number rose to 74 percent. Individual online registrations became available in 2004.

An AKC pilot program launched in July 2006 made it easier for breeders to individually register all puppies in a litter. The Full Litter Registration Application enables breeders to register a litter and individually register each puppy at the same time, using one application form.

COMMUNICATION–SPREADING THE WORD

In the first decade of the twenty-first century, the AKC increased its emphasis on building an effective communication network to establish ongoing awareness of what the American Kennel Club is and what the club does. The AKC focused on becoming more relevant to the general purebred pet owner. With this in mind, and with the creative help of Doner Advertising, the club developed its first-ever television and print advertising campaign. The campaign featured two thirty-second spots,

ABOVE: Dennis B. Sprung established the DOGNY program following the attacks of September 11, 2001. Here Dennis is surrounded by a pack of sculptures honoring New York City's fallen heroes. Displayed at firehouses around the city, the sculptures were greeted with tributes, both emotional and floral.

BELOW, LEFT: Sculpture *All Breeds and Bones,* painted by Beata Szpura. **BELOW, RIGHT:** Mary Fragapane painted this sculpture *Brave New World* to capture the "resounding sense of patriotism" in the country following the terrorists' attacks.

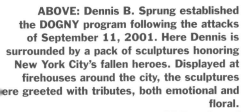

The heroes of 9/11 were both two-footed and four! German Shepherd Dogs' excellence as search and rescue workers cannot be overstated.

ABOVE: Search and rescue dogs are rigorously trained for their job. Here's a beautifully trained Boxer working on a practice search. BELOW: Volunteers from the Suffolk County SPCA assisted in the daily upkeep and care of the brave search and rescue dogs at Ground Zero.

one highlighting the AKC as an organization and the other emphasizing the excitement, education, and enjoyment that can be shared by all ages through participation in AKC events. Among other initiatives, the televised broadcast of the AKC/Eukanuba National Championship spread the word about all of the AKC's available services to the public at large.

Following the tragic events on September 11, 2001, Dennis B. Sprung, then Vice-President of Corporate Relations, established the

In service to humankind: no questions asked. The unconditional relationship of dogs and their owners resonates profoundly and is unmistakable in the noble expression of this Rough Collie.

Military Working Hero Award

The American Kennel Club's participation in the 2004 *Intrepid* Foundation's Fleet Week celebration marked the first time that military dogs were honored at this annual event.

AKC Chairman Ron Menaker presented the city of New York with the original bronze DOGNY statue in tribute to America's search and rescue dogs, now on permanent display as part of The *Intrepid* Sea-Air-Space Museum's "The *Intrepid* Remembers 9/11" exhibit.

Acknowledging the vital contributions of military working dog teams in the service of our country, Menaker also presented the first DOGNY Heroic Military Working Dog Award to Sergeant Herman Haynes and Frenke, a seven-year-old German Shepherd Dog with an outstanding record of service in Afghanistan and Iraq.

Sergeant Herman Haynes and seven-year-old German Shepherd Dog Frenke distinguished themselves with exceptional meritorious service in Afghanistan during Operation Enduring Freedom. Currently, Sgt. Haynes and Frenke are deployed in Baghdad in support of Operation Iraqi Freedom-2. Their dedication, commitment to excellence, and selfless service to the Armed Forces and our nation in support of the global war on terrorism are an inspiration to us all. Working with his trainer Sgt. Haynes since May 2001, Frenke is certified in explosive detection and patrol and has saved countless lives. With sound temperament and loyalty to his handler, Frenke stands ready to assist, protect, and defend our national interests.

DOGNY program, which was launched by Mayor Michael Bloomberg at City Hall. The centerpiece of this effort involved 112 DOGNY sculptures, created by professional artists, which were displayed throughout New York City.

ALL THE BEST FOR YOUR PUREBRED PET

AMERICAN KENNEL CLUB familydog

Reading
Your Dog's
Vital Signs

Vaccines:
Which Ones
& How Often?

DEAN KOONTZ
on his beloved Trixie

WINNER
BEST
MAGAZINE

SEPTEMBER/OCTOBER 2008
$3.95

AKC's newest periodical, *Family Dog* magazine was first published in 2003.

The program had immeasurable public relations value. In total contributions, sponsorships, merchandising, and the auction of these statues at the end of the program, more than $3 million was raised for professional and volunteer canine search and rescue organizations throughout our nation. Highlights included a commemorative book, as well as DOGNY Day at Yankee Stadium, a salute on Broadway's Great White Way in Shubert Alley, the only display in Saks Fifth Avenue's otherwise blacked-out windows on the 9/11 anniversary, and many appearances on major television networks.

THE PRINTED WORD

In 2002, work began on a concept for a new communication tool, *Family Dog* magazine, aimed at the new or casual purebred dog owner. Initially a quarterly publication, this new outreach facilitated communication between the AKC and more of its registrants than ever before while sharing messages of responsible dog ownership and the benefits of competing in AKC events. First published in 2003, this popular periodical is now a bimonthly publication.

PUBLIC SERVICE PROGRAMS

Public education and communication remained at the forefront of AKC's goals. In many respects, Delegates played a more important role than ever before in AKC history, in part by encouraging the nationwide network of more than 4,000 volunteer Public Education Coordinators and Canine Ambassadors who distributed materials about AKC programs and initiatives.

In keeping with public outreach, the AKC Library launched a searchable online version of its massive catalog at www.akc.org in December 2004. A Public Service Announcement (PSA) focusing on the importance of responsible dog ownership was also created. It was aired more than 3,300 times and watched by more than 8 million viewers.

Part of this key communication strategy was AKC Responsible Dog Ownership (RDO) Day, launched in 2003. This annual event spotlights the importance of responsible ownership for all dog owners and educates the public about the many ways that the AKC helps pet owners enhance their relationship with their dogs. On September 17, the month and day of the AKC's founding in 1884, RDO Day festivities took place in New York and Raleigh. In 2008, more than 600 AKC Clubs and other organizations held similar events around the country.

LEGISLATION AND GRASSROOTS EFFECTIVENESS

The AKC Legislative Department hosted the first-ever "Lobby Day" in Washington, DC. The event gave our nationwide legislative liaisons the opportunity to network, expand their lobbying skills, and learn more about the AKC's federal agenda. The AKC met with great success in maintaining access to air travel for people and their dogs. The department also worked with fanciers to persuade American Airlines to rescind a breed-specific shipping ban and led a grassroots campaign to convince United Airlines to lift an embargo on shipping pets as excess cargo. AKC lobbying helped move the United States

Through annual events, its Web site, and its many programs, AKC continues to reach out to all dog owners, providing education, assistance, and support.

New Exhibitor Mentoring Program

The AKC's New Exhibitor Mentoring Program provides expert guidance for novices entering the sport of purebred dogs. Seasoned handlers and exhibitors share their expertise, answer questions, and provide encouragement to introduce new exhibitors to the world of dog shows and familiarize them with the AKC environment.

Owners of AKC-registered dogs considering involvement in dog sports can request a mentor through the New Exhibitor Mentoring Program. After completing an application, the potential dog fancier is paired with an experienced fancier who volunteers to serve as a mentor through AKC-affiliated clubs. Since the program's inception in October of 2008, 350 mentors have participated in fulfilling approximately 550 match requests.

The AKC also provides an introduction to the sport of purebred dogs through an AKC Canine Experience, a day-long, multiclub, multisport event to welcome and educate owners of newly AKC-registered puppies. These events feature educational presentations and opportunities for potential owners to be mentored by experienced exhibitors prior to an afternoon match, in which they can practice their newly learned skills. Only licensed and member clubs are eligible to host an AKC Canine Experience.

In 2005, the AKC established a scholarship program for Veterinary Technician students with Hartz as the original sponsor. Since its inception, the program, sponsored by Bayer Healthcare's Animal Health Division beginning in 2007, has awarded a total of $132,000.

SPECIAL SERVICES

To better service the core fancy, the Special Services Department was created and staffed with a group of subject-matter experts with in-depth knowledge of the dog sport. Questions from Delegates, Club Officers, judges, and fanciers are directed to this department and dealt with by its experienced staff members.

INTERNAL CONSULTING GROUP

In 2003, the AKC created the Internal Consulting Group. At the direction of Chairman Ron Menaker, the AKC began developing a three-part program to ensure that experienced, versatile individuals are identified and cultivated for careers within the company. This group was intended to bring in additional people from outside the company as well and create a team of employees working together on companywide initiatives and department-specific programs. The team was to improve services as well as efficiency and generate additional revenue. The goal was to groom those in this group for future leadership roles at the AKC. In 2004, newly appointed Chief Operating Officer John Lyons assumed a major role in advising this group as they moved forward.

SUMMER INTERN PROGRAM

This program enables college-age fanciers to work for two months at paid assignments; opportunities are available in both the Raleigh and New York offices. The jobs are project-focused so that the interns gather real-life work experience. The program allows the AKC to identify potential employees with professional skills and knowledge of the sport.

AKC UNIVERSITY

In 2003, the American Kennel Club launched AKC University, an in-depth employee development and training program. Seminars are offered so that all employees can broaden their knowledge of AKC events and departments and stay abreast of ongoing changes and improvements to programs and policies. The program also offers general educational opportunities for all employees.

HURRICANE RELIEF 2005

The year 2005 will long be remembered as the year of the Gulf Coast hurricanes. The AKC immediately appointed a team, coordinated by the Public Relations Department, to address the needs in this dire situation. AKC and AKC/CAR staff visited shelters and staging areas that were temporarily housing animals in Mississippi, Louisiana, Alabama, and Texas to meet with relief workers and determine where assistance was needed. The AKC sent shipments of food, water, crates, dog bowls, and exercise pens to the disaster areas. Donations from the AKC/CAR Support and Relief Fund went to help reimburse the expenses of veterinary schools that served as temporary shel-

Your AKC

While serving as COO, Dennis Sprung requested that an online newsletter be created for communication with AKC constituents to satisfy the public's growing demand for information and content on the purebred dog. More than 1.2 million individuals have chosen to receive this complimentary monthly email newsletter.

Disaster Preparedness

Volunteers from the AKC Disaster Relief team are shown removing abandoned dogs from a New Orleans airlift following Hurricane Katrina.

The AKC Web site provides in-depth guidelines to help dog owners prepare for emergency evacuation, including links to the Red Cross.

The AKC also provides direct support for displaced pets during disasters through the AKC/CAR Canine Support and Relief Fund. Since its formation in 2001, AKC/CAR has provided disaster relief to displaced pets throughout the country from the California wildfires, multiple hurricanes, and floods in Iowa.

The AKC's unique network of resources and expertise allows it to respond quickly and effectively in a multitude of situations as was seen in their response to Hurricane Katrina.

Following Hurricane Katrina, AKC/CAR donations were used to purchase essential supplies and coordinated their delivery through a network of local kennel club members. AKC/CAR personnel worked with local kennels and shelters to arrange temporary care for displaced pets. AKC inspectors made on-site visits to the facilities to assess conditions and offer assistance. AKC/CAR coordinated airlifts to take displaced pets to safety and utilized their record-keeping expertise to ensure that all pets were clearly identified and could be later reunited with their owners.

In addition to AKC/CAR Katrina Relief fund donations used for pets, $25,000 from the AKC/CAR Canine Support and Relief Fund was given to Take the Lead Katrina Disaster Fund to aid those in the fancy who were affected by the disaster.

Two rescued dogs from Hurricane Katrina with volunteers from an AKC rescue mission.

Recognizing that excellent veterinary care is essential to responsible dog ownership, AKC offers affordable pet health insurance to all dogs and cats meeting underwriting criteria including a complimentary sixty-day trial AKC Healthcare Plan for newly registered dogs.

All AKC Pet Healthcare plans cover medically necessary services including surgical procedures, prescription medications, diagnostic and laboratory tests, cancer diagnosis and treatment, and hospitalization.

Essential Plans provide coverage for unexpected accidents, injuries, and illnesses. Wellness Plans provides higher coverage for unexpected accidents, injuries, and illnesses, plus preventive-care coverage.

No veterinary exam or records are required, and applications can be completed by telephone, mail, or e-mail. Premiums can be paid monthly or annually. Insured pets can be treated by any licensed veterinarian in the United States or Canada.

The claim-filing process provides direct reimbursement for covered services within fifteen days of receipt of all necessary paperwork. A staff of professionally qualified veterinary technicians and insurance adjusters is available by phone and e-mail, including evenings and Saturdays.

ters. The AKC also coordinated eight airlifts of displaced dogs to shelters around the country, including St. Hubert's Animal Welfare Center's Katrina K-9 Center in Mendham, New Jersey.

In total, the AKC/CAR received more than $1.1 million in donations. In a heartfelt gesture of goodwill, The Kennel Club (England) and The Kennel Club Charitable Trust contributed a combined 10,000 British pounds to the relief effort.

THE AKC PET HEALTHCARE PLAN

The American Kennel Club Pet Healthcare Plan by Pet Partners, Inc., was begun in 2003. The insurance program further expands the array of services that the AKC offers to fanciers and pet owners. As a value-added component to AKC registration, all AKC-registered dogs are eligible for a complimentary sixty-day pet healthcare insurance policy.

THE AKC HUMANE FUND

The AKC Humane Fund, Inc. was incorporated in 2008 to promote and foster responsible ownership among pet lovers of all kinds. Activi-

FAITH

At the site of the Oklahoma City bombing, this search and rescue dog returns for the unveiling of the memorial.

ties of the fund focus on education, outreach, and grant-making for the benefit of dogs and the people who love them. The Fund awards grants to clubs that perform breed rescue, shelters that permit pets to accompany victims of domestic abuse, and other organizations that share the Fund's mission. The Fund also creates and supports educational programs that celebrate the human-canine bond, such as the Hall of Fame for the sport of dogs and the previously mentioned ACE awards. Donations to the AKC Humane Fund, Inc., are tax deductible under section 501(c)(3) of the IRS code.

ACE Awards

In 2000, the AKC instituted the American Kennel Club Awards for Canine Excellence (ACE) to acknowledge the many ways that dogs contribute to human health and well-being.

ACE awards are open to AKC-registered or -registerable dogs that have performed exemplary acts to benefit a community or individual. One annual award is given in five categories: law enforcement, search and rescue, therapy, service, and exemplary companion dog. Each recipient receives a cash award of $1,000 and an engraved sterling silver collar medallion at the AKC/Eukanuba National Championship. Their names are also engraved on a plaque that hangs permanently in the American Kennel Club Library.

GOOD SPORTS

As a result of the Chairman's Committee on Conflict of Interest, in 2006 the Board of Directors approved the first-ever written Code of Sportsmanship for the sport

The memorial at Oklahoma City, being visited by one of the search and rescue dogs who responded to the call.

Branded!

The value of the AKC brand was cultivated and developed into a licensing program as a means to create an alternative revenue source. The program was a huge success, bringing AKC brand merchandise to dog lovers across the country. Major licensees managed by 4 Sight Licensing Solutions include Jakks Pets, Aspen, and Steiff. In 2008, Jakks won the Licensing Industry Merchandisers Association award for best Corporate Brand Licensee for its work with AKC brand products.

of purebred dogs. This Code of Sportsmanship, drafted by the Hon. David Merriam, reflected the input of the Delegates at the January 2006 Forum in Tampa. The Board unanimously voted to adopt the Code presented to them during the February session.

NEW AND IMPROVED

Rally® is the new dog sport that has taken the nation by storm from its inception in 2005. This is a sport in which the dog and handler complete a course that has been designed by the Rally judge. The Rally course is made up of a number of stations, and each station has

Completing a full circle to the right, this Australian Shepherd and his exhibitor, competing at a Rally event.

Rally

In January 2005, Rally was approved as an AKC event. The objective was to provide a transitional step from basic training to obedience or agility through an activity combining the fun of dog sports with experience in a competitive situation. Rally combines aspects of rally car racing, agility, and obedience. Rather than a stepping stone for novices, this unique blend of challenge, excitement, and fun proved to be overwhelmingly popular with agility, obedience, and conformation exhibitors alike.

Dog/handler teams move at their own pace through a course with the dog heeling at the handler's left side. At each station, the team performs an exercise according to instructions posted on a sign. Teams are judged on coordination, communication, problem-solving skills, and strategy rather than on speed or rigorous precision.

Rally is open to all AKC-registered dogs six months of age or older, including ILP/PAL- and approved FSS-registered dogs meeting eligibility requirements.

Judges design a unique course for each trial. Exhibitors receive a map and can walk the course before the judging. Teams begin with 100 points and must complete the course with a minimum score of 70 points to qualify. Three qualifying scores are required to earn titles at each level.

Rally Novice (RN) competition consists of ten to fifteen on-lead exercises designed to demonstrate the dog's understanding of basic commands.

Rally Advanced (RA) competition consists of twelve to seventeen exercises to demonstrate responsiveness and control off lead.

Rally Excellent (RE) competition consists of fifteen to twenty challenging off-lead exercises to demonstrate precision and coordination between dog and handler.

RE-titled dogs can earn Rally Advanced Excellent (RAE) titles by qualifying ten times in both Advanced B and Excellent B at the same trial. Titles at this level are numbered to reflect how many times it has been earned (i.e., after the twentieth leg, title will be RAE2; after the thirtieth, it will be RAE3, etc.).

Labrador Retriever and his exhibitor walking a Rally course prior to the start of the event. Winning teams exhibit the best communication and coordination rather than speed.

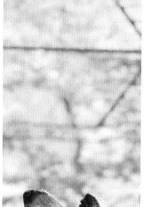

AKC Coonhound
events have become
increasingly popular
in the new century.

Treeing Walker Coonhound winning at an AKC Bench Show.

a sign that provides instructions regarding the skill that is to be performed. Intended as a successful stepping-stone from the AKC Canine Good Citizen® program to the world of Obedience or Agility, Rally was designed with the traditional pet owner in mind but can still be very challenging for those who enjoy higher levels of competition. The main objective of Rally is to produce dogs that have been trained to behave in the home, in public places, and in the presence of other dogs, in a manner that will reflect positively on the sport of Rally at all times and under all conditions.

The AKC offers a newly expanded and developed Coonhound Events Program that was started in 2005. Bench Shows, Field Trials, Nite Hunts, and Water Races are competitive events that provide owners with

An enthusiastic beginning to a Coonhound Field Trial.

Coonhounds

In 2007, AKC's Coonhound Events department sanctioned 1,723 events in which 444 Coonhounds earned titles. The staff of experienced coon hunters also focuses resources on legislative efforts to protect the sport and a youth program to ensure its future. For information, visit www.akc-coonhounds.org or call 1-888-4-DOG-HUNT.

AKC Coonhound events are open to all AKC-registered American English Coonhounds, Black and Tan Coonhounds, Bluetick Coonhounds, Plotts, Redbone Coonhounds, and Treeing Walker Coonhounds six months or older.

AKC offers three levels of Bench Show, Field Trial, Nite Hunt, and Water Race titles.

Bench Shows
Bench Show Championships (CCH)
Bench Show Grand Championships
  (CGCH)
Bench Show Supreme Grand
  Championships (CSG)

Water Races
Water Race Champion (CWC)
Grand Water Race Champion
  (CGW)
Supreme Grand Water Race
  Champion (CSGW)

Field Trials
Coonhound Field Champion (CFC)
Grand Field Champion (CGF)
Supreme Grand Field Champion
  (CSGF)

Nite Hunts
Nite Champion (CNC)
Grand Nite Champion (CGN)
Supreme Grand Nite Champion
  (CSGN)

In 2007, 5,241 dogs competed at 523 AKC Coonhound Bench Shows, resulting in 140 CCH, 84 CGCH, and 55 CSG titles. AKC Nite Hunts are one of the most popular dog sports in the nation. Dogs are evaluated in actual competitive hunting situations, although no firearms are permitted and no game taken. In 2007, 8,717 Coonhounds competed in 1,113 AKC Nite Hunts, earning 121 CNC, 28 CGN, and 7 CSGN titles.

AKC also encourages Coonhound excellence through the World Coonhound Nite Hunt and Bench Show Championship, an annual six-day event for the nation's top-winning Coonhounds. In 2008, more than four hundred Coonhounds from six Coonhound breeds competed for prestigious titles and top prize money.

To become a World Nite Champion, a Coonhound must demonstrate superior abilities to strike a track, run, and tree wild raccoons in a series of consecutive Nite Hunts. A Coonhound must compete through successive elimination rounds of breed judging. Six World Champions of Breed represent each breed in the final challenge for AKC World Bench Show and Reserve World Bench Show Champion.

the opportunity to demonstrate the beauty and natural abilities of the several breeds of purebred Coonhounds. At the same time, deserving dogs achieve AKC recognition by acquiring championship titles on three different levels in each activity. These activities also benefit Coonhound clubs by increasing memberships and providing an atmosphere of comaraderie and sportsmanship.

The AKC Board of Directors approved a series of recommendations from the AKC Obedience Advisory Committee, including changes designed to improve the overall Obedience program and offer exhibitors more chances to compete. The majority of these changes became effective on January 1, 2009, while other changes will become active in 2010 or 2011. In addition, clubs began to have the option of offering new Optional Titling Classes and Non-Regular Classes starting in 2009.

Global Service

The AKC's new Global Services program is designed to provide record-keeping and registration processing to foreign kennel clubs. Its first project is the development of an accurate purebred registry and competition records for the National General Kennel Club (NGKC) of China. Through AKC Global Services, the AKC can contribute to the worldwide betterment of purebred dogs by sharing its expertise as the world's largest purebred registry.

AKC Gazette's Photo Contest, Third Place Color, 2006, photographer Kim Mach.

Looking forward to the next challenge and shining horizon...

EPILOGUE

Very few companies can enjoy enduring success for 125 years. It is a testament to the AKC's heritage, clubs, and great leaders of the past, as well as the collective efforts of the dedicated purebred dog community and the AKC's commitment to maintaining its core values. The commitment to upholding tradition has consistently been coupled with sound business practices in daily operations. As the AKC has expanded its services into the new millennium, the club can remain proud of remaining true to its mission and dedicated to serving the needs of a varied and ever-expanding constituency.

Horatio Henry Couldery's *The President*, 1868, was on display at first exhibition at The Dog Museum of America. This oil on canvas painting was the gift of Frank T. Sabella.

APPENDIX A:

AMERICAN KENNEL CLUB PRESIDENTS

MAJOR JAMES M. TAYLOR

Major James M. Taylor was one of that small group of men who met in Philadelphia in September 1884 when the American Kennel Club began. Major Taylor's extensive activities in this and other related sports gave him a clear view of the dog sport in America. He knew that there was some cheating at dog shows, such as substituting one dog for another, and was aware of attempts to intimidate judges. He also knew that a reliable Stud Book was needed.

Years before the American Kennel Club was founded, Major Taylor was a busy judge, both at Bench Shows and at Field Trials. He judged at Westminster a number of times. His well-known tall bearded figure was seen at shows in Boston; Rutherford, New Jersey; and other cities. He judged numerous breeds, mainly Sporting Dogs and Hounds. He continued judging into the first decade of the twentieth century.

Major Taylor's name appeared frequently in the *American Field*. The November 1884 issue reports the adoption of the AKC Constitution and Bylaws and the election of Taylor as AKC President. At that time, he was the Delegate from the Cincinnati Bench Show Association. The *American Field* in October 1885 reports on Taylor's speech at the National Sportsmen's Convention. He was in favor of outlawing spring shooting in order to preserve game birds and animals by giving the young a chance to grow to maturity. Major Taylor not only was active in Bench Shows and Field Sports but also was ahead of his time in conservation.

His presidency lasted approximately fourteen months, until December 1885. We know that Major Taylor continued to serve the American Kennel Club in various capacities for the rest of his life. He became the Delegate from the Kansas City Kennel Club, later represented the Saint Louis Kennel Club, and ultimately represented the Columbus Fanciers' Club. He remained as the Columbus club's Delegate through March 1909, the year before his death.

In 1894, 1895, and 1896, Major Taylor was a member of the AKC Advisory Committee, a forerunner of the Board of Directors, and he took an active part. In 1894, he was a member of an AKC committee that was to confer with Representatives of the Canadian Kennel Club concerning an agreement of cooperation between the two organizations. At one time, he offered to resign from the Advisory Committee because illness was temporarily preventing him from carrying out his duties. His resignation was not accepted.

Any view of Major James Taylor's career must include his work as a sporting journalist. His articles appeared in various sporting publications for many years. Perhaps his most important achievement was *Field Trial Records of Dogs in America*, published in 1907. When we review the statistical section of that book, we find accuracy and completeness. It is an astonishing accomplishment for one man, keeping Field Trial records from 1874 through the first half of 1907. Major Taylor died at his home in Rutherford, New Jersey, on September 1, 1910.

ELLIOT SMITH

Elliot Smith became the American Kennel Club's second President in December 1885 and served until 1887. He was one of the group that met in Philadelphia in 1884 whose actions resulted in the founding of the American Kennel Club. On the original slate of officers, he was First Vice-President.

When his presidency ended, he remained active in AKC affairs. He was a Collie fancier and represented several dog clubs as Delegate, beginning in 1889 with the Pacific Kennel Club. From February 1896 through January 1897, he was the Delegate of the Westminster Kennel Club. He then became the Delegate of the Oakland Kennel Club for a very brief period. On September 17, 1894, a luncheon party was held at Delmonico's in New York City to celebrate the AKC's tenth anniversary. One of the toasts offered was to former officers of the club. Elliot Smith made a gracious response to the toast and gave some insight into the tenure of his presidency. In part, he said: "Everything was novel; we had no example to follow or avoid. Everyone had a different view to be discussed."

The Westminster Kennel Club shared Smith's time and energy with the AKC. From 1892 to 1896, he was a member of the Bench Show Committee and the Westminster Kennel Club Board of Governors. In 1896, he served as Show Chair for the annual Westminster Kennel Club Dog Show.

WILLIAM H. CHILD

In 1887 and in the early part of 1888, William H. Child was chosen as President of the American Kennel Club, succeeding Elliot Smith. Child was selected after having served first as Second Vice-President and then First Vice-President.

Less information has survived concerning the third American Kennel Club President than any other AKC President. He was a native of Philadelphia and served as AKC Delegate from the Philadelphia Kennel Club between February 1891 and November 1891. Soon thereafter, all mention of his name faded from American Kennel Club records, with the exception of the registered kennel name that he owned for some years, Oakview. Time has obscured the rest of the details of his life.

AUGUST BELMONT, JR.

August Belmont, Jr., had a heritage of business and public service. His mother was the daughter of Commodore Matthew Perry, who opened Japan to Western trade, and his father came to the United States at the age of twenty-four as an agent of the House of Rothschild. Operating brilliantly on behalf the Rothschilds and himself as well, he was soon a millionaire.

Although the first August Belmont had stopped formal schooling at fourteen, he had extraordinary intelligence and discrimination ability. He became an art collector, an opera patron, and a successful breeder of Thoroughbred horses. He admired the political system of his adopted country enough to devote time and money to politics.

When August Belmont, Jr., became the fourth President of the American Kennel Club in 1888, he was the head of the international banking firm that his father founded. Even so, he addressed the problems of the four-year-old AKC as though nothing else required his attention.

August Belmont, Jr., came to the position as a dog lover and breeder of Fox Terriers. An 1886 report shows a balance of $49.15 in the AKC Treasury. The nature of the club's operation had not yet been defined, and some assumed it would be a gentlemen's social club for eating, drinking, and talking. From the beginning, however, August had a clear-eyed perception of what the organization had to become, and he directed it steadily toward that goal. He suggested that an official publication chronicling AKC actions was needed. Thus began the *Gazette* in 1889, with President Belmont personally guaranteeing $5,000 each year for five years against possible losses. The AKC has always been proud that not a penny of the President's money needed to be used.

August Belmont, Jr., also supervised the incorporation of the American Kennel Club in 1906. In 1908, a special charter was secured from the State of New York, clearly defining the club's right to regulate dog shows and the Stud Book. He also negotiated with organizations in other countries, particularly Canada and Great Britain, setting up reciprocal agreements. When August Belmont, Jr., resigned as President in 1916, the AKC was recognizable as the organization that exists today. It supervised the sport of purebred dogs, it was financially solid, and its integrity was respected.

Mr. Belmont's twenty-eight-year tenure has never been duplicated. He died in 1924, but through August Belmont, Jr., the AKC is linked to a fascinating and significant era in the social history of America.

HOLLIS H. HUNNEWELL

Hollis Horatio Hunnewell became the fifth President of the AKC after the departure of August Belmont, Jr., in 1916. He came from a Massachusetts family whose lives reflected respect for the traditions of a gracious and solidly established way of life. The family was based on an estate famous for its beautiful gardens. He graduated from Harvard in 1890 and was then able to pursue his personal interests as a sportsman. Despite his background, he was not a dilettante. His father had a philosophy of "do your damndest," and it was a principle that Hunnewell followed. One of his hobbies was the indoor game of racquets (squash). He became a nationally known player and built the first United States squash court on the Hunnewell estate in Wellesley.

His consuming interest was the sport of dogs. He began to breed Fox Terriers, and in 1892, two years after graduating from college, he was granted the registered kennel name Hill Hurst. He became Secretary of the American Fox Terrier Club in 1898 and its AKC Delegate in 1899. He remained as their Delegate until his death.

Mr. Hunnewell held many positions with the AKC. His committee assignments were numerous, and in 1901 he became an AKC Vice-President, then First Vice-President in 1909, and finally President in 1916. His presidency was capable and orderly, representing a smooth transition to a new era. He resigned in 1921 because of poor health, and died the following year.

HOWARD WILLETS

The Willets family first came to America from England in 1638, a generation after the Pilgrims. They settled on Long Island in an area that has since become part of Queens. Today, Willets Point Boulevard runs adjacent to Shea Stadium and the site of two World's Fairs.

Howard Willets, the sixth President of the American Kennel Club, was born in New York in April 1861. He began his business career as a commission merchant. His partnership in Willets and Company began in 1885 and lasted until his death more than a half a century later.

Howard Willets had an abiding interest in animals, including horses, cattle, and dogs. In 1898, he purchased from the Gedney family the famous 250-acre Gedney Farms estate in Westchester County, where he maintained a herd of prize Jersey cattle. He also raised dogs and harness horses, and Gedney Farms became his registered kennel name in 1904. In those days, Mr. Willets could often be seen driving a carriage and horses, with Dalmatians running under the coach. Both horses and dogs were bred at Gedney Farms. It was a prized local spectacle. He was also an expert horseman and owned the world champion high jumper Heatherbloom.

Mr. Willets began his association with the AKC when it was founded. He held various AKC positions, culminating in his presidency in 1921. He served until 1923, when he found that his personal responsibilities did not permit him to devote adequate time to his AKC duties. However, he did continue as a Delegate

Howard Willets died in 1938, at age seventy-seven. His second wife, Elyse Young Willets, had been associated with the AKC in 1923, when they were mar-

ried. One of his sons, J. Macy Willets, also served as an AKC Delegate.

JOHN E. DE MUND, MD

The only American Kennel Club President who was a physician was John E. De Mund. His term lasted from 1923 to 1932. Documents of that time refer to his uncommon decisiveness and energy. With his help, the AKC managed to avoid disaster during the first terrible years of the Depression.

While Dr. De Mund was President, the AKC initiated a significant court case, suing an Illinois organization calling itself the American Kennel Club. The Illinois organization's defense was that the AKC's New York charter, which had been secured by August Belmont, Jr., was valid in New York but nowhere else. The Illinois court found in favor of the American Kennel Club in 1924, enjoining the Illinois organization from imitating the American Kennel Club in any way, including use of the initials, seal, and certificates. This landmark decision confirmed the legal right of the AKC to regulate the registration and showing of purebred dogs all over the United States.

John E. De Mund was born in Brooklyn in 1866. He graduated from Rutgers College and the College of Physicians and Surgeons at Columbia University, then practiced medicine between 1890 and 1912. An otolaryngologist, he was a member of the staff of the New York Eye and Ear Hospital. His father, Dr. Frederick Cornell De Mund, was also a well-known physician. AKC President Dr. De Mund's career acquired a startling, cloak-and-dagger dimension when the United States Department of Justice enlisted his help as a secret agent during Word War I.

Dr. John De Mund retired from medicine in 1912 to devote himself to other interests, particularly purebred dogs and yachting. As chairman of the Brooklyn Yacht Club, Dr. De Mund sponsored one of the first long-distance ocean races for small craft. He himself sailed several times on the American challengers in the Lipton Cup yachting races. He was the AKC Delegate from the Russian Wolfhound (Borzoi) Club of America for many years and was AKC Second Vice-President and First Vice-President before becoming President. He died from a heart attack in November 1933.

CHARLES TOPPING INGLEE

The eighth President of the American Kennel Club was Charles Topping Inglee, born in Brooklyn in December 1877. Because of his poor health as a child, he spent a lot of time in the country, reaping the benefits of fresh air and sunshine and developing an interest in dogs.

He owned his first gundog when he was twelve. He first showed dogs, English Setters, at a Long Island Kennel Club show in 1895 at a skating ring in Brooklyn. However, he soon turned his attention to Gordon Setters.

No breeder has been more closely identified with a particular breed of dog than Charles Inglee was with Gordon Setters. He did not introduce them to America; this was done by Daniel Webster, who acquired a pair from the Duke of Gordon (Scotland) in 1842. Inglee, however, bred Gordons so successfully at his Inglehurst Kennels that he became known as "the Father of the American Gordon." He founded the Gordon Setter Club of America and was its AKC Delegate during the 1920s.

Charles Inglee's business career was centered in real estate. He had one daughter, Jean, who became the wife of artist Edwin Megargee, famous for his precise and sensitive drawings of dogs as well as the beautiful AKC bookplate that can be seen at the AKC Library in New York.

By 1928, Mr. Inglee was Second Vice-President of the American Kennel Club. He became First Vice-President in January 1932 and President in September of that year. Soon after, there was an extensive reorganization of the AKC administration. Mr. Inglee resigned the presidency after only five months in office and accepted the newly created post of Executive Vice-President, a position he held until his death in April 1941.

RUSSELL H. JOHNSON, JR.

Russell Hampden Johnson, Jr., was President of the American Kennel Club from 1933 to 1940. Born in Pennsylvania in 1878, he was educated at private schools in the Philadelphia area. After finishing school, he joined Lawrence Johnson and Company, dealers in hides and goatskins, a business founded by his two uncles. Russell Johnson, Jr., was associated with this company for the remainder of his life and served as its President for many of those years.

His love of purebred dogs began early, and Russell Johnson, Jr., was never without a dog from the age of four. This has almost always been true of those who have become prominent in the sport. Someone who had visited another AKC President as a boy recalled shuffling along a floor "ankle deep in puppies."

A powerful, impressive figure, Mr. Johnson was also active in sports. As a boy, he played football at school. A few years later,

D. Read, who shared his abiding interest in dogs and subsequently became very active in the Devon Dog Show Association.

Lafore was a Lieutenant Commander in the United States Navy during World War II. Afterward, he became active in politics. He served four consecutive terms in the Pennsylvania State Legislature, from 1950 to 1957. In 1957, he was called upon to fill an unexpired term in the United States House of Representatives for the 13th District of Pennsylvania. He was then elected to a full term as Congressman and served on the Congressional Ways and Means Committee.

In addition, he maintained a business career. He was President of the Kellett Aircraft Corporation of Willow Grove, Pennsylvania, and financial Vice-President of Day and Zimmerman of Philadelphia.

Even while he was busy in community service and business, Mr. Lafore became increasingly more involved in the world of purebred dogs. He and Mrs. Lafore began to breed Collies under the Chantwood prefix. In 1956, their attention became focused on the Keeshond. His varied dog club affiliations reflected his growing interest. He was, at different times, District Director of the Collie Club of America, a First Vice-President and President of the Keystone Collie Club, a Director of the Keeshond Club of America, and President of the Keeshond Club of Delaware Valley. In addition, he was a Director of the Chester Valley Kennel Club.

As early as 1953, Mr. Lafore was a Delegate to the American Kennel Club, representing the Devon Dog Show Association. He became a Member of the AKC Board of Directors in 1963. The Board elected him Executive Vice-President in 1968, and then AKC President in 1971.

Under his leadership, a definitive step was taken to cope with the avalanche of paperwork that threatened to engulf the AKC.

This was a result of the huge spurt in registrations and show activity that occurred after World War II. The computerization of American Kennel Club records began.

Mr. Lafore also guided another movement toward the future, as female Delegates were accepted, and the AKC named its first female Vice-President during his presidency.

When John Lafore, Jr., retired as AKC President in 1978, he did not retire from service to the American Kennel Club. Many years later, people who read *Pure-Bred Dogs/American Kennel Gazette* could still see the name of the genial, competent man who had been the AKC's thirteenth President listed as Delegate and Director.

WILLIAM F. STIFEL

William Fredrick Stifel was elected the fourteenth President of the American Kennel Club in March 1978. Mr. Stifel was born in June 1922 in Toledo, Ohio, and studied at Western Reserve Academy and Harvard University. During World War II, he served in the United States Coast Guard. He married Carolyn Graham in 1957, and they have two daughters.

Mr. Stifel joined the AKC staff as a part-time typist in August 1957 and became a full-time employee three weeks later. He became Supervisor of the Show Plans and Show Records Departments and served in this capacity until 1964, when he was elected Executive Secretary. He was Chairman of the Beagle Advisory Committee from 1969 to 1977. In 1976, he became Executive Vice-President and in 1978 was elected President. He was elected to the Board of Directors in 1977.

He is a member of the Westminster Kennel Club, the Westchester Kennel Club, and the Greater St. Louis Training

Club. He has served as Delegate from the San Francisco Dog Training Club, after which he represented the Greater St. Louis Training Club. As of this writing, he is the AKC Delegate from the Westminster Kennel Club.

In 1982, William F. Stifel received the Fido Award as Man of the Year from the Gaines Dog Research Center. The citation singled out his work in lifting the American Kennel Club to "greater heights than ever before" and, specifically, "his direction in bringing about major changes in the judge selection process and the standards for judges."

Mr. Stifel represented the American Kennel Club at the First World Conference of Kennel Clubs held in London in 1978 and the Second World Congress of Kennel Clubs in Edinburgh in 1981. He was Chairman of the Third World Congress of Kennel Clubs, which was hosted by the American Kennel Club in Philadelphia in 1984. Mr. Stifel was also founding President of the American Kennel Club Foundation, which established the Dog Museum of America in 1980.

KENNETH A. MARDEN

Kenneth A. Marden became AKC President in May 1987 and assumed office in July of that year. He was elected to the Board in 1986, having been the Delegate from the German Shorthaired Pointer Club of America since 1974.

He had long been involved in Conformation, Field Trials, and Obedience and he handled eleven dogs of his own breeding to Show Championships. He also helped to develop the AKC's Hunting Test for Pointing Breeds. Club memberships included the German Shorthaired Pointer Club of America, Eastern German Short-

haired Pointer Club, Long Island German Shorthaired Pointer Club, Diamond State German Shorthaired Pointer Club, Kennel Club of Philadelphia, and Princeton Dog Training Club.

Mr. Marden was with Johnson and Johnson for twenty years, holding a variety of marketing positions. From 1980, he served as Vice-President of Viacom-FCB, a Philadelphia advertising agency.

During his tenure as President, the AKC added several new sports, specifically Agility, Lure Coursing, Earthdog, and Herding. For his accomplishments, Mr. Marden received the Lifetime Achievement Award in 2007.

LOUIS AUSLANDER

In May 1990, Louis Auslander, the AKC Board Chairman, was appointed as interim President, being the only individual to hold both positions. (See additional information in Mr. Auslander's Chairman's biography later in this Appendix.)

ROBERT G. MAXWELL

Robert G. Maxwell was elected as AKC President in 1991. He began as Comptroller in 1969 and was named Vice-President of Administration in 1985. In 1988, he became Senior Vice-President and was elected Executive Vice-President and Chief Executive Officer in 1990.

As CEO, Mr. Maxwell oversaw the relocation of all registration-related services from New York to Raleigh, North Carolina. During his administration, the registration inspection program was greatly expanded. DNA testing was introduced into the registry, and microchipping procedures for dog identification were adopted.

APPENDIX B:

AKC CHAIRMEN OF THE BOARD

Chairman of the Board was a position created in 1972, with the President then becoming the Chief Executive Officer. Prior to that, the President had acted as the (amateur) Chairman of the Board.

ALEXANDER FELDMAN

Alexander Feldman became the AKC's first Board Chairman, having been active in the sport for over thirty-five years. Mr. Feldman became a Delegate in 1957 and a Board member in 1964. He owned St. Bernards, Doberman Pinschers, and Cocker Spaniels, but his principal interest was Great Danes. He bred and exhibited many Great Dane Champions and held several offices in the Great Dane Club of America, including President and AKC Delegate. He also belonged to the Westbury Kennel Association and the Saw Mill River Kennel Club.

Mr. Feldman was the third-generation head of his family's newspaper distribution business, founded prior to 1900. He was President of Crescent News Distributors and Woodhaven News Co., as well as President of the Evening Newspaper Wholesalers Association. He attended Columbia University and received an LLB degree from St. Lawrence University Law School.

AUGUST BELMONT

August Belmont became Chairman in March 1979. He was the grandson of August Belmont, Jr., AKC President from 1888 to 1916. He became a Board Member in 1968 and AKC Treasurer in 1972. The Delegate from the American Chesapeake Club, he bred and competed with both Chesapeake Bay and Labrador Retrievers in Retriever Field Trials. He chaired the Retriever Advisory Committee and held office in the National Amateur Retriever Club, the American Chesapeake Club, the Long Island Retriever Club, and the Maryland Retriever Club. He also served as First Vice-President of the Orthopedic Foundation for Animals.

A graduate of St. Marks School and Harvard University, he was Special Assistant to the Under Secretary of the Navy during World War II and held the rank of Lieutenant Commander, winning the Bronze Star.

He retired as Chairman of Dillon Read and Company investment bankers, serving as company President from 1962 to 1970. He was also a Trustee of the American Museum of Natural History and Presbyterian Hospital of New York City.

HAWORTH HOCH

Haworth Hoch served as Board Chairman from 1979 to 1982 and as a Board Member from 1970 to 1984. Mr. Hoch owned and exhibited a number of breeds, beginning in 1934 with Collies. He also had Labrador Retrievers, English Springer Spaniels, Beagles, Pointers, Shetland Sheepdogs, and Cardigan Welsh Corgis. He exhibited Shetland Sheepdogs from 1940 to 1969. He was an officer of Mississippi Valley Kennel Club, St. Louis Collie Club, and Greater St. Louis Shetland Sheepdog Club. From 1963 to 1970, he served as President of the American Shetland Sheepdog Association. He was also a multiple-Group judge.

Graduating from the University of Michigan in 1930, he became associated with McCourtney-Breckenridge and Company, an investment banking firm in St. Louis. He served on the Midwest Stock Exchange Board of Governors and that of the Harrisonville Telephone Company, as well as numerous committees of the Investment Bankers Association and the National Association of Securities Dealers.

HON. WILLIAM H. TIMBERS

The Hon. William H. Timbers became Chairman of the Board in March 1982. He was Chief Judge of the United States District Court, Connecticut, from 1968 until his appointment to the United States Court of Appeals in 1971, where he became a Senior Judge of the Second Circuit United States Court of Appeals.

He had served as Chairman of the AKC New York Trial Board from 1965 to 1968, when he became an AKC Director.

Judge Timbers bred and exhibited Norwegian Elkhounds. He was a member of the Ox Ridge Kennel Club and the Norwegian Elkhound Club of America, serving as President of the latter from 1960 to 1965.

He graduated from Dartmouth in 1937 and Yale Law School in 1940. From 1953 to 1956, he served as General Counsel for the United States Securities and Exchange Commission. Prior to his judicial appointment, he was a partner in the law firm of Spadden, Arps, Slate, and Timbers.

WILLIAM ROCKEFELLER

William Rockefeller served as Chairman from 1984 to 1987, having been a Member of the Board since 1979 and a Delegate since 1957.

Mr. Rockefeller served as President of the Westminster Kennel Club from 1975 until 1984. He had also been President of the ASPCA from 1956 to 1969 and Chairman of the Geraldine Rockefeller Dodge Foundation and the Baker Institute at Cornell University. Mr. Rockefeller was a graduate of Yale University and of Columbia University Law School. He practiced law in New York City and was a partner in the firm of Shearman and Sterling.

Mr. Rockefeller also served the community in many capacities, including as Chairman of the Metropolitan Opera Association, Secretary and Trustee of Memorial Sloan-Kettering Cancer Center, Trustee of Paul Smith College, Chairman of the Yale Alumni Board, Trustee of St. John the Divine Cathedral, and Vestryman and Warden of Christ's Church, Rye, New York.

LOUIS AUSLANDER

In 1987, Louis Auslander was elected Chairman after having served on the Board since 1985. Involved in the sport since 1964, he bred and showed Miniature Schnauzers, Whippets, and both Smooth and Wire Fox Terriers. He became an AKC-approved judge in 1970.

He is the Delegate from the International Kennel Club of Chicago and a member of the American Whippet Club, the American Miniature Schnauzer Club, the American Fox Terrier Club, and Park Shore Kennel Club. Mr. Auslander was a member of the AKC Museum of the Dog Board of Directors and served as Chairman of their Steering Committee.

Mr. Auslander was President of a Chicago construction company and had an interest in an insurance/adjusting firm.

In May 1990, Mr. Auslander was appointed interim AKC President, still retaining the title of Chairman. This was done while the AKC Bylaws were amended to remove the requirement that the AKC President must be a Board Member. He is the only individual in the AKC's history to simultaneously hold both titles.

JOHN S. WARD

John S. Ward was elected Chairman in March 1988, having served on the Board since 1974 and as AKC Treasurer since 1979. Mr. Ward graduated from the University of Notre Dame. He was a Naval Communications Officer during World War II, after which he worked as a research chemist before entering government service in 1950.

Mr. Ward and his family raised, trained, and showed Cocker Spaniels in Conformation and Obedience, and he became an Obedience judge in 1952. He was a member of Old Dominion Kennel Club of Northern Virginia, Mount Vernon Dog Training Club, Capital City Cocker Club, and the American Spaniel Club. He also served as President of the Association of Obedience Clubs and Judges.

In 2001, Mr. Ward was presented with the American Kennel Club Lifetime Achievement Award for a half century of contributions to the sport.

JAMES W. SMITH

James W. Smith was elected Chairman in March 1994. Smith became involved in Dalmatians in 1956 and later began breeding and exhibiting Smooth Fox Terriers. He served as Secretary and President of the American Fox Terrier Club and has been Delegate from the Dalmatian Club of America since 1986. He became an AKC-approved judged in 1972.

Mr. Smith graduated from Washington and Lee University and is President of American Wire Tie, Inc.

DR. ROBERT J. BERNDT

Dr. Robert J. Berndt became Board Chairman in March 1995, having served on the Board since 1994. Under Dr. Berndt's tenure, the AKC pursued the idea of consolidating all operations in Durham, North Carolina. Property was purchased for this purpose, but the Board later voted to maintain a New York headquarters while having an Operations facility in Raleigh, North Carolina.

Involved in purebred dogs since 1958, Dr. Berndt finished thirty champions in several breeds and showed dogs in every Group. He is an all-breed judge, initially gaining approval in 1970. A member of the Illinois Capital Kennel Club, he served on the Board of Directors of both the American Maltese Association and the American Lhasa Apso Club. A longtime member of the Ozarks Kennel Club, he was its Delegate from 1980 to 1996. He is also a member of the Dog Writers' Association of America and has written numerous articles and several dog books.

HON. DAVID C. MERRIAM

Elected Chairman in March 1997, David C. Merriam had bred and exhibited Bull Terriers since 1953. He handled his first Specialty winner at age fifteen. He was show chairman for the Kennel Club of Riverside and held office in the Golden Gate State Bull Terrier Club and Bull Terrier Club of America. He chaired the AKC Los Angeles Trial Board and is approved to judge the Terrier Group.

First appointed to the Board in 1979 to fill a vacancy in the Class of 1980, Judge Merriam served on the Board three different times: 1979 to 1985, 1992 to 1996, and 1997 to 2009. Before becoming Chairman, Judge Merriam served briefly as AKC Executive Vice-President and CEO.

Judge Merriam graduated cum laude from Claremont Men's College and was a National Defense Fellow at Stanford University, where he received a master's degree. After graduation from UCLA School of Law, he was admitted to the California Bar in 1967. Prior to becoming a judge, he was a deputy district attorney and a partner in the firm of Naylor, Hyde, and Merriam.

RONALD H. MENAKER

Ronald H. Menaker became AKC Board Chairman in March 2002. He had been involved with purebred dogs for more than thirty-five years, having bred and showed Giant Schnauzers, Bedlington Terriers, and Norfolk Terriers. He became an AKC-approved judge in 1994. Mr. Menaker was first elected to the Board in 1997 to fill a one-year vacancy. He was elected to serve his first full four-year term in 2000.

Active in a number of clubs, Mr. Menaker held several offices, including President, Director, and Delegate in the Bedlington Terrier Club of America and Show Chairman for the Westminster Kennel Club.

Mr. Menaker was President and a Director of JP Morgan Services, as well as a Managing Director and Group Head of JP Morgan, an affiliate of JP Morgan Services.

During his career, he has served on many Boards, including New York Downtown Hospital and New York University Medical Center. He was President of the AKC Museum of the Dog and a Trustee of both St. Hubert's Giralda Animal Welfare and Education Center and the Morris Animal Foundation.

APPENDIX C:
2009 AKC BOARD OF DIRECTORS

Class of 2010

Dr. Carmen L. Battaglia
Delegate, German Shepherd
   Dog Club of America

Dr. William R. Newman
Delegate, Mastiff Club of
   America

Nina Schaefer
Delegate, Back Mountain
   Kennel Club, Inc.

Class of 2011

Dr. Patricia Haines
Delegate, Cincinnati Kennel
   Club, Inc.

Ken Marden
Delegate, German Shorthaired
   Pointer Club of America

Patti Strand
Delegate, Dog Fanciers
   Association of Oregon, Inc.

Class of 2012

Dr. Thomas M. Davies, Vice
   Chairman
Delegate, Springfield Kennel
   Club, Inc.

Walter F. Goodman
Delegate, Skye Terrier Club of
   America

Ronald H. Menaker, Chairman
Delegate, Rockford-Freeport
   Illinois Kennel Club

Class of 2013

Lee Arnold
Delegate, Southern Colorado
   Kennel Club

Carl C. Ashby, III
Delegate, United States Kerry
   Blue Terrier Club

Alan Kalter
Delegate, American Bullmastiff
   Association

Dr. Robert D. Smith
Delegate, Memphis Kennel
   Club

Ex Officio: Dennis B. Sprung

APPENDIX D:

AMERICAN KENNEL CLUB STATISTICS
Dog and Litter Registrations

Year	Breeds	Dogs	Litters	Year	Breeds	Dogs	Litters
1878–1884	8	1,416	-	1915	66	22,127	-
1885	26	1,896	-	1916	59	14,161	-
1886	26	2,085	-	1917	57	15,552	-
1887	38	2,202	-	1918	57	13,409	-
1888	49	4,457	-	1919	57	18,479	-
1889	39	4,217	-	1920	57	23,453	-
1890	37	2,866	-	1921	59	29,960	-
1891	36	4,308	-	1922	59	29,119	-
1892	37	4,469	-	1923	63	39,721	-
1893	38	4,028	-	1924	70	49,579	-
1894	37	3,667	-	1925	69	54,172	-
1895	36	3,473	-	1926	71	59,455	-
1896	37	3,512	-	1927	72	57,560	-
1897	42	3,738	-	1928	74	52,762	-
1898	49	3,649	-	1929	79	48,160	-
1899	46	4,351	-	1930	83	48,147	-
1900	43	4,881	-	1931	83	46,724	-
1901	43	5,445	-	1932	81	47,112	29,200
1902	45	6,319	-	1933	85	51,497	44,309
1903	46	6,595	-	1934	93	60,196	50,891
1904	51	7,396	-	1935	96	72,390	52,520
1905	49	8,276	-	1936	100	84,475	57,225
1906	53	9,730	-	1937	103	84,156	54,925
1907	52	10,496	-	1938	102	82,797	56,925
1908	57	10,676	-	1939	100	79,989	53,425
1909	54	10,790	-	1940	105	83,345	53,950
1910	61	10,819	-	1941	99	87,968	55,300
1911	60	9,955	-	1942	99	89,383	53,250
1912	69	10,311	-	1943	100	78,200	46,025
1913	57	10,243	-	1944	98	77,400	47,275
1914	66	10,608	-	1945	97	147,707	73,089

Year	Breeds	Dogs	Litters	Year	Breeds	Dogs	Litters
1946	100	206,978	92,662	1977	122	1,013,650	380,050
1947	100	235,720	110,092	1978	123	980,299	371,500
1948	105	227,647	115,384	1979	124	965,250	371,900
1949	106	241,811	119,493	1980	125	1,011,799	382,350
1950	104	251,812	113,557	1981	125	1,033,849	404,599
1951	104	264,415	123,788	1982	125	1,037,149	405,850
1952	105	294,240	139,550	1983	128	1,085,248	415,799
1953	105	326,234	142,551	1984	128	1,071,299	422,098
1954	102	346,525	152,475	1985	129	1,089,149	439,548
1955	104	359,900	159,684	1986	129	1,106,399	453,100
1956	104	430,900	188,482	1987	130	1,187,400	496,900
1957	106	436,600	192,262	1988	130	1,223,500	525,400
1958	107	446,625	207520	1989	130	1,257,700	550,300
1959	106	460,300	216,975	1990	131	1,253,214	557,237
1960	109	442,875	226,447	1991	134	1,379,544	567,763
1961	111	493,300	238,525	1992	136	1,528,392	540,581
1962	115	516,800	250,925	1993	137	1,422,559	514,187
1963	115	568,300	270,750	1994	137	1,345,941	523,368
1964	115	640,300	292,675	1995	140	1,277,039	533,630
1965	115	722,800	319,925	1996	143	1,333,568	558,227
1966	115	804,400	351,025	1997	145	1,307,362	564,165
1967	115	885,800	379,775	1998	146	1,220,951	555,964
1968	115	909,300	404,175	1999	147	1,119,620	527,023
1969	116	973,100	421,125	2000	148	1,175,473	506,727
1970	116	1,056,225	446,025	2001	150	1,081,335	461,863
1971	116	1,129,200	451,675	2002	150	958,800	440,641
1972	118	1,101,943	430,700	2003	151	915,668	423,761
1973	120	1,099,850	420,749	2004	154	958,641	437,504
1974	121	1,103,249	418,150	2005	154	920,804	421,128
1975	121	1,022,849	397,950	2006	155	870,192	413,957
1976	122	1,048,648	406,550	2007	157	812,452	392,334
				2008	158	716,195	352,136

Events
1884–1925

Year	All-Breed Shows	Specialty Shows	Field Trials
1884	11	0	-
1885	11	0	-
1886	18	1	-
1887	11	1	-
1888	11	1	-
1889	14	0	-
1890	12	0	-
1891	25	1	-
1892	22	2	-
1893	20	0	-
1894	17	0	-
1895	12	0	-
1896	19	0	-
1897	23	0	-
1898	18	2	-
1899	22	5	-
1900	24	3	-
1901	22	0	-
1902	26	1	-
1903	32	4	-
1904	35	7	-
1905	55	6	-
1906	57	6	-
1907	72	8	-
1908	84	13	-
1909	91	12	-
1910	79	20	-
1911	71	29	-
1912	75	27	-
1913	70	28	-
1914	71	27	-
1915	77	27	-
1916	76	33	-
1917	72	37	-
1918	38	32	-
1919	52	33	-
1920	70	46	-
1921	73	48	-
1922	96	64	-
1923	128	78	18
1924	157	87	22
1925	169	103	22

Events
1926–1967

Year	All-Breed Shows	Specialty Shows	Field Trials	Independent Obedience Trials	Tracking Tests	Obedience Trials with Shows
1926	164	115	30	-	-	-
1927	183	109	30	-	-	-
1928	177	84	36	-	-	-
1929	166	93	36	-	-	-
1930	145	95	35	-	-	-
1931	125	93	39	-	-	-
1932	121	100	39	-	-	-
1933	128	103	41	-	-	-
1934	166	110	53	-	-	-
1935	188	110	68	-	-	-
1936	181	121	82	-	-	-
1937	196	121	83	-	-	-
1938	212	124	98	4	-	-
1939	222	104	97	1	4	-
1940	223	112	111	11	9	-
1941	234	117	119	14	16	-
1942	164	60	103	13	13	-
1943	130	59	96	12	10	-
1944	196	100	115	16	15	-
1945	138	76	136	27	12	-
1946	254	178	168	26	21	-
1947	272	212	204	26	19	-
1948	305	214	231	37	12	-
1949	331	227	265	42	13	-
1950	361	273	309	59	15	-
1951	367	257	348	74	14	190
1952	382	269	386	87	15	206
1953	375	272	416	96	20	227
1954	384	304	473	110	21	241
1955	402	322	524	120	21	268
1956	411	317	592	128	20	282
1957	432	322	659	127	20	316
1958	440	337	699	136	22	331
1959	449	361	729	144	26	354
1960	459	392	737	143	26	382
1961	476	404	753	141	23	396
1962	480	421	752	142	31	406
1963	488	399	754	152	32	421
1964	496	421	773	154	34	428
1965	511	432	819	158	37	444
1966	520	456	833	159	41	454
1967	537	473	846	170	50	466

Events
1968-2008

Year	All-Breed Shows	Specialty Shows	Field Trials	Independent Obedience Trials	Tracking Tests	Obedience Trials with Shows
1968	545	512	851	176	48	489
1969	557	546	887	178	54	500
1970	569	599	902	190	56	511
1971	586	646	941	197	62	538
1972	606	690	974	196	62	569
1973	625	771	1,000	216	66	620
1974	656	838	993	215	73	679
1975	703	950	1,032	226	88	772
1976	732	1,050	1,069	230	92	844
1977	775	1,136	1,106	235	101	901
1978	815	1,198	1,096	247	105	952
1979	823	1,238	1,113	264	110	940
1980	844	1,272	1,119	254	132	1,030
1981	877	1,302	1,138	263	161	1,087
1982	915	1,339	1,145	270	181	1,133
1983	961	1,360	1,134	276	173	1,165
1984	989	1,414	1,141	282	191	1,196
1985	1,015	1,465	1,151	324	211	1,214
1986	1,039	1,487	1,129	337	203	1,241
1987	1,056	1,501	1,150	344	201	1,268
1988	1,072	1,539	1,157	364	222	1,308
1989	1,090	1,544	1,192	365	215	1,358
1990	1,110	1,608	1,196	377	225	1,413
1991	1,139	1,666	1,223	392	248	1,478
1992	1,155	1,733	1,238	404	255	1,538
1993	1,177	1,828	1,300	414	263	1,616
1994	1,220	1,860	1,384	455	272	1,672
1995	1,245	1,954	1,416	467	267	1,722
1996	1,266	1,966	1,415	490	271	1,724
1997	1,295	1,994	1,441	507	290	1,764
1998	1,331	1,970	1,391	500	265	1,745
1999	1,365	1,997	1,444	540	304	1,746
2000	1,415	2,049	1,508	579	326	1,766
2001	1,444	2,067	1,525	592	320	1,776
2002	1,455	2,118	1,534	602	340	1,755
2003	1,477	2,150	1,562	640	338	1,742
2004	1,474	2,140	1,593	672	347	1,726
2005	1,490	2,194	1,591	754	388	1,718
2006	1,519	2,225	1,612	824	392	1,722
2007	1,540	2,202	1,629	858	408	1,647
2008	1,534	2,258	1,670	903	420	1,584

Hunting Tests	Herding Events	Lure Coursing Events	Agility Events	Earthdog Events	Coonhound Events	Rally Events
-	-	-	-	-	-	-
-	-	-	-	-	-	-
-	-	-	-	-	-	-
-	-	-	-	-	-	-
-	-	-	-	-	-	-
-	-	-	-	-	-	-
-	-	-	-	-	-	-
-	-	-	-	-	-	-
-	-	-	-	-	-	-
-	-	-	-	-	-	-
-	-	-	-	-	-	-
-	-	-	-	-	-	-
-	-	-	-	-	-	-
-	-	-	-	-	-	-
-	-	-	-	-	-	-
-	-	-	-	-	-	-
-	-	-	-	-	-	-
-	-	-	-	-	-	-
13	-	-	-	-	-	-
64	-	-	-	-	-	-
175	-	-	-	-	-	-
329	-	-	-	-	-	-
440	-	-	-	-	-	-
535	69	0	-	-	-	-
609	109	33	-	-	-	-
643	120	209	-	-	-	-
696	152	262	-	-	-	-
738	198	343	23	5	-	-
762	254	441	121	37	-	-
809	226	395	255	47	-	-
852	229	353	377	53	-	-
756	242	261	401	70	-	-
759	259	324	681	78	-	-
765	318	324	877	98	-	-
815	335	325	1,002	96	-	-
822	379	329	1,139	104	-	-
846	406	306	1,379	121	-	-
842	509	288	1,668	140	221	-
886	586	315	1,812	138	374	1,066
929	637	391	1,956	139	777	1,708
944	619	431	2,014	135	1,723	2,021
978	681	475	2147	144	2,387	2,060

Dogs in Competition
1951–1981

Year	Shows	Obedience Trials	Tracking Tests	Field Trials
1951	167,687	13,936	74	36,897
1952	171,412	16,358	90	39,391
1953	178,007	18,154	129	44,778
1954	190,461	22,224	115	50,805
1955	200,908	24,351	112	58,794
1956	208,764	24,611	107	66,383
1957	223,205	28,275	132	72,477
1958	225,756	30,316	164	76,655
1959	231,954	31,051	199	80,188
1960	246,200	31,874	177	81,301
1961	258,000	32,116	131	80,433
1962	270,168	33,360	195	82,467
1963	294,895	36,718	224	79,637
1964	322,299	38,661	226	82,436
1965	360,500	38,032	259	86,797
1966	398,752	41,292	311	88,844
1967	440,299	44,877	381	89,243
1968	490,471	50,500	352	94,597
1969	539,929	49,781	420	104,911
1970	597,174	56,524	452	104,111
1971	658,247	63,506	479	108,976
1972	705,117	66,490	537	112,755
1973	750,920	71,792	550	113,165
1974	789,612	75,890	627	113,240
1975	853,591	84,951	740	118,019
1976	894,934	86,989	805	122,965
1977	991,159	93,530	941	122,318
1978	947,473	91,033	946	116,937
1979	938,898	90,290	934	115,600
1980	949,053	91,547	1,053	111,694
1981	1,008,830	91,829	1,191	115,286

Dogs in Competition
1982–2008

Year	Shows	Obedience Trials	Tracking Tests	Field Trials	Hunting Tests
1982	1,050,863	100,846	1,236	113,853	-
1983	1,117,682	103,850	1,217	113,979	-
1984	1,133,084	103,501	1,310	114,204	-
1985	1,180,040	97,700	1,274	117,529	681
1986	1,222,481	95,691	1,216	116,398	3,777
1987	1,278,991	95,525	1,251	116,657	9,532
1988	1,307,106	99,460	1,346	114,978	15,792
1989	1,362,655	104,677	1,306	119,973	20,247
1990	1,411,219	107,068	1,327	125,393	23,856
1991	1,438,266	104,689	1,390	128,831	26,815
1992	1,444,862	104,871	1,390	129,861	28,404
1993	1,475,940	104,698	1,399	130,645	29,606
1994	1,493,325	110,217	1,385	135,458	31,909
1995	1,525,788	106,232	1,395	136,221	34,313
1996	1,522,734	103,787	1,220	137,432	38,501
1997	1,553,668	103,859	1,425	141,127	40,477
1998	1,533,607	110,603	1,347	143,049	41,329
1999	1,532,471	122,273	1,425	146,602	42,760
2000	1,524,492	118,526	1,502	148,598	44,312
2001	1,525,056	120,337	1,463	147,470	46,479
2002	1,534,893	118,518	1,581	147,397	49,153
2003	1,554,668	117,792	1,600	149,640	50,157
2004	1,549,752	116,092	1,621	150,448	50,559
2005	1,535,723	113,701	1,802	146,750	51,264
2006	1,532,131	109,868	1,851	148,858	51,617
2007	1,509,240	104,290	1,861	145,735	49,698
2008	1,422,933	100,381	1,925	142,399	50,123

Herding Events	Lure Coursing Events	Agility Events	Earthdog Events	Coonhound Events	Rally Events
-	-	-	-	-	-
-	-	-	-	-	-
-	-	-	-	-	-
-	-	-	-	-	-
-	-	-	-	-	-
-	-	-	-	-	-
-	-	-	-	-	-
-	-	-	-	-	-
1,601	-	-	-	-	-
1,647	1,608	-	-	-	-
1,694	3,704	-	-	-	-
2,423	6,446	-	-	-	-
3,237	6,470	1,800	230	-	-
2,920	5,923	11,323	2,347	-	-
3,711	6,380	28,651	3,218	-	-
4,366	6,803	59,032	2,936	-	-
4,983	6,025	65,831	2,083	-	-
5,834	6,821	186,598	4,284	-	-
6,560	7,934	261,385	4,758	-	-
7,330	8,438	324,195	4,742	-	-
7,675	8,185	407,309	5,881	-	-
8,121	8,374	492,723	6,043	-	-
9,508	9,175	573,813	7,049	2,906	-
10,805	8,981	613,909	7,014	2,941	65,116
11,109	11,390	674,706	7,706	6,866	90,737
12,031	12,369	747,715	8,326	14,345	93,021
12,098	13,901	758,351	8,488	17,593	78,909

Field Trials by Type
1923–1950

Year	Basset Trials	Beagle Trials	Foxhound Trials	Dachshund Trials	Pointing Breed Trials	Retriever Trials	Spaniel Trials
1923	-	17	1	-	1	-	-
1924	-	20	1	-	1	-	-
1925	-	22	-	-	-	-	-
1926	-	28	1	-	-	-	1
1927	-	26	1	-	-	-	4
1928	-	29	1	-	-	-	3
1929	-	30	1	-	-	-	3
1930	-	25	2	-	-	-	4
1931	-	31	2	-	1	1	5
1932	-	30	2	-	2	2	4
1933	-	30	2	-	3	2	4
1934	-	38	1	-	3	3	5
1935	-	44	1	2	7	4	12
1936	-	47	1	3	9	9	13
1937	1	48	1	3	5	10	15
1938	2	49	1	3	10	17	14
1939	1	50	1	3	7	17	17
1940	2	52	1	3	9	23	21
1941	1	63	1	1	6	23	25
1942	1	67	-	1	3	16	15
1943	1	70	-	1	2	13	9
1944	1	82	-	1	2	17	11
1945	2	92	-	1	6	22	12
1946	1	109	-	1	10	31	20
1947	2	135	-	-	15	35	16
1948	2	154	-	-	17	39	18
1949	2	170	-	-	22	49	21
1950	1	198	-	-	35	49	27

Field Trials by Type
1951–1981

	Basset Hounds		Beagles		Dachshunds	
Year	# of Trials	# of Starters	# of Trials	# of Starters	# of Trials	# of Starters
1951	2	38	220	29,813	1	18
1952	2	41	243	31,588	1	13
1953	2	51	259	36,109	1	22
1954	2	83	286	39,510	1	17
1955	3	116	313	45,612	1	26
1956	3	154	342	50,024	1	25
1957	4	267	372	53,858	1	33
1958	6	507	380	56,249	1	30
1959	7	583	406	57,996	2	33
1960	11	759	399	57,322	1	16
1961	11	771	397	54,778	1	26
1962	12	867	400	56,308	1	27
1963	13	932	401	53,576	1	26
1964	12	787	403	54,619	1	31
1965	15	978	411	56,861	1	30
1966	15	1,029	407	57,193	1	25
1967	15	1,186	411	55,859	2	53
1968	15	1,151	412	57,394	2	53
1969	17	1,113	408	60,485	2	51
1970	19	1,212	395	59,665	2	54
1971	19	1,216	405	61,197	3	87
1972	22	1,353	413	60,244	3	85
1973	24	1,600	402	57,651	3	65
1974	24	1,811	386	55,890	3	58
1975	30	2,017	394	56,611	3	75
1976	29	1,735	390	56,993	3	73
1977	31	1,599	397	53,881	3	117
1978	31	1,541	382	50,266	3	68
1979	31	1,478	387	49,152	5	124
1980	32	1,349	391	47,735	7	133
1981	35	1,544	391	50,082	8	195

Pointing Breeds		Retrievers		Spaniels	
# of Trials	# of Starters	# of Trials	# of Starters	# of Trials	# of Starters
42	1,759	54	3,974	29	1,295
51	2,204	59	4,106	30	1,439
61	2,700	61	4,518	32	1,378
82	4,183	71	5,565	31	1,447
104	5,933	73	5,447	30	1,528
125	6,706	88	7,588	33	1,886
148	7,736	100	8,742	34	1,841
170	8,731	106	9,404	36	1,734
173	9,673	108	10,236	33	1,667
181	10,681	111	10,727	34	1,796
195	11,950	115	11,130	34	1,778
186	11,741	119	11,754	34	1,770
184	12,615	123	12,153	32	1,830
196	13,550	126	11,727	35	1,720
225	15,182	135	12,226	32	1,520
236	15,740	140	13,265	34	1,592
244	17,307	139	13,235	35	1,603
255	19,392	134	15,019	33	1,588
282	24,522	138	16,865	40	1,875
310	24,241	139	17,351	37	1,588
329	26,155	144	18,735	41	1,586
355	29,184	144	20,241	37	1,648
380	29,589	152	22,497	39	1,763
386	30,603	156	23,177	38	1,701
407	32,164	165	25,430	33	1,668
428	34,429	173	27,546	46	2,189
445	35,567	184	29,115	46	2,039
446	34,058	190	28,929	44	2,075
453	34,463	192	28,298	45	2,085
454	32,783	191	27,585	44	2,109
464	33,071	192	27,939	48	2,455

Field Trials by Type
1982–2008

Year	Basset Hounds # of Trials	Basset Hounds # of Starters	Beagles # of Trials	Beagles # of Starters	Dachshunds # of Trials	Dachshunds # of Starters
1982	37	1,464	393	49,345	9	175
1983	38	1,561	402	49,106	10	206
1984	37	1,532	406	48,981	14	346
1985	38	1,373	400	50,435	13	307
1986	38	1,437	400	51,016	13	325
1987	37	1,456	422	51,005	14	406
1988	38	1,352	422	49,875	15	442
1989	40	1,350	441	51,882	21	604
1990	39	1,333	436	54,547	22	658
1991	40	1,247	450	56,012	28	798
1992	39	1,214	445	56,169	30	873
1993	39	1,179	466	55,894	36	1,131
1994	40	1,326	493	58,680	39	1,254
1995	39	1,197	501	58,935	41	1,102
1996	39	1,174	511	58,802	40	1,021
1997	37	1,178	526	60,356	40	1,305
1998	32	1,239	527	59,014	43	1,847
1999	36	1,205	563	61,272	48	2,434
2000	39	1,237	610	61,931	53	2,683
2001	36	1,077	633	61,501	53	2,974
2002	37	1,040	646	61,659	55	3,186
2003	37	1,089	669	63,468	59	3,719
2004	35	891	688	62,913	68	4,448
2005	36	967	686	59,897	70	4,285
2006	36	948	700	60,100	64	4,301
2007	38	932	719	58,244	65	4,474
2008	34	679	723	56,104	75	4,720

Pointing Breeds		Retrievers		Spaniels	
# of Trials	# of Starters	# of Trials	# of Starters	# of Trials	# of Starters
462	33,230	195	27,219	49	2,420
435	32,029	201	28,639	48	2,438
434	32,064	203	28,869	47	2,412
442	32,608	212	30,416	46	2,390
420	31,009	211	29,937	47	2,674
413	30,097	215	30,734	49	2,959
406	29,613	220	30,281	56	3,415
408	30,603	226	31,570	56	3,964
415	32,670	228	32,254	56	3,931
414	33,184	227	33,340	64	4,250
431	34,373	225	32,975	68	4,257
453	35,130	229	33,048	77	4,263
485	37,426	239	32,812	88	3,960
497	38,884	241	31,946	97	4,157
490	39,807	236	31,385	100	5,243
495	40,167	240	32,214	103	5,907
460	41,078	236	33,242	93	6,629
464	40,726	231	33,995	100	6,970
463	40,160	233	35,634	112	6,953
449	38,922	237	35,954	117	7,042
446	37,209	235	36,539	118	7,764
432	36,004	239	37,771	126	7,589
437	36,909	243	37,591	123	7,696
431	34,829	241	38,930	127	7,842
426	35,656	256	39,623	130	8,230
415	34,546	268	39,385	124	8,154
425	34,318	284	38,491	129	8,087

PHOTOGRAPHY CREDITS

The American Kennel Club has been indebted to the talents and expertise of a legion of photographers for many decades. The superb work of the following photographers, much of it specifically commissioned by the AKC, is represented in this new volume: the AKC and Publisher greatly appreciate how vast their individual and collective contribution is toward making this anniversary volume the very special book it is. Photographs presented in this book from the AKC's *Gazette* Photo Contest are credited on the pages on which they appear.

John Ashbey
Debbie Asher
Anne Beck
George Berger
Laura Berger
Nancy Best
Carol Beuchat
Charles Blessis
Mary Bloom
William Brown
Kerrin and Dale Churchill
Lisa Croft-Elliott
Kent Dannen
Paul Dantuomo
D. Davis
Tara Darling
Jack Dewitt
Brian Drumm
Nina Fatula
Ed and Candy Ferner
Jim Fredericks
Christina Freitag
Dan Gauss
William Gilbert
Phyllis Gilman
Gay Glazbrook
Mike Godsil
Earl Graham
Tilly Grassa
Jennifer Greenberg
Beth Hanson
Jeannie Hedgecorth
Lori Herbel
Sheryl Hess
Ed Huff
Rhonda S. Jacobs
Chet Jezierski
Percy T. Jones
Diane Lewis

Meghan Lyons
John T. Marvin Collection
Dean Keppler
Melody Kist
Jeanne Kowalewski
Kathi Lamm
Linda Leeman
Karen Leshkivich, DVM
Danielle Levy
Diane Lewis
Judy Linden
Long Beach Convention
    and Visitors Bureau
Vicki W Lowrimore
Ben Mancuso
Dr. Janet C. Moyer
Debby Palleschi
Eric Palmer
Melinda Peters
Don Ploke
Sue Richey
Kit Rodwell
A. H. Rowan
Jan Schlobohm
Bill Schumacher
Evelyn Shafer
Signal Corps
Sirius Photography
Cheryl Snyder
Nancy Spelke
Phillip Steinkraus
Karen and Ian Stewart
Judith E. Strom
Steve Surfman
Harry Van Vliet
Diane Vasey
Marjorie J. White
A. C. Wilmerding
Robert Young

INDEX

NOTE: Page numbers or ranges in bold indicate a photograph or other graphic.